W9-DAY-637

Modern Language Association of America

Approaches to Teaching
World Literature

Joseph Gibaldi, Series Editor

1. Joseph Gibaldi, ed. *Approaches to Teaching Chaucer's* Canterbury Tales. 1980.
2. Carole Slade, ed. *Approaches to Teaching Dante's* Divine Comedy. 1982.
3. Richard Bjornson, ed. *Approaches to Teaching Cervantes'* Don Quixote. 1984.
4. Jess B. Bessinger, Jr., and Robert F. Yeager, eds. *Approaches to Teaching* Beowulf. 1984.
5. Richard J. Dunn, ed. *Approaches to Teaching Dickens'* David Copperfield. 1984.
6. Steven G. Kellman, ed. *Approaches to Teaching Camus's* The Plague. 1985.
7. Yvonne Shafer, ed. *Approaches to Teaching Ibsen's* A Doll House. 1985.
8. Martin Bickman, ed. *Approaches to Teaching Melville's* Moby-Dick. 1985.
9. Miriam Youngerman Miller and Jane Chance, eds. *Approaches to Teaching* Sir Gawain and the Green Knight. 1986.
10. Galbraith M. Crump, ed. *Approaches to Teaching Milton's* Paradise Lost. 1986.
11. Spencer Hall, with Jonathan Ramsey, eds. *Approaches to Teaching Wordsworth's* Poetry. 1986.
12. Robert H. Ray, ed. *Approaches to Teaching Shakespeare's* King Lear. 1986.
13. Kostas Myrsiades, ed. *Approaches to Teaching Homer's* Iliad *and* Odyssey. 1987.
14. Douglas J. McMillan, ed. *Approaches to Teaching Goethe's* Faust. 1987.
15. Renée Waldinger, ed. *Approaches to Teaching Voltaire's* Candide. 1987.
16. Bernard Koloski, ed. *Approaches to Teaching Chopin's* The Awakening. 1988.
17. Kenneth M. Roemer, ed. *Approaches to Teaching Momaday's* The Way to Rainy Mountain. 1988.
18. Edward J. Rielly, ed. *Approaches to Teaching Swift's* Gulliver's Travels. 1988.
19. Jewel Spears Brooker, ed. *Approaches to Teaching Eliot's Poetry and Plays.* 1988.
20. Melvyn New, ed. *Approaches to Teaching Sterne's* Tristram Shandy. 1989.
21. Robert F. Gleckner and Mark L. Greenberg, eds. *Approaches to Teaching Blake's* Songs of Innocence and of Experience. 1989.
22. Susan J. Rosowski, ed. *Approaches to Teaching Cather's* My Ántonia. 1989.
23. Carey Kaplan and Ellen Cronan Rose, eds. *Approaches to Teaching Lessing's* The Golden Notebook. 1989.
24. Susan Resneck Parr and Pancho Savery, eds. *Approaches to Teaching Ellison's* Invisible Man. 1989.
25. Barry N. Olshen and Yael S. Feldman, eds. *Approaches to Teaching the Hebrew Bible as Literature in Translation.* 1989.
26. Robin Riley Fast and Christine Mack Gordon, eds. *Approaches to Teaching Dickinson's Poetry.* 1989.
27. Spencer Hall, ed. *Approaches to Teaching Shelley's Poetry.* 1990.

28. Sidney Gottlieb, ed. *Approaches to Teaching the Metaphysical Poets*. 1990.
29. Richard K. Emmerson, ed. *Approaches to Teaching Medieval English Drama*. 1990.
30. Kathleen Blake, ed. *Approaches to Teaching Eliot's* Middlemarch. 1990.
31. María Elena de Valdés and Mario J. Valdés, eds. *Approaches to Teaching García Márquez's* One Hundred Years of Solitude. 1990.
32. Donald D. Kummings, ed. *Approaches to Teaching Whitman's* Leaves of Grass. 1990.
33. Stephen C. Behrendt, ed. *Approaches to Teaching Shelley's* Frankenstein. 1990.
34. June Schlueter and Enoch Brater, eds. *Approaches to Teaching Beckett's* Waiting for Godot. 1991.
35. Walter H. Evert and Jack W. Rhodes, eds. *Approaches to Teaching Keats's Poetry*. 1991.
36. Frederick W. Shilstone, ed. *Approaches to Teaching Byron's Poetry*. 1991.
37. Bernth Lindfors, ed. *Approaches to Teaching Achebe's* Things Fall Apart. 1991.
38. Richard E. Matlak, ed. *Approaches to Teaching Coleridge's Poetry and Prose*. 1991.
39. Shirley Geok-lin Lim, ed. *Approaches to Teaching Kingston's* The Woman Warrior. 1991.
40. Maureen Fries and Jeanie Watson, eds. *Approaches to Teaching the Arthurian Tradition*. 1992.
41. Maurice Hunt, ed. *Approaches to Teaching Shakespeare's* The Tempest *and Other Late Romances*. 1992.
42. Diane Long Hoeveler and Beth Lau, eds. *Approaches to Teaching Brontë's* Jane Eyre. 1993.
43. Jeffrey B. Berlin, ed. *Approaches to Teaching Mann's* Death in Venice *and Other Short Fiction*. 1992.
44. Kathleen McCormick and Erwin R. Steinberg, eds. *Approaches to Teaching Joyce's* Ulysses. 1993.
45. Marcia McClintock Folsom, ed. *Approaches to Teaching Austen's* Pride and Prejudice. 1993.
46. Wallace Jackson and R. Paul Yoder, eds. *Approaches to Teaching Pope's Poetry*. 1993.
47. Edward Kamens, ed. *Approaches to Teaching Murasaki Shikibu's* The Tale of Genji. 1993.
48. Patrick Henry, ed. *Approaches to Teaching Montaigne's* Essays. 1994.
49. David R. Anderson and Gwin J. Kolb, eds. *Approaches to Teaching the Works of Samuel Johnson*. 1993.

Approaches to Teaching
Montaigne's *Essays*

Edited by
Patrick Henry

The Modern Language Association of America
New York   1994

© 1993 by The Modern Language Association of America
All rights reserved. Printed in the United States of America

Library of Congress Cataloging-in-Publication Data

Approaches to teaching Montaigne's Essays / edited by Patrick Henry.
      p.   cm.—(Approaches to teaching world literature ; 48)
  Includes bibliographical references and index.
  ISBN 0-87352-719-4 (cloth)—ISBN 0-87352-720-8 (paper)
  1. Montaigne, Michel de, 1533-1592. Essais. 2. Montaigne, Michel
de, 1533-1592—Study and teaching. I. Henry, Patrick, 1940- .
II. Series.
PQ1643.A83   1993
844'.3—dc20   93-34507

Cover illustration of the paperback edition: 16th-cent. portrait of Montaigne, by Thomas de Leu, Musée Condé, Chantilly.

An earlier version of the essay by Raymond C. La Charité appeared in *Le parcours des Essais: Montaigne 1588–1988*, ed. Marcel Tetel and G. Mallary Masters (Paris: Aux Amateurs de Livres, 1989), under the title "Montaigne's Silenic Text: 'De la phisionomie.'" Used by permission.

Published by The Modern Language Association of America
10 Astor Place, New York, New York 10003-6981

Printed on recycled paper

Dedicated to the memory of

Donald M. Frame
(1911–91)

translator and interpreter of Montaigne
teacher and friend of the contributors to this volume

CONTENTS

PREFACE TO THE SERIES

In *The Art of Teaching* Gilbert Highet wrote, "Bad teaching wastes a great deal of effort, and spoils many lives which might have been full of energy and happiness." All too many teachers have failed in their work, Highet argued, simply "because they have not thought about it." We hope that the Approaches to Teaching World Literature series, sponsored by the Modern Language Association's Publications Committee, will not only improve the craft—as well as the art—of teaching but also encourage serious and continuing discussion of the aims and methods of teaching literature.

The principal objective of the series is to collect within each volume different points of view on teaching a specific literary work, a literary tradition, or a writer widely taught at the undergraduate level. The preparation of each volume begins with a wide-ranging survey of instructors, thus enabling us to include in the volume the philosophies and approaches, thoughts and methods of scores of experienced teachers. The result is a sourcebook of material, information, and ideas on teaching the subject of the volume to undergraduates.

The series is intended to serve nonspecialists as well as specialists, inexperienced as well as experienced teachers, graduate students who wish to learn effective ways of teaching as well as senior professors who wish to compare their own approaches with the approaches of colleagues in other schools. Of course, no volume in the series can ever substitute for erudition, intelligence, creativity, and sensitivity in teaching. We hope merely that each book will point readers in useful directions; at most each will offer only a first step in the long journey to successful teaching.

Joseph Gibaldi
Series Editor

PREFACE TO THE VOLUME

Montaigne has always been a giant of French letters. His essays, the only authentically modern literary form produced by the sixteenth century in France, constitute the first example of a major new literary genre and originate the moralist tradition in France. They have been debated in past centuries by the greatest French writers—including Descartes, Pascal, Bossuet, Voltaire, Rousseau, Flaubert, and Sainte-Beuve—and discussed in the twentieth century by French authors like André Gide and Michel Butor.

Central to the French tradition, Montaigne's *Essays* is one of only a handful of great works of the Renaissance that have been judged seminal to the whole development of Western culture. Accordingly, the *Essays* can now be read even in Russian, Polish, Turkish, and Japanese. Montaigne has become a universal phenomenon; the lover of travel and citizen of Rome would be pleased to learn that his book has a worldwide readership four hundred years after his death in 1592.

Most recently, the growing interest in genre and gender studies, autobiography, rhetoric, reader response, intertextuality, and all aspects of critical theory not only has changed the nature of the teaching of the *Essays* in French language classrooms, where it has remained a classic at all levels of instruction, but has catapulted the *Essays* , through the superb translation of Donald Frame, into an impressive number of different courses that span the undergraduate curriculum. The author's popularity, however, has not made him any easier to teach. His language, extensive incorporation of sources, oblique presentation of ideas, baroque structure, and fondness for paradox make him tough going for undergraduates reading him in the original or in translation.

The aims of this volume are to present information on the large body of critical material published on the work and its background, to provide specific approaches and interpretations by specialists, and to offer successful experiences in teaching the *Essays* in a variety of disciplines and on different undergraduate levels. Although the book is primarily intended for nonspecialists and undergraduate instructors, it is hoped that even established scholars will find the contents useful for classroom preparation.

Approaches to Teaching Montaigne's Essays is divided into two sections. Part 1 evaluates French and English editions and classroom texts of the *Essays* as well as reference works and audiovisual aids. It then enumerates the specific essays taught at various undergraduate levels and courses. This is followed by a discussion of the ways our survey respondents present the *Essays* and the difficulties encountered in teaching it. The last section, "The Instructor's Library," lists the major books and articles on the *Essays*, its background, and the author's biography. The information in this section is based on the fifty responses to a questionnaire sent out in 1989 to instructors who teach the *Essays* to American undergraduates.

Part 2 contains twenty essays by Renaissance scholars who have taught the *Essays* in a variety of colleges and universities and who offer their reflections on specific aspects of their experiences. These essays examine a host of different ways of reading the *Essays* and contain individual pedagogical strategies that have proved helpful in the classroom. A list of survey participants, the bibliography of works cited, and an index conclude the volume.

From the outset, this has been a collective endeavor, and I acknowledge with gratitude all those who have helped me and who, with me, believe in the integrity and usefulness of this scholarly venture. I thank the fifty respondents to the survey, without whom the "Materials" section would be nonexistent, and the twenty contributors who wrote the "Approaches" section. In addition, I deeply appreciate the support given me by the MLA staff, particularly Joseph Gibaldi, Adrienne Ward, and Elizabeth Holland, who offered excellent advice and helped me through some rough spots. I would be remiss if I didn't mention Sally Hooker and June Ellis, who prepared the manuscript with great care and patience. Finally, as always, my greatest debt is to Mary Anne O'Neil and our daughter, Anne, who have made the project both possible and worthwhile.

Patrick Henry
Whitman College

Part One

MATERIALS

Editions and Texts

The standard French edition of Montaigne's complete works is the *Œuvres complètes* in the Pléiade volume edited by Albert Thibaudet and Maurice Rat. The initial 1962 printing contains many errors in strata indicators, most of which have been corrected in subsequent printings. Another French edition of the complete works well worth consulting is that of Arthur Armaingaud. The best French edition of the *Essais* is the Pierre Villey edition, reprinted under the supervision of V. L. Saulnier. There are two excellent editions of the original 1580 edition of the *Essais*, one long out of print, by Reinhold Dezeimeris and H. Barckhausen, that contains the minor variants of the 1582 and 1587 editions, and the current two-volume photographic reproduction, by Daniel Martin, that supplies variants of the 1582, 1587, 1588, and 1595 editions. Marcel Françon has edited a photographic reprint of the 1582 edition of the *Essais* and Martin a photographic reproduction of the 1588 edition. Pierre Michel's richly documented paperback edition of Montaigne's *Journal de voyage en Italie* is by far the best available.

No English translation of the *Essays* can compete with Donald Frame's. Jacob Zeitlin's is worth consulting and John Florio's Renaissance translation remains for some a sentimental favorite, but Frame's is, finally, the most faithful and most consistently eloquent. Hence his is the standard edition of the complete works of Montaigne in English, as well as the standard single-volume edition of the complete *Essays*. His handsomely published paperback edition of *Montaigne's Travel Journal* is the first separate publication of this work in English.

The choice of a French classroom text is complicated because the deluxe editions are expensive and because no undergraduate class reads all the essays. With the sole exception of lower-division courses that survey all of French literature in two semesters, instructors teaching Montaigne in French use relatively inexpensive paperback editions. The French survey courses use either Morris Bishop's *A Survey of French Literature* or Henri Clouard and Robert Leggewie's *Anthologie de la littérature française*, thus limiting the reading of Montaigne in the first instance to "To the Reader" and a slightly abridged version of "Of Cannibals" and, in the second, to an embarrassingly short seven-page extract from "Of the Education of Children."

Many of these instructors choose texts that offer extracts, such as the Nouveaux Classiques Larousse edition; the Bordas edition; the Lagarde et Michard edition; Frank Chambers's *Prosateurs français du XVIe siècle*, which contains "Of Friendship," "Of Cannibals," and "Of Repentance"; and *Montaigne: Selected Essays*, edited by Arthur Tilley and A. M. Boase. By far the most popular text in this genre is Frame's *Montaigne's* Essays *and Selected Writings*. This rich five-hundred-page paperback volume contains extracts and complete texts (in French and in English) from all three books of essays in addition to related writings of Montaigne. Preferred by approximately one-quarter of the respondents, it is generally used in upper-division courses where the essays are studied for three, four, or five weeks.

Many respondents, however, refuse to teach extracts and have their students buy the complete *Essays* in paperback volumes. While only a couple of these instructors prefer either the Pierre Michel edition because it is in modern French or that of Michel Butor because of its brilliant introductions, most, again about one-quarter of the respondents, use the Garnier Flammarion edition, which provides the strata indicators, introductions, notes, a glossary, somewhat modernized spelling, and non-French quotations translated into French. Recently, a new text edited by Camilla Nilles and Ian Winter, *Rebelais et Montaigne: Chapitres choisis*, has appeared. In addition to containing selections from *Gargantua* and *Pantagruel*, introductions to both authors, and a detailed description of sixteenth-century French grammar, this volume contains Montaigne's "To the Reader" and the complete original French text of eight of the most commonly studied essays: "Of Idleness," "That to Philosophize Is to Learn to Die," "Of the Education of Children," "Of Friendship," "Of Practice," "Of the Art of Discussion," "Of Vanity," and "Of Experience."

Seventy-five percent of the respondents who teach Montaigne in English use the Donald Frame edition of the complete *Essays*. Three instructors, all of whom teach Montaigne in Western civilization and philosophy courses, use the Penguin edition, translated by John M. Cohen. Although this translation is inferior to Frame's and does not provide the strata indicators, it is chosen, as one respondent claims, because it "provides a good selection of essays in complete form in English and is less expensive than the Frame volume." Montaigne is also taught in English in lower-division survey courses using the *Norton Anthology of World Masterpieces* (gen. ed., Maynard Mack), which contains the complete text of "Of Cannibals" and "Of the Inconsistency of Our Actions" and very brief extracts from "Apology of Raymond Sebond" and "Of Repentance," all translated by E. J. Trechmann.

Reference Works

Montaigne criticism has reached enormous proportions. The most useful guide for the teacher and scholar is *A Critical Bibliography of French Literature*, volume 2: *The Sixteenth Century* (1965), edited by Alexander H. Schutz, and its revised 1985 edition, edited by Raymond La Charité. The annual *MLA International Bibliography* should be consulted for more current critical works, and one must also be aware of the two major journals dedicated to Montaigne: *Bulletin de la Société des Amis de Montaigne* (1913 to the present; general editor, Claude Blum) and the recently founded *Montaigne Studies: An Interdisciplinary Forum*, edited by Philippe Desan, of the University of Chicago, and published by the University of Chicago. Roy Leake's *Concordance des Essais de Montaigne* is a godsend that has already established itself as an indispensable scholarly tool, while Randle Cotgrave's *A Dictionarie of the French and English Tongues* and Edmond Huguet's *Dictionnaire de la langue française au seizième siècle* are invaluable lexicological aids.

Montaigne in the Classroom

Courses Taught

Perhaps the most satisfying result of the survey was to discover how broadly Montaigne is being taught at the undergraduate level both in English and French. It was not uncommon to learn that a single respondent might even teach the author of the *Essays* in three different courses: a survey course in French, an advanced literature course in French, and one other, such as a great works freshman course, a comparative literature course, or an advanced senior seminar dedicated to Montaigne.

At the lower-division level, selections from the *Essays* are taught in French in the traditional two-semester survey of French literature course where, generally, three or four classes are dedicated to them. At the mid-range level, Montaigne is read, again for three or four classes, in the introduction to French literature course and the history of French civilization course, whereas he occupies two full weeks of study in various classics of French literature courses. At this same level, Agnes Scott College alone offers an introductory course on literary genres where two weeks are spent on the *Essays*. At the upper-division level, Montaigne is read for two weeks as background material in a course on seventeenth-century moralists, for two or three weeks in the medieval-Renaissance course, for four weeks in the French Renaissance course, for five weeks in several French Renaissance prose courses, for eight weeks in the very popular Rabelais-Montaigne seminar, and for an entire semester at Duke University and Boston College in senior seminars dedicated solely to the *Essays*.

In English, the range is even greater, and it is heartening for admirers of the *Essays* to learn of the growing importance of this work throughout the entire undergraduate curriculum. At the freshman level, Montaigne's text is studied for a week in the medieval-Renaissance core at Washington University and for the same time in the humanities core at Columbia, Vanderbilt, and the University of Montana. It also constitutes two weeks of study in the sophomore honors course at Fordham University. More generally, the essays are read for a week or two in various courses such as Introduction to Comparative Literature, Intellectual Traditions in the West, Masterpieces of French Literature in Translation, and Masterpieces in the Romance Languages in Translation. Montaigne is read for three weeks in courses on world literature of the Renaissance at Whitman College, Vanderbilt, Fordham, and the University of Montana and, again for three weeks, in an introduction to philosophy course at the College of Wooster. At the upper-division level, the essays are studied for three weeks in an autobiography course at the University of Montana, a course on the literature of the self at Fordham University, and a course on literature and psychoanalysis at Dartmouth College. Finally, there are fourteen- to sixteen-week senior seminars on Montaigne offered by literature departments at Whitman and Dartmouth Colleges and by the political science department at the College of the Holy Cross.

Essays Taught

It goes without saying that the number and nature of essays taught are contingent on personal taste and the type of course in which they are studied. In lower-division courses where neither anthologies nor texts of extracts are used and where Montaigne is read for a week or two, instructors generally photocopy material from either the standard French or English texts. While these choices understandably remain diverse, several patterns emerge. Where students of French are not advanced enough to tackle the longer chapters, a popular series of three rather short essays, "Of Idleness," "Of Practice," and "Of Cripples," is read. One also finds a more ambitious pattern consisting of "Of the Education of Children," "Of Cannibals," and "Of Repentance." At the mid-range level and in the upper-division courses where two to three weeks are spent on the *Essays*, "To the Reader" and "Of Experience" are often added to the latter series. In any event, "Of the Education of Children," "Of Cannibals," "Of Repentance," and "Of Experience" are the four most widely read essays at the undergraduate level, even though philosophers and historians tend to substitute "That to Philosophize Is to Learn to Die" for one of the above-mentioned essays, and courses devoted exclusively to the essayist's study of self normally emphasize only essays in the third book.

At the level where the essays are studied anywhere from four to eight weeks, it is difficult to uncover neat patterns, but larger ones emerge nevertheless. Those using the Frame bilingual edition of the *Essays* read in whole or in part seventeen essays: from book 1, "Of Idleness," "That to Philosophize Is to Learn to Die," "Of the Education of Children," "Of Cannibals," "Of Solitude," and "Of Democritus and Heraclitus"; from book 2, "Of the Inconsistency of Our Actions," "Of Practice," "Apology for Raymond Sebond," "Of Presumption," "Of Giving the Lie," and "Of the Resemblance of Children to Fathers"; from book 3, "Of Repentance," "Of Vanity," "Of Husbanding Your Will," "Of Physiognomy," and "Of Experience." When we compare Frame's selections with those chosen by the instructors who have their students buy all three volumes in paper and thus have all the essays at their disposal, we see how truly representative Frame's selections are. Almost invariably each of the essays in Frame's collection is also read by those who do not use his edition. In fact, when we add to Frame's selections the following nine titles, which are also popular at this upper-division level, we have the twenty-six Montaigne essays most commonly read by American undergraduates: from book 1, "Of Pedantry" and "Of Friendship"; from book 2, "Of the Affection of Fathers for Their Children," and "Of Books"; and from book 3, "Of Three Kinds of Association," "On Some Verses of Virgil," "Of Coaches," "Of the Art of Discussion," and "Of Cripples."

In the six seminars dedicated solely to Montaigne offered in English and French, instructors assign anywhere from fifty to all of the essays. They all, however, assign the first, middle, and final chapters of the three books; all essays in book 3; the "Apology for Raymond Sebond" in its entirety; and ten essays not yet mentioned from the first two books. From the first book, these essays are "That Intention Is Judge of Our Actions," "Of Liars," "That the Taste of Good and Evil Depends in Large Part on the Opinion We Have of Them," "That Our Happiness Must Not Be Judged Until After Our Death," "Of the Power of the Imagination," "Of Custom, and Not Easily Changing an Accepted Law," and "It Is Folly to Measure the True and False by Our Own Capacity"; from the second book, "A Custom of the Island of Cea," "Of Cruelty," and "Of Three Good Women."

Approaches and Difficulties

The course titles already enumerated give some indication of the diversity of interest in the *Essays*. Indeed our survey records a whole spectrum of approaches emanating from traditional humanism and contemporary critical theory. Many of these approaches are discussed in detail in the second half of this book. While no single volume could contain detailed examples of all of the approaches outlined by the survey respondents, the following summary should nonetheless indicate the rich plurality of readings of Montaigne's classic work at the undergraduate level.

There are, first of all, many varieties of historical approaches to the *Essays*. Often Montaigne is read in the tradition of Castiglione as a representative of Renaissance society in courses that survey the period from Rabelais to Shakespeare. Here his humanist concerns for language, religion, modes of social interaction, and education are highlighted. Western civilization courses also read the *Essays* as history and tend to depict Montaigne as an example of late Renaissance skepticism. These teachers often stress in addition his appropriation of Stoical models at a time of great social upheaval. Socio-critical approaches insist upon a detailed discourse analysis of Montaigne's text in the sociological context of late Renaissance France, while the politics of the *Essays* are habitually elucidated by comparing them with the writings of contemporary and ancient political philosophers and by a close textual analysis of the author's "defensive writing" in an age of strict censorship.

The rhetorical approaches to Montaigne's work have also taken multiple forms. The more traditional approach views the *Essays* against the background of the Ciceronian rhetorical tradition while the newer technique envisions rhetoric as the textual strategies employed by the author to generate his text. Whereas the former depicts Montaigne's deep-seated antipathy toward the rhetorical tradition, the latter has affirmed the dialogical nature of the *Essays* and the central role of paradox. Other formalist approaches analyze the specifics of Montaigne's style, his ambivalence toward closure, and his philological brilliance. While Montaigne is in fact taught as a philosopher in the Socratic tradition, he is more frequently placed by our respondents in the moralist tradition. Here his ideas are related to Catholicism, Jewish thought, and the Renaissance commonplace tradition, and his "way of life"— as opposed to a "body of thought"—is explored.

Approximately forty percent of the respondents spend some class time attempting to define the essay as a genre. This is sometimes accomplished by comparing Montaigne's chapters with the writings of Plutarch, Seneca, and Erasmus. Other teachers indicate the specificity of Montaigne's essays by comparing them with those of Bacon and Emerson. The recent appearance of the following three volumes indicates the growing interest in the essay: Alexander Butrym, editor, *Essays on the Essay: Redefining the Genre*; Graham Good, *The Observing Self: Rediscovering the Essay*; Réda Bensmaïa, *The Barthes Effect: The Essay as Reflective Text*. Other modern approaches outlined by our respondents include the very popular analysis of the author's self-portrait, the connection between Montaigne's book and the visual arts, psychoanalysis or the textual unconscious, the author's radical and conservative statements on gender, his view of the reading process, and the deconstructionist approach that underscores how the text continually puts into question the meanings it posits.

The time allotted to Montaigne in each specific course dictates not only the number of essays read but, to some extent, what is and what is not done with the text. Our survey indicates, for example, that only in the advanced courses where Montaigne is studied for five or more weeks is much attention paid to the quotations within the text. While many teachers may point to the quotations in order to stress the importance of Seneca, Lucretius, Ovid, Horace, and Virgil as sources of Renaissance thought, most feel compelled to spend their limited time on more basic approaches. Only at the advanced level do we find an attempt to elucidate the poetics of quotation and to define the function of the quotations within Montaigne's text. Similarly, eighty percent of the respondents noted that they do not teach the architecture of the *Essays*. Here again, time constraints do not permit most teachers to pay attention to the place occupied by an essay in its book. It is primarily, but not exclusively, in the senior seminars dedicated solely to Montaigne that the order of the essays is analyzed. All those teaching such courses specifically noted, for example, that they teach the first, middle, and last essay of all three books. Several other teachers mentioned that they emphasize that the essay on friendship is found at the center of book 1.

Although it would certainly be true to say that time constraints also preclude the teaching of the strata of composition in the *Essays*, it is only fair to point out that much more is at stake on this question. There were three major editions of the *Essays* in the sixteenth century: the 1580 edition, which contained the 94 chapters of books 1 and 2; the 1588 edition, which also included the 13 chapters of book 3 and 600 additions to the first two books; and the posthumous edition of 1595, which had no new chapters but 1,000 additions to the text of 1588, additions that make up approximately one-fourth of the entire work (see over). Montaigne never made any attempt to denote the different strata of composition. His text was not divided into paragraphs, and nothing indicated to the reader what parts of any given chapter dated from 1580, 1588, or 1595. Readers of the *Essays* had to wait three hundred years for Fortunat Strowski, Pierre Villey, and the Darwinian influence on literary criticism to offer texts that indicated the three major editions and allowed the scholar a glimpse at the evolution of the essayist's work. Ever since Villey and Strowski, all major editions have indicated the strata, and it has become customary to use them to teach both the evolution of specific essays and the general evolution of the entire book. As with the phenomenon of intertextuality and the order of the essays, many respondents claimed that they simply do not find time to treat the strata of composition. Others said that they refer to them "on occasion" or "often" to depict the author's changing views and his habit of rewriting or adding to his text. But on this point, as on no other in our survey, many respondents felt compelled to take a stand. Donald Stone, for one, argued that if we don't need the strata "to read" the *Essays*, they nonetheless help us "to study" them. Jerome Schwartz, typifying a common view, noted, "I use them but do not abuse them." Craig Brush remarked that "Montaigne worked to make the strata more or less invisible; so why should we work to make them obvious?" David Schaefer refuses to use them because "Montaigne didn't present his work in this fashion," while another respondent, Raymond La Charité, said that "the strata should be avoided at the undergraduate level." He went on to applaud "Michel Simonin's intention to bring out a critical edition of the *Essays* without strata indicators." While Donald Stone may be right to assert that the strata help us to study the *Essays*, for they do indeed allow us to watch the essayist reflecting and adding to his text as much as twenty years after he began writing, there is no getting around the fact that Montaigne did not intend his book to be read in this manner. This, of course, should not be construed to mean that it isn't fair game to compare, say, early

A page from the 1588 (Bordeaux exemplar) edition of "That the Taste of Good and Evil Depends in Large Part on the Opinion We Have of Them" (1.14), showing, in the author's handwriting, additions that would appear in the posthumous 1595 edition of the *Essays*. (Photograph from *Reproduction en phototypie de l'exemplaire avec notes manuscrites marginales des Essais de Montaigne appartenant à la ville de Bordeaux*, Paris: Hachette, 1912).

essays in book 1 with those in book 3 for either philosophical or stylistic development.

Montaigne is a ferociously difficult author to teach to undergraduates. *Every* respondent made this point abundantly clear. His sixteenth-century French is tough going even for graduate students, and his oblique method of presenting ideas, his digressions, and his open-ended discourse, which happens to contain over twelve hundred Latin quotations, present a formidable challenge even to our most dedicated and intelligent students. Then there is the question of genre. Students have at least some idea of what to expect from unfamiliar poems, novels, and plays, but they come to the *Essays* unprepared. It is, moreover, no help to have read modern essays because, although Montaigne founded the genre, his essays break all the rules of modern essay writing. Once more, he confirms student perplexity when he refers to his essays in "Of Friendship" as "grotesque and monstrous bodies, pieced together of divers members, without definite shape, having no order, sequence, or proportion other than accidental" (135; 1.28).[1] In addition, some respondents noted that, for today's students, the essayist "talks too much about himself" and appears "too jaded," "too pessimistic," "too male chauvinist," "too intellectually radical and too politically conservative." Others expressed difficulty in getting students to appreciate the author's ideas on love, his stoical humanist (elitist) stance, the feminist side of his book, the importance of the quotations and digressions, the dialogical structure, obscure short chapters, paradox, irony, and role of the reader. Finally, and more ambitiously, another group of respondents told how they struggled in their effort to teach: how history and fiction are woven together in the text; that the essayist's view from the tower is not a cop-out; that Montaigne critiques European humanism; how his conservatism and liberalism come together in his realization of self; that he creates a persona; how, despite the contradictions and oppositions, one can draw conclusions about the author's positions, even though no absolute answers are given. Most ambitiously of all, one respondent finds his greatest difficulty "in getting students to write like Montaigne." Many of these points of difficulty are dealt with directly in the twenty essays in this volume.

Respondents were also asked to note the specific methods they employ in their teaching of the *Essays*. A good number of them hand out short lists of three or four study questions for each essay read in class. Starting with these questions and following the essayist's own pedagogical strategy of "sometimes letting [the student] clear his own way" (110; 1.26), one student or two present the form and content of each essay before a general discussion begins. Despite the overwhelming tendency to keep critical commentary out of the classroom, two respondents reported that students read two accounts of each essay, one by a formalist critic, the other by a social historian. By far the most popular teaching method is the explication de texte. Indeed, over sixty percent of the respondents use this line-by-line analysis of key passages as their major way of entry into the *Essays*. It is essential to realize that this standard French pedagogical strategy is not only important for traditional intentionalist critics in their attempt to show how the author says what he says and what images he uses, but it has also proved indispensable to socio-critics, philological critics, and deconstructionists. George Hoffmann related perhaps the most imaginative strategy for teaching the author's manner of composing: "I cut up one medium-length essay, 'Of Cruelty,' for example, and have students rearrange this 'mystery' chapter into the order they best see fit and pick a title for it. Back in class, we discuss the merits and justifications of their order of the essay as a preliminary to discussing Montaigne's principles of composition and structure." Finally, I find nothing more fruitful than Frame's reflection, made after almost fifty years of teaching the *Essays* at all levels: "If I were to start all over," he noted at the end of his four-page single-spaced response to our survey written during the last months of his life, "at the undergraduate level, I would try more to arouse curiosity than to confer information."

Audiovisual Aids

Most respondents were apprehensive about using audio or visual materials to help teach the *Essays*. Those who do so, however, speak so positively about their experience that all instructors should at least be aware of these possibilities.

The most frequently used audiovisual aids are slides depicting Montaigne's château and library, La Boétie's residence in Sarlat, emblems of the period, and pages of the Bordeaux exemplar of the *Essays* that contain the author's marginal additions to the 1588 edition of his book. Videos on the Renaissance and on the most celebrated self-portraits of the period, James Burke's series *The Day the Universe Changed*, Kenneth Clark's *Civilization* episode on Montaigne and Shakespeare, and the film *The Return of Martin Guerre*, have also been successfully integrated into classroom teaching.

One instructor, Tom Conley, has a particularly original and dynamic audiovisual approach to the teaching of the *Essays*: "I have a photographic collection of pages from the Angelier edition; close-ups of titles, headings, and individual sentences or syntagms; a collection of paintings and emblems that furnish information about the allegorical bases of the *Essays* (especially from the Fontainebleau tradition: Rosso, Primaticcio, Fantuzzi, etc.); architecture (from flamboyant to flamboyant-Italian in both ecclesiastical and secular forms: stairwells, entries, windows, lucarnes, etc.); grotesques in their development in architecture and in book illustration (e.g., La Perrière, Corrozet, Holbein, de Bry, Testu); cartography (I have taken pictures from collections at the James Ford Bell and Newberry Libraries), especially for gaining a sense of the dynamics of the *Essays* as a living map; perspective (Jean Cousin and the materials that Panofsky puts forward in *Early Netherlandish Painting*). I find that this aspect of the teaching of the *Essays* counts among the most crucial for imparting a drive to taste and to take pleasure in the form and substance of the work. My courses use these traditions substantially."

Required and Recommended Reading for Undergraduates

As noted earlier, the overwhelming tendency is to avoid secondary readings for undergraduate students and to concentrate solely on the text of the *Essays*. Most teachers limit the outside reading to the introduction to the edition used in class. Some even specifically advise students not to read any criticism and to spend whatever extra time they might have reading other essays of their choice. Even those who recommend outside reading insist that no reading of secondary materials should precede the completion of the essays about which they are written. A small number of teachers noted emphatically that, at the undergraduate level, it is far more important to have students familiarize themselves with texts that were of significance to Montaigne than to have them read critical studies of the *Essays*. These teachers encourage their students to read sections from classical and Renaissance texts such as Plato's *Dialogues*, the poetry of Lucretius, the *Moralia* of Plutarch, the epistles of Seneca, Thomas More's *Utopia*, Machiavelli's *The Prince*, and Castiglione's *The Book of the Courtier*. While some teachers at the advanced level did in fact mention specific secondary texts that they recommend but do not require, no text was mentioned with sufficient regularity to qualify it as a popular guide for student reading. The only required text at the undergraduate level for the study of Montaigne is the *Essays*.

The Instructor's Library

Teachers of Montaigne are availing themselves of the very large number of critical studies of the *Essays* and books and articles related to their study. Indeed, our survey unearthed over three hundred different books and articles read in class preparation. Under the categories of background and biography, book-length studies, collections of essays, and articles, this section lists the most commonly cited studies that our respondents find useful.

Background and Biography

Aside from ancient and contemporary authors, our respondents cite the following secondary books and articles as helpful background sources. For general historical background, they singled out *Histoire de la civilisation française*, by Georges Duby and Robert Mandrou, while for a deep historical sense of the period during which Montaigne wrote the following volumes were noted: A. G. Dickens, *Reformation and Society in Sixteenth-Century Europe*; Abel Lefranc, *La vie quotidienne au temps de la Renaissance*; Donald R. Kelley, *Foundations of Modern Historical Scholarship: Language, Law and History in the French Renaissance*; and Hiram Hayden, *The Counter-Renaissance*. In addition, Robert Mandrou's *Introduction à la France moderne, 1500–1640* was lauded for depicting "la psychologie historique," or collective spirit, of the time, as were J. R. Hale's *Renaissance Europe: Individual and Society, 1480–1520* for its panoramic initiation to the "mentalité" of the early sixteenth century and George Huppert's *Les bourgeois gentilhommes: An Essay on the Definition of Elites in Renaissance France* for illuminating the ways of access for the new gentry class in Renaissance society to which Montaigne belonged. For the religious wars, our respondents pointed to James W. Thompson, *The Wars of Religion in France, 1559–1576*; Philippe Erlanger, *Le massacre de Saint-Barthélemy*; Georges Livet, *Les guerres de religion*; and Robert M. Kingdon, *Myth and Massacre in Sixteenth Century Europe: Reactions to St. Bartholomew's Massacres of 1572*. In the same vein, J. H. M. Salmon's *Society in Crisis: France in the Sixteenth Century* was praised for faithfully recording the changes in the economic, social, and religious life of France during the civil wars. Finally, the two most commonly mentioned historical works, both written by Géralde Nakam—*Montaigne et son temps: Les événements et les* Essais: *L'histoire, la vie, le livre* and *Les* Essais *de Montaigne: Miroir et procès de leur temps*—not only paint the background and portray Montaigne in it but also, by their rich insights and historical precision, help to elucidate many individual essays.

For philosophical background, respondents turned most often to Richard Popkin's accomplished and learned *The History of Scepticism from Erasmus to Spinoza* and Henri Busson's *Le rationalisme dans la littérature française de la Renaissance*, which studies the application of rational methods to religious topics. Two other often noted sources of general philosophical background were Nannerl O. Keohane's *Philosophy and the State in France* and Huppert's *The Idea of Perfect History: Historical Erudition and Historical Philosophy in Renaissance France*. For religious background, our respondents regularly mentioned Walter Ong, *The Presence of the Word: Some Prolegomena for Cultural and Religious History*; D. P. Walker, *The Ancient Theology: Studies in Christian Platonism from the Fifteenth to the Eighteenth Century*; Emile G. Léonard, *Histoire générale du protestantisme*; H. Outram Evennett, *The Spirit of the Counter-Reformation*; and Augustin Renaudet, *Humanisme et Renaissance*, a collection of stimulating and important articles that paint the religious climate of the period and indicate the changing aspects of humanism. Other cultural works frequently cited include Natalie Zemon Davis, *Society and Culture in Early Modern France*; William Kerrigan and Gordon Braden, *The Idea of the Renaissance*; Davis Bitton, *The French Nobility in Crisis, 1560–1640*; Eugene Rice, *The*

Renaissance Idea of Wisdom; Paul Porteau, *Montaigne et la vie pédagogique de son temps*; Franco Simone, *Culture et politique à l'époque de l'humanisme et de la Renaissance*; Paul Oskar Kristeller, *Renaissance Thought: The Classic, Scholastic, and Humanist Strains*; and Philippe Desan, editor, *Humanism in Crisis: The Decline of the French Renaissance*, a collection of penetrating and original essays that analyze the decline of humanism from 1580 to 1630.

In addition to the original classical and Renaissance literary works, survey respondents commonly referred to the following secondary texts as extremely useful for literary background essential to the teaching of the *Essays*: Denis Hollier, editor, *A New History of French Literature*; Pierre Brunel et al., *Histoire de la littérature française*; Ernst Robert Curtius, *European Literature and the Latin Middle Ages*; Daniel Ménager, *Introduction à la vie littéraire du XVIe siècle*; Jean Plattard, *La Renaissance des lettres en France, de Louis XII à Henri IV*; Ian McFarlane, *Renaissance France, 1470–1589*; J. E. Seigel, *Rhetoric and Philosophy in Renaissance Humanism, Petrarch to Valla*; Harry Levin, *The Myth of the Golden Age in the Renaissance*; Margaret M. McGowan, *Ideal Forms in the Age of Ronsard*; Richard Lanham, *The Motives of Eloquence: Literary Rhetoric in the Renaissance*; Walter J. Ong, *Ramus: Method, and the Decay of Dialogue*; Antoine Compagnon, *La seconde main; ou, Le travail de la citation*; and two classics by Rosalie Colie, *Paradoxia Epidemica: The Renaissance Tradition of Paradox* and *The Resources of Kind: Genre-Theory in the Renaissance*.

When compared with later historical and literary figures such as Voltaire, Rousseau, Diderot, and Hugo, Montaigne has elicited few biographies. As with Shakespeare, his contemporary, there is much speculation about important parts of his life. In any event, although works such as Géralde Nakam's contain important biographical material, only two genuine biographies were mentioned in our survey. Frame's *Montaigne: A Biography*, published in 1965, is certainly the most complete and fully satisfying biography ever to appear on the author of the *Essays* and is to be published in French by Champion. It should be noted nonetheless that Roger Trinquet's *La jeunesse de Montaigne*, published in 1972, occasionally corrects Frame's earlier volume on significant points and supersedes it for the first twenty-five years of the author's life. It is certainly the best we have on Montaigne's family and on his education at the Collège de Guyenne.

Books on the Essays

Ten critical volumes on the *Essays* were clearly singled out by our respondents as the most useful for class preparation. Although deemed "challenging for the beginning instructor," Hugo Friedrich's richly documented and immensely learned analysis of the essayist, his book, and his predecessors was often cited as the best single volume on Montaigne. Friedrich's *Montaigne* originally appeared in German in 1949, then in French in 1968 and in

English in 1991. This is obviously a rare feat for a book of criticism and a testimony to its lasting value. Easier to read and less forbidding than Friedrich's *Montaigne*, and the only other candidate for the best single volume on the essayist, is Richard Sayce's *The* Essays *of Montaigne: A Critical Exploration*. His study is particularly good at examining the art, unity of thought, and conservative and revolutionary aspects of the *Essays*. Pierre Villey's *Les sources et l'évolution des* Essais *de Montaigne* is still considered essential for the dating and sources of individual essays even if it projects the now questioned theory of philosophical evolution from Stoicism to skepticism to Epicureanism. Following Villey's evolutionary theory, *Montaigne's Discovery of Man: The Humanization of a Humanist*, by Frame, leads the reader from the essayist's hedonism and Stoical humanism through skeptical revolt to ultimate liberation and the discovery of human solidarity. Marcel Tetel's *Montaigne*, although limited by the format of the Twayne series, is a succinct and helpful comprehensive introduction with an annotated bibliography. To a large extent, the other five most popular works of criticism on the *Essays* strive more to cover one aspect of the book than provide a total picture of the man and his work. Floyd Gray's *Le style de Montaigne*, for example, published in 1958, is still the essential study of the essayist's style, while Mary McKinley's recent *Words in a Corner: Studies in Montaigne's Latin Quotations* was lauded as a rich and illuminating intertextual analysis of the essayist's borrowings from Ovid, Horace, and Virgil, one that opens new ground and perceptively incorporates the context of the borrowed quotation into its meaning and function within the *Essays*. Richard Regosin's *"The Matter of My Book"*: *Montaigne's* Essais *as the Book of the Self*, already a classic, offers rich insights into friendship, self-portrait, rhetoric, and writing in the *Essays*. It is perhaps the best attempt we currently possess to reconcile the historical and fictional approaches to Montaigne's book. *Lectures de Montaigne*, by Jules Brody, presents close readings of several key essays that the author depicts advancing philologically rather than logically. He stresses the literary and metaphorical aspects of the *Essays* and the author's craft as process rather than product. Many respondents reported that his explications de texte are so compelling that it is impossible to teach the essays he has analyzed without incorporating his observations. Finally, Jean Starobinski's *Montaigne en mouvement*, recently translated into English as *Montaigne in Motion*, is an authoritative compilation of twenty-five years of phenomenological, literary, and psychological reflection on the *Essays*. Surveying a vast array of topics—appearance and reality, the body, self-awareness, custom, death, politics, religion, and the relation to others—Starobinski portrays the circular movement of Montaigne's thought, a logical but not necessarily chronological movement from dependence to independence and ultimately to synthesis, that enables the essayist to change an initially unhappy consciousness into a happy one. This is perhaps the richest book on the essayist for the modern and postmodern reader.

A second group of ten critical studies, whose titles often reveal their specific approach, were also frequently mentioned: Carol Clark, *The Web of Metaphor: Studies in the Imagery of Montaigne's* Essais; Margaret McGowan, *Montaigne's Deceits: The Art of Persuasion in the* Essais; Barbara Bowen, *The Age of Bluff: Paradox and Ambiguity in Rabelais and Montaigne*; Lawrence Kritzman, *Destruction/découverte: Le fonctionnement de la rhétorique dans les* Essais *de Montaigne*; Frieda Brown, *Religious and Political Conservatism in the* Essais *of Montaigne*; Raymond La Charité, *The Concept of Judgment in Montaigne*; Terence Cave, *The Cornucopian Text: Problems of Writing in the French Renaissance*; Michaël Baraz, *L'être et la connaissance selon Montaigne*; Donald Frame, *Montaigne's* Essais: *A Study*; and Jean-Yves Pouilloux, *Lire les* Essais *de Montaigne*.

Our respondents also singled out four short introductions to the *Essays* particularly suited for the beginning teacher of Montaigne: Peter Burke's *Montaigne*; Frank Bowman's *Montaigne:* Essays; Marie-Luce Demonet's *Michel de Montaigne: Les* Essais; and Dorothy Gabe Coleman's *Montaigne's* Essais. There is, finally, an additional group of books that were simply cited too often in our survey not to be recorded here: Robert Cottrell, *Sexuality/Textuality: A Study of the Fabric of Montaigne's* Essais; James J. Supple, *Arms versus Letters: The Military and Literary Ideals in the* Essais *of Montaigne*; Frederick Rider, *The Dialectic of Selfhood in Montaigne*; Albert Thibaudet, *Montaigne*; Michel Butor, *Essais sur les* Essais; Gérard Defaux, *Marot, Rabelais, Montaigne: L'écriture comme présence*; André Tournon, *Montaigne: La glose à l'essai*; M. A. Screech, *Montaigne and Melancholy: The Wisdom of the* Essays; François Rigolot, *Les métamorphoses de Montaigne*; Ian Winter, *Montaigne's Self-Portrait and Its Influence in France, 1580–1630*; Floyd Gray, *La balance de Montaigne: Exagium/essai*; Alfred Glauser, *Montaigne paradoxal*; Michel Beaujour, *Miroirs d'encre*; Antoine Compagnon, *Nous, Michel de Montaigne*; Marcel Gutwirth, *Michel de Montaigne ou le pari d'exemplarité*; and Gisèle Mathieu-Castellani, *Montaigne: L'écriture de l'essai*.

Collections of Essays on the Essays

While there have been close to two dozen quality collections and festschriften published on Montaigne over the past twelve or thirteen years, commemorating various publication dates in the history of the *Essays*, three of these volumes particularly stand out in our survey as reference points for undergraduate teachers of Montaigne. *O un amy! Essays on Montaigne in Honor of Donald M. Frame*, edited by Raymond La Charité, contains the following pieces: "Montaigne et l'idéal de l'homme entier," by Michaël Baraz; "'De mesnager sa volonté' (3.10): Lecture philologique d'un essai," by Jules Brody; "'Si le chef d'une place assiegée doit sortir pour parlementer' and 'L'heure des parlemens dangereuse': Montaigne's Political Morality and Its Expression in the Early Essays" by Frieda S. Brown; "What Montaigne Has to Say about Old Age" by Craig B. Brush; "Montaigne's Pyrrhonism" by

Floyd Gray; "Les *Essais*, et la manière de s'en servir" by Marcel Gutwirth; "The Ethics of Montaigne's 'De la cruauté'" by Philip P. Hallie; "A Prose Poem: Montaigne's 'Mother Virtue'" by John C. Lapp; "Paper and Ink: The Structure of Unpredictability" by Lino Pertile; "The Visual Arts in Montaigne's *Journal de Voyage*" by R. A. Sayce; "'La Conscience d'un Homme': Reflections on the Problem of Conscience in the *Essais*" by Jerome Schwartz; "Man Humbled and Exalted: Montaigne's 'Apologie de Raimond Sebond' and a Passage of Plato's *Timaeus*" by Isidore Silver; "Montaigne et l'argent" by Roger Trinquet; and "Language, Truthfulness, and the Self-Portrait of Michel de Montaigne" by Dilys Winegrad. *Montaigne: Essays in Reading*, edited by Gérard Defaux, includes these articles: "Dangerous Parleys—*Essais* 1.5 and 6," by Thomas M. Greene; "A Long Short Story: Montaigne's Brevity," by Antoine Compagnon; "Self-Interpretation in Montaigne's *Essais*," by André Tournon; "Readings of Montaigne," by Gérard Defaux; "Lessons of the New World: Design and Meaning in Montaigne's 'Des Cannibales' (1.31) and 'Des coches' (1.6)," by Edwin M. Duval; "L'Etre et l'Autre: Montaigne," by Tzvetan Todorov; "Montaigne's Purloined Letters," by François Rigolot; "Guesswork or Facts: Connections between Montaigne's Last Three Chapters (3.11, 12 and 13)," by Marianne S. Meijer; "'By Diverse Means . . .' (1.1)," by Marcel Gutwirth; "Montaigne: The Paradox and the Miracle—Structure and Meaning in 'The Apology for Raymond Sebond' (*Essais* 2.12)," by Catherine Demure; "The Affirmation of Paradox: A Reading of Montaigne's 'De la phisionomie' (3.12)," by Joshua Scodel; "'Du repentir' (3.2): A Philological Reading," by Jules Brody; and "The Body's Moment," by Jean Starobinski. Finally, *Montaigne: Essays in Memory of Richard Sayce*, edited by I. D. McFarlane and Ian Maclean, incorporates seven critical studies: "Considerations on the Genesis of Montaigne's *Essais*," by Donald M. Frame; "The Evolution of the *Essais*," by David Maskell; "The Art of Transition in the *Essais*," by Margaret McGowan; "Talking about Souls: Montaigne on Human Psychology," by Carol Clark; "The Concept of Virtue in Montaigne," by I. D. McFarlane; "*Le païs au delà*: Montaigne and Philosophical Speculation," by Ian Maclean; and "Problems of Reading in the *Essais*," by Terence Cave.

Articles on the Essays

In addition to the articles in the collections noted above, our respondents repeatedly stressed the relevance of the following group of articles to their teaching. Here I limit myself to listing only the twenty-five most commonly cited pieces, beginning with two classic studies. Erich Auerbach's "L'Humaine Condition" examines "Of Repentance" and elucidates the discontinuity of the essayist's style, while "Montaigne's Notion of Experience," by Will Moore, stresses the ultimate importance of the nonintellectual in living a fully human life. Regarding the early essays, Raymond La Charité indicates their personal aspects in "Montaigne's Early Personal Essays," while Edwin Duval explicates their rhetorical strategies in "Rhetorical Composition and 'Open Form' in Montaigne's Early Essays." Two pieces examine the specific nature of friendship in the *Essays*: "The Rhetoric of Friendship in Montaigne's *Essais*," by Barry Weller, and Beryl Schlossman's "From La Boétie to Montaigne: The Place of the Text." Two other popular essays in book 1 are studied by Steven Rendall and Frieda Brown. Rendall's "Dialectical Structure and Tactics in Montaigne's 'Of Cannibals'" treats the author's art of persuasion, and Brown's "'De la Solitude': A Re-examination of Montaigne's Retreat from Public Life" depicts the essayist's evolving notion of retirement. Donald Stone, in "Death in the Third Book," rejects Villey's evolutionary theory of Montaigne's concept of death, and Vivien Thweatt's "L'art de conferer: Art des *Essais*, art de vivre" elucidates the centrality of debate within the *Essays*. Two other articles dispute the meaning of "Of Coaches." Richard Sayce denotes its baroque structure in "Baroque Elements in Montaigne" while René Etiemble responds in "Sens et structure dans un essai de Montaigne" by insisting on its ideological clarity. On the origins of self-study in the *Essays*, respondents cited Craig Brush's "Montaigne Tries Out Self-Study" and for self-portraiture, they recommended the following three pieces: Donald Frame, "Specific Motivation for Montaigne's Self-Portrait"; Richard Regosin, "Figures of the Self: Montaigne's Rhetoric of Portraiture"; and Steven Rendall, "The Rhetoric of Montaigne's Self-Portrait: Speaker and Subject." On the concept of reading and critical theory, one would do well to consult Rendall's "*Mus in pice*: Montaigne and Interpretation" and Cathleen Bauschatz's "Montaigne's Conception of Reading in the Context of Renaissance Poetics and Modern Criticism." Finally, and more generally, the following articles were named as helpful guides to teaching the *Essays*: Anthony Wilden, "'Par Divers Moyens On Arrive à Pareille Fin': A Reading of Montaigne"; Marc Eli Blanchard, "'Of Cannibalism' and Autobiography"; Richard Regosin, "Sources and Resources: The 'Pretexts' of Originality in Montaigne's *Essais*"; Craig Brush, "The Essayist Is Learned: Montaigne's *Journal de voyage* and the *Essais*"; Steven Rendall, "Montaigne under the Sign of *Fama*"; Timothy Hampton, "Montaigne and the Body of Socrates: Narrative and Exemplarity in the *Essais*," recently incorporated into his *Writing from History: The Rhetoric of Exemplarity in Renaissance Literature*; and Richard Regosin, "Recent Trends in Montaigne Scholarship: A Post-structuralist Perspective."

NOTE

[1]Throughout both parts 1 and 2 of this book, references to Montaigne's work in English are to *The Complete* Essays *of Montaigne*, translated by Donald Frame, and in French to *Les* Essais *de Michel de Montaigne*, edited by Pierre Villey and V. L. Saulnier. Book and essay numbers follow page numbers.

Part Two

APPROACHES

Introduction

The second part of this volume, consisting of twenty essays written by seasoned instructors of Montaigne, begins with the section "Montaigne and the Renaissance." In the opening essay, "Our Troubles: The Essays' and Their Backgrounds," Timothy Hampton delineates the relation between the essayist, his historical background, and textual tradition, while suggesting that our role, as teachers of the *Essays*, is to evoke these backgrounds and traditions without turning Montaigne's book into a museum piece. More specifically, Hampton paints, as background, the inherited humanist culture of rhetoric, history, and moral philosophy, and its radical transformation during the collapse of civil order in late sixteenth-century France. This is highlighted within the context of the public-private dichotomy by a discussion of freedom, custom, and tyranny in La Boétie and Montaigne. Barbara C. Bowen, in "The Rhetoric of the *Essays*," also attempts to put Montaigne back into his century. She describes his subtle and idiosyncratic use of rhetoric throughout the *Essays* against the background of the Ciceronian rhetorical tradition and the reading and writing exercises familiar to Renaissance schoolchildren.

The next section, "General Approaches," opens with "The *Essays*: An Overall View," by Gérard Defaux, who warns us to avoid three dangers: the obsession with the referent, the temptation to anthologize, and the confusion of voices and levels of discourse. He calls for a critical analysis based on intertextuality, mimesis, representation, and "la maniere, non . . . la matiere du dire" (928; 3.8). Marianne Meijer's "The Essays in the Context of the *Essays*" makes the case for reading the essays, not as separate entities, but as they relate to one another. Taking Montaigne's cue—"My stories take their place according to their timeliness, not always according to their age" (736; 3.9)—she analyzes clusters of essays, showing that, when read in the context of contiguous chapters, certain meanings change or become clearer. Finally, Colin Dickson's "Montaigne's Style" elucidates the essayist's use of parataxis, occasional laconism, irony, shifting voices, metaphor, simile, and general sentence structure and word play. Dickson ends by discussing the problematics of closure in a book whose author remarked, "Who does not see that I have taken a road along which I shall go, without stopping and without effort, as long as there is ink and paper in the world?" (721; 3.9).

The third section is composed of four interdisciplinary studies. "Montaigne and Politics," by David Lewis Schaefer, maintains that Montaigne's *Essays* is best understood as a work of political philosophy, one in which the author endeavors to accomplish a transformation in the way human beings live and are governed. Inspired by Leo Strauss's *Persecution and the Art of Writing* and following Arthur Armaingaud, Schaefer portrays the essayist's defensive writing and methods of subterfuge and establishes him as one of the earliest philosophic architects of modern liberal politics. T. A. Perry zeroes in on the value of *non*doing—*in*action—in "Just Say No: Montaigne's Negative Ethics." Perry admits that this is only one aspect of the author's ethics, but a very important and neglected one. He outlines Montaigne's habit of negative definition (and self-definition) and his often stated view—originating perhaps in Sephardic wisdom—that good is the absence of evil. The essayist thus encourages, rather than the pursuit of justice, the avoidance of injustice. Here inaction and restraint can attain the highest form of human action. In "The *Essays* and the Visual Arts," Tom Conley depicts how Montaigne writes in and through the plastic arts, accounting for them yet distorting them, in his printed book, published in an age that did not make the distinctions between painting, architecture, and literature that we do. Montaigne relies on portraiture to convey the nature of his autobiography; he applies the art of perspective of the Italian masters to the verbal form of his work; he develops a tactic of association linked to practices of framing in mannerist painting; and, finally, many of his essays are written in tandem with iconic representation of themes contemporary to the author. Lastly, Philippe Desan, in "For a Sociology of the *Essays*," studies the interaction between text, author, and society by a close analysis of the language of the *Essays*. The sixteenth century witnessed the invasion of accounting, banking, and mercantile terms into its social discourse, and this new commercial discourse (of economic materialism) ultimately came to replace the older nobiliary (idealistic and atemporal) one. Desan recounts how the essays depict the struggle between the commercial and nobiliary discourses, and his study culminates in a close explication de texte of the revealing "Of the Useful and the Honorable," where the two types of discourse come together to reflect the crisis of language in late Renaissance France.

"Contemporary Critical Approaches" brings together six critical ways of entry into the *Essays*: autobiography, reader-oriented perspective, psychoanalysis, intertextuality, gender, and deconstruction. Richard L. Regosin's "The *Essays*: Autobiography and Self-Portraiture" begins by showing how undergraduates can feel at home reading Montaigne for, like them, perhaps, he felt pressured by established authority and the weight of conventional values, fought against being totally absorbed by the outside world, and was concerned with articulating and forming a self. It is precisely this active and endless forming of a self, the dynamics of autobiography, that Regosin stresses in his teaching, rather than the portrait of the settled and serene Renaissance humanist. Regosin finds the term *autobiography* always, in some sense, appropriate to Montaigne's book, for even when the essayist discusses other matters, he is testing his judgment and writing. The essay ends with a discussion of "Of Physiognomy," which presents the author's portrait of Socrates as his own ideal self-portrait. In "A Reader-Oriented Approach to Teaching Montaigne," Cathleen M. Bauschatz faithfully records her students' personal reactions in reading the *Essays*. Like most "real" readers, as opposed to academic ones, they read Montaigne "to find out about him" and, additionally, keep an account in a journal of the differences and similarities they discover between themselves and the essayist. Bauschatz concludes by emphasizing that this reader-oriented approach actually fulfills Montaigne's pedagogical ideal whereby a dialogue is created between reader and text. "Montaigne and Psychoanalysis," by Lawrence D. Kritzman, performs an in-depth analysis of a short piece by Jacques Lacan—"The Mirror Stage As Formative of the Function of the I As Revealed in Psychoanalytic Experience"—and Montaigne's essay "Of Friendship." The study shows that while Lacan's text theorizes the genesis of the human subject due to the reflection of the self found in the visual perception of the mirror, "Of Friendship" figurally represents the undoing of the self through the shattering of an ideal union. More generally, however, Kritzman proves not only that psychoanalytic criticism can be used as a heuristic device for reading and interpreting the essays but also that the essays themselves are literary fictions that project psychoanalytic positions in their own right. Mary B. McKinley's "The *Essays* as Intertext" relates how the author's writing is intimately linked with his reading, and how his book, in an age that extolled *imitatio*, became a mosaic of quotations. In addition, she shows convincingly that some of the most auto-biographical passages in the *Essays* are in part skillful reworkings and rhetorical imitations of antecedent texts, thus indicating that, in the final analysis, the essayist's book exhibits a felicitous blend of intersubjectivity and intertextuality. "En-gendering the *Essays*," by Julia Watson, examines what it means to speak of gender in Montaigne's book: the absence and the treatment of literary and historical women, the representation of masculinity, and the author's relation to his own body as a (de)gendered site/text. Watson points out that the acknowledged marginality of women in the *Essays* as a "gynephobic discourse" needs to be read against other discourses in the book that obliquely destabilize the hierarchy of gender and the privilege of masculinity. She encourages her students to read the *Essays* as a nondominating discourse and to rethink the book's gynephobic blindspots in the light of a method of writing that, four centuries before Virginia Woolf, was interested in "breaking the sentence, breaking the sequence." Finally, Jerome Schwartz's "Montaigne and Deconstruction" affirms the challenge of the essayist's skepticism to the Platonic foundation of Western metaphysics and examines specific "deconstructive moments" in the *Essays* where he finds undecidability, the dismantling of certain ideas that would indicate an absence of a recoverable point of origin that might serve as a solid foundation of knowledge, and the consequent endless postponement of full meaning. Schwartz admits nonetheless that Montaigne's book remains resolutely mimetic, Pyrrhonian skepticism having subverted the project of self-portrayal but not precluded it. In writing essays, Montaigne both deconstructs other texts and constructs a self as a text that resists closure.

The final segment of the "Approaches" section consists of five articles on the teaching of specific essays. In "'By Diverse Means We Arrive at the Same

End': Gateway to the *Essays*," Frieda S. Brown shows convincingly that the first essay in the volume is a true path to those that follow. Similar to but not one of the earliest written pieces, it contains key ideas found in all three books—the inconstancy of human behavior, the human propensity for violent revenge, and the author's hatred of cruelty—as well as structural and rhetorical strategies of the mature artist, such as presenting an example or a view and immediately undercutting it. "'Of the Education of Children': Knowledge and Authority," by Steven Rendall, describes how Montaigne outlines, perhaps for the first time, a conception of discourse as the representation, not of what is true, but of what the speaker "believes" to be true when he says it. The essayist thereby inaugurates modern autobiographical writing by shifting the reference of discourse from its object to its subject. This conception of the essayist, Rendall indicates, closely resembles what the author prescribes for his ideal pupil: the concentration on the cultivation of individual judgment and the notion that books are primarily pretexts for the student's self-discovery. Rendall concludes by pointing out the irony in the fact that students are taught today to look for the image of the essayist in the text—as Montaigne himself tells Mme de Duras to do (595; 2.37)—rather than to follow the pedagogy he proposes in "Of the Education of Children." John Lyons's "'Of Three Kinds of Association': In the Library, Looking Out" not only examines the essayist's portrayal of his relationships with men, women, and books but also underscores the centrality of place, from the very placement of the chapter itself—as chapter 3, in book 3, with three kinds of association—to the author's library on the third floor of his tower where he goes to read, walk, and look out on the world. Here we discover that the author's books are windows, just as his windows are books—Lyons finds him "paging through his house" from this solitary place of refuge that offers him interaction with books, the world outside, and himself. "'Of the Art of Discussion': A Philological Reading," by Jules Brody, argues most convincingly that, if we read this chapter as a metaphorical construct generated by certain tendencies of Montaigne's language—its redundancies, antitheses, repetitions, recurrent images, Latin quotations, and various contextual meanings of certain key words—we will find a coherence seldom apparent in the usual content-centered, ideological readings of the *Essays*. Lastly, Raymond C. La Charité, in "'Of Physiognomy': The Staging and Reading of Facial Narrative," evokes the coherence of this essay by portraying its essential theatricality in the staging of faces and surfaces to be read in a veritable *theatrum mundi* infiltrated by disease, hypocrisy, and civil war. In this contrastive configuration of faces, which includes Socrates's and the common people's, the author unmasks his own.

The diversity of approaches and interpretations found in these studies testifies to the growing importance of the *Essays* in the undergraduate curriculum. Written by many of the most eminent Montaigne scholars in America today, the essays in this volume all have a pedagogical focus. Their delineation of teaching strategies and techniques that have proved effective in the classroom challenges the traditional notion of a dichotomy between research and teaching. Whether these instructors teach Montaigne traditionally or apply current critical theories to his book, they are unanimous in their belief in the accessibility of the *Essays* to undergraduates at all levels and of all majors. It is hoped, therefore, that their reflections will be a fruitful source of inspiration to all those, specialists and nonspecialists, who teach the *Essays* in the undergraduate classroom.

PH

MONTAIGNE AND THE RENAISSANCE

Our Troubles: The Essays and Their Backgrounds

Timothy Hampton

It is probably fair to say that no one who has ever tried to teach the *Essays* has escaped the troubling problem of relating Montaigne's work to its various textual and historical backgrounds. For one of the remarkable paradoxes of Montaigne's text is the way in which it blends the depiction of a sensibility that appears thoroughly modern, and thus easily recognizable to the twentieth-century reader, with extended references to contexts and traditions—minor incidents from Roman history, fine points of Renaissance political strategy, and so on—that often seem arcane even to the specialist, not to mention the average undergraduate. What is most perplexing about this situation is that these two facets of the text are linked. Much of the interest of Montaigne's portrait of himself lies in the ways he overturns or transforms traditions of writing about such dusty topoi as, say, anger or friendship. To study Montaigne's text without evoking those traditions, or to read it apart from its literary history, is to divorce it from the source of much of its originality and rhetorical power. Yet, conversely, to root Montaigne's text too firmly in its various contexts by burdening students with background on such subjects as the Battle of Dreux or the career of Dionysius of Syracuse is to turn this most lively of books into a museum piece.

The question of background involves both a historical problem (the relation of a given text to its social and political context) and a discursive problem (the relation of a given text to the literary traditions, generic conventions, and commonplaces on which it draws). To try to link the *Essays* to these two problems is to address nothing less than the emergence of the essay itself as a historically defined literary form. Moreover, this confrontation between a textual tradition that endures through time and a specific social or political moment is thematized in Montaigne's very project. His famous claim that he and his book are one and the same, that text and self create and define each other, means that issues involving the book—problems of writing and representation, questions of literary history, and so on—are constantly shading over into the domain of issues involving the man, questions concerning the political and social position of a rural aristocrat in the sixteenth century. Montaigne's dual concern for self and book means that the backgrounds of the *Essays* must be read as related both to questions of writing and language and to issues of self-exploration and definition. To read Montaigne as a writer concerned exclusively with either the existential problems of a sage philosopher or the slipperiness of language is to reduce the complexity of his project.

According to theorists of the rise of the novel, new modes of experiencing historical time in the Renaissance had a profound effect on literary narrative (Bakhtin, "Forms"; Weimann). For an approach to the essay—a literary form not structured temporally—one might consider a different question. Walter Benjamin once pointed out that the form of the essay wavers between the ephemeral impressionism of the fragment and the deductive reasoning of the treatise (see, too, Adorno). The essay thus moves between two types of knowledge, the specific, personal knowledge produced by the momentary impressions of the essayist and the collective experience of larger social groups as it is encapsulated in tradition and registered in the language of the community. In schematic terms, this means that a reading of the essay must begin with the tension between private experience and public language. A study of Montaigne's essays and their backgrounds must look at those fragments of discourse that most clearly bear the imprint of the confrontation of public and private (Reiss).

The essays are marked in important ways by the massive crisis of public life that characterizes late sixteenth-century France. Many of the most celebrated passages depicting the author's own actions vividly evoke the political and social upheaval of the religious wars between Protestants and Catholics, or what he calls "our troubles." The much studied episode in "Of Practice," in which Montaigne faints after a fall from his horse, is seen against the background of "our third trouble, or our second (I do not quite remember which)" (268; 2.6). And the well-known scene in "Of Physiognomy," in which Montaigne's castle is invaded and its master taken prisoner, is carefully placed in the same political context.

On one level, this crisis of French public life may be understood as a crisis of language, of the language that mediates between private subjects and public life. When public life begins to unravel, new models of discourse are produced that make possible the eruption of a new type of subjectivity into language. Indeed, just as Montaigne, in the final pages of "Of Physiognomy," finds the safe retreat of his castle invaded by the "troubles" of political unrest, so is the language of the public world "invaded" by the way in which Montaigne's subjectivity redefines its terms from within its own vocabulary.

The tension between public life and private life is articulated in the opening lines of one of the chapters in the first book of the *Essays*, the short text entitled "Of Not Communicating One's Glory." "Of all the illusions in the world," begins Montaigne, "the most universally received is the concern for reputation and glory" (187; 1.41). Yet once Montaigne has expressed this commonplace, he goes on to denounce it. He quotes a passage from *Jerusalem Delivered*, the epic poem by his Italian contemporary Tasso. The Italian lines say that glory is merely a dream, an illusion that charms men away from the real essence of life. In Tasso's poem these lines are spoken by the wicked temptress Armida, whose design is to lure otherwise virtuous knights away from their duty and into a trap of idleness. By adopting the perspective of the female who wants to draw men away from their epic concern with glory, Montaigne defines his distance from the public world. At the same time, the critique of glory helps to suggest the anxious relation of the discourse of the essays to the generally sanctioned ideals of the culture that provides their background.

The epic concern with glory or earthly fame is a cornerstone of the Renaissance humanism that forms much of the background to the *Essays* (see Burckhardt). Montaigne assumes that his mostly male readers—men "of understanding" (177; 1.39)—would be familiar with the conventions and cultural commonplaces of humanist culture that were developed in Italy and transformed in northern Europe during the first decades of the sixteenth century. The humanist culture that Montaigne and his readers inherit is an essentially public culture, in which the pursuit of glory or political fame was understood to be the goal of all human activity. The great fifteenth- and sixteenth-century Italian humanists defined their project of resuscitating the culture of the classical world as essential to the civic life of the city-state (Burke, *Italian Renaissance*, ch. 5). To prepare young men for active participation in this life, the humanist schools promoted the study of those arts that might facilitate virtuous and prudent public action. Specifically, the humanist curriculum was built around the study of rhetoric and the study of history. Rhetoric, the science of persuasion, was aimed at developing the oratorical skills of young men who would later become ambassadors and civic leaders. At the same time (and especially for those of less exalted birth) it taught students to develop a good Latin prose style so that they could pursue careers of public service in mercantile states such as Florence and Venice (Kahn; Grafton and Jardine).

If the study of rhetoric facilitated political and diplomatic discourse, the study of history (and principally ancient history) aimed to teach young men the art of prudent political action. Studying the words and deeds of the illustrious Greeks and Romans allowed students to test and hone the faculty of judgment, and examples were considered for imitation or avoidance (Kahn; Hampton, *Writing*). These questions of judgment and prudence were explored with unmatched subtlety in the works of the two great Florentine political philosophers of the early sixteenth century, Niccolò Machiavelli and Francesco Guicciardini. The two writers are among the three or four Italians whose work Montaigne knew very well and with whom he assumed his readers would be familiar. Their interest in the establishment of laws of history forms a backdrop to Montaigne's fascination with the principles that motivate human action.

The two disciplines of rhetoric and history, a science of persuasion and a science of action, were joined by another topic of study that would take on extreme importance for Montaigne. This is the vast and somewhat shapeless body of moral philosophy and advice literature produced both during antiquity and during the late fifteenth and early sixteenth centuries. These treatises, on every subject from marriage to table manners, formed the staple of much humanist culture. As court society in Italy and France became more refined, humanist writers turned their attention to classical treatises on forming or transforming the self through philosophical and moral discipline. The moral treatises of Cicero and, later, Seneca and Plutarch became models for humanist writers concerned with advising their noble patrons on proper behavior. The most famous Renaissance example of this literature is Castiglione's *Book of the Courtier*, which Montaigne alludes to throughout the *Essays*. Thus in addition to the traditions of historiography and rhetoric, Montaigne would have assumed his readers to know moral philosophy, or what might be called a science of the self (Burckhardt, pt. 2, ch. 2).

The urbane court culture and political reflection that characterize the Italian Renaissance were imported into France during the first half of the sixteenth century under the patronage of Francis I. Francis's interest in Italian culture was matched only by his desire to unify France. As he embarked on ambitious plans to create uniform networks of judicial and fiscal authority throughout his kingdom, he created a bureaucracy requiring precisely the type of humanist intellectual responsible for so much of the important Italian Renaissance writing (Knecht). Within the ambit of the splendid Valois court there was thus produced a new type of Gallic humanism. The philological and political writings of such figures as Guillaume Budé sought to rival Italian humanists and promote the glory of Francis. The young king's patronage of the arts and interest in Italian poetry helped to ensure the wide diffusion of the great Italian literary innovators such as Petrarch, Boccaccio, and Ariosto. These writers, whom Montaigne alludes to throughout his work, were rivaled by such French writers as Clément Marot, Marguerite de Navarre, Joachim du Bellay, and Pierre de Ronsard. Thus Montaigne's interest in poetry, which he claims has particular power over him, involves not only the great classical Latin poems but also more recent works in the lyric traditions. His references in the first book of the *Essays* to the Petrarchan sonnets of his friend Etienne de La Boétie suggest this interest. At the same time, however (and more important for the question of public and private), there is the Christian humanism of Erasmus, which posited a more universal, Christ-centered moral philosophy and political ethos and enjoyed great currency throughout France. Erasmian doctrines inform, for example, the prose narratives of Rabelais, which all of Montaigne's readers would have known. The works of Rabelais offer yet another version of the humanist concern with virtue in public life as they narrate the development of gigantic protagonists from youthful folly to maturity, from adolescent self-involvement to dedication to political and civic duty.

If the political and intellectual fabric of the court of Francis I seemed to reproduce and redefine the humanist culture of the Italians, this period of Gallic humanism was short-lived. After the deaths of Francis I in 1547 and Henry II in 1559 the country was plunged into a civil war between increasingly fanatic factions of Protestants and Catholics. Montaigne (who says in "Of Liars" that he hates obstinacy almost as much as he hates falsehood [24; 1.9]) allied himself with the moderate Politiques group. This loose collection of intellectuals, whose members might be said in many ways to share the commitment to ethical moderation and dialogue that characterizes the ideals of much humanist thought, sought to mediate between the two increasingly intransigent adversaries (Kelley).

Under the pressure of this crisis of public life, the various fields of study that formed the core of the humanist project—history, rhetoric, and moral philosophy—all underwent radical transformations (Desan). Interpreting the nature of these transformations is crucial both for understanding and teaching the *Essays* and for imagining the type of reader that Montaigne might have had in mind. The rhetorical ideals of the Italian humanists and of the early sixteenth-century French humanists had been predominantly Ciceronian. Ciceronian rhetorical style, with its balanced periods and its elevated tone, had its origins in the public life and law courts of Rome; it offered the perfect ideal for a political and cultural movement that saw itself as trying to revive the Roman imperial or republican ideal. Moreover, its very roots in the spoken declamation reflected a model of political life in which human action was transparent and comprehensible to a specific community of like members. By the late sixteenth century, however, this public rhetorical ideal and the understanding of political life that it connoted had begun to be replaced by alternative models taken from the writings of Seneca and Tacitus. The "intimate" and friendly style of Seneca's *Letters to Lucilius* offered an alternative to the high-flown bombast of Cicero. Montaigne's discussion of Seneca praises the way in which "his virtue shows forth so live and vigorous in his writings" (545; 2.32). Similarly, the style of Tacitus, with its emphasis on the "point" or clever turn of phrase and the oblique witticism, seemed more attuned to the spirit of a time in which the public sphere and the clichés of Ciceronianism had been appropriated by increasingly shrill Protestant and Catholic extremist propaganda. As J. H. M. Salmon writes:

> In the new climate of absolutist politics Cicero, *pater eloquentiae*, yielded place to Tacitus, *pater prudentiae*. . . . The intellectual climate of the religious wars in France . . . at first encouraged the application of Ciceronian rhetoric to political debate, but as the wars intensified the Ciceronian emphasis upon the active participation of the citizen no longer seemed appropriate.   ("Cicero" 307, 323)

Montaigne's own suspicion of Ciceronian rhetoric stems from both his frustration at the excesses of propagandists and what seems to be an intense dislike of the personality of Cicero himself, who, says Montaigne, seemed to be interested only in fame and to concern himself with virtue only to the extent that it might win him glory. Thus, to return to "Of Not Communicating One's Glory," when Montaigne decries the thirst for glory he responds both to ideals of renown that now seem outdated in a time of political disarray and to a style of language that has been appropriated by propagandists.

The study of history, too, underwent a transformation during the period. Montaigne's interest in the rhetorical model of Tacitus is matched by his fascination for the method and matter of Tacitean historiography. Whereas the humanist historiographer Machiavelli had sixty years earlier devoted himself to writing a commentary on the histories of Livy, with their emphasis on the rise and political triumphs of Rome, Montaigne takes an interest in the Tacitean account of Roman decadence. This shift in interest suggests that the lessons of political prudence and wisdom illustrated in Tacitus seemed particularly relevant to political life in the dark times of the civil wars. The poisonings and intrigues recounted by Tacitus offered a mirror of French fortunes.

But if one can assume a general knowledge of the histories of Tacitus among those whom Montaigne might have hoped would be his readers, Montaigne himself seems interested in the Roman historian's modes of analysis and judgment as well. The genius of Tacitus, like the genius of Plutarch in his *Lives* (another text that Montaigne's readers would have known well), lies in the fact that he moves beyond an interest in heroic public deeds to analyze the customs and private habits of those he studies. Montaigne says in "Of the Art of Discussion" that Tacitus's form of history is "the most useful" (719; 3.8), since it tells of the effects the acts of tyrants have on their subjects, instead of merely focusing on heroic lives and deaths. For Montaigne, fascinated with his own foibles and with those of his contemporaries, this more "intimate" or private type of history writing was extremely attractive.

This turn to the private, which I have pointed to in both historiography and rhetoric, might be noted as well in the domain of moral philosophy. The close connection between court society and the cultivation of the perfect nobleman that was assumed by Castiglione's famous *Book of the Courtier* had itself become a source of scandal by the time of Montaigne. The French court was assumed—and not only by the austere provincial nobleman who sat down to write the *Essays* in the 1570s—to be a place of overrefinement, foppery, and effeminacy. The failure of royal will that characterized the reigns of both Henry III and Charles IX was seen to go hand in hand with the presumed decadence of court life. Against ideals of court life, Montaigne and many of his contemporaries turned to a new interest in Stoic thought, privileging the virtue of constancy as the key to survival in difficult times. For Montaigne, the interest in Stoicism was accompanied by a fascination with the moral writings of such late antique philosophers as Seneca and Plutarch. Their interest in the cultivation of the body, in personal health and hygiene, in diet, and so on, offered material for a kind of private moral reflection during a moment of national crisis when the very possibility of effective political praxis seemed in doubt.

My point here is that each of the three important domains that helped form the fabric of humanist culture in the fifteenth and early sixteenth centuries underwent a transformation in the late 1500s under the weight of the political and social disintegration of France. The turn to more intimate, personal, or private modes of understanding and valuing human experience was accompanied and fostered by a new interest in texts and traditions that had only been of minor importance earlier. This is not to claim that Montaigne's readers suddenly stopped reading Cicero, Livy, and Castiglione to focus exclusively on Seneca, Tacitus, and Plutarch. Rather, it is to suggest that the older public humanist tradition had in many ways calcified into cliché and been discredited. As Montaigne claims in his essay on the education of children, schooling had come to consist of the lifeless repetition of classical models, with no concern for the ethical, moral, and political choices that would face a young man whose life is dedicated to "conducting a war, governing a people, or gaining the friendship of a prince or a foreign nation" (109; 1.26). Thus the cultural context within which the *Essays* took form (and with which Montaigne assumed his readers to be familiar) was a kind of archaeological site, a space of several sedimented layers, in which humanist commonplaces jostled against new texts and traditions that were emerging into the forefront of intellectual fashion.

The year 1571, in which Montaigne began his famous "retirement" from the world to work on the *Essays*, was an auspicious year for Christendom. It was the year during which Spanish forces under Don Juan of Austria defeated the Turks at the Battle of Lepanto, thereby putting an effective halt to decades of Saracen threats to the security of Europe. It was, however, a terrible year for France. And it was surpassed in its horrors by the following year, which witnessed the Massacre of Saint Bartholomew, when hundreds of unsuspecting Protestants were murdered in their beds by Catholic troops—possibly at the instigation of the queen mother, Catherine de Médicis herself. The butchery sparked violence all across France (Salmon, *Society*). When Montaigne claims that he hates obstinacy only slightly less than he hates lying, his anger is doubtless directed both at those whose political fanaticism leads them to acts of butchery and cruelty and at those whose political and ideological inflexibility lead them to the abuse of language in the name of higher goals. In the essay "Of Liars" Montaigne laments the abuse of language by the people of his day. And he cautions, "We are only men, and only hold on to each other, by the word" (23; 1.9). With characteristic semantic richness Montaigne's phrase covers philosophical, political, and moral registers; human beings are distinguished from animals by their speech ("we are only men . . ."). And yet it is only when that speech becomes a "word," an ethically defined speech act (the word of a gentleman, for example), that it can offer the ground for political and social order. Clearly, in this melancholy pronouncement about humanity's dependence on the word, the confident humanist ideals of political rhetoric that informed the education of Montaigne and his readers seem fragile indeed.

Thus the backgrounds that operate most powerfully in Montaigne's dual project of contemplating himself and articulating a new mode of writing are those political problems and textual traditions involving the relation of public life to private life. Since Montaigne's essays work so extensively against clichés of moral philosophy, rhetoric, and historiographical discourse, simply to read Montaigne in a vacuum, as is often done in so-called great books courses, or to present him as a kind of inconsistent precursor to Descartes, as philosophy departments tend to do, fails to do justice to the troubling power of the *Essays*.

My undergraduate teaching of Montaigne's *Essays* takes place in both upper-level seminars on the French Renaissance and great books courses. In both contexts (though obviously with greater detail in the more specialized course) we attempt to read the *Essays* against the background of fundamental changes in the relation between the public and the private spheres. To suggest the ways in which the *Essays* appropriates and redistributes the terms of these struggles, we begin by focusing on a cultural problem that parallels the problem of political crisis. This is the theme of innovation. My students and I read two influential humanist treatises from the early sixteenth century, Machiavelli's *The Prince* and Erasmus's *On Good Manners for Boys*. Both these texts raise issues about the definition of the self, its deeds, and their role in the sphere of public action. Both texts address the relation between innovation and tradition in a number of contexts, including politics, society, and religion. Machiavelli, particularly in his third chapter, offers an analysis of the ways in which the prince can manipulate his subjects' desires for either change or permanence in order to consolidate his power. Erasmus focuses on the ways in which the self rejects its own bad habits and the customs of those around it in order to create itself as an aesthetically and ethically whole being able to act virtuously in civic life.

After we have studied these two analyses of the relation of present action to tradition and custom, we turn to a much more problematic example, but an example of great moment for the study of Montaigne. Both the political question of how to define the relation between private subjects and public life and the historical problem of the fragmentation of the public sphere during the wars of religion are raised by the reception of the work of Montaigne's best friend, Etienne de La Boétie. La Boétie seems to have been a kind of mentor to Montaigne, and his early death is lamented throughout the *Essays* (Rigolot, "Letters"). Yet La Boétie's destiny has more than a psychological importance for Montaigne. His major work, a political treatise criticizing the power of tyrants and entitled *Discourse on Voluntary Servitude*, was appropriated after its author's death by Protestant propagandists. They changed its name to *Contr'un* 'Against One,' and many of its discussions of human political behavior were recast, through judicious substitution of a few words here and there, as discussions of the troubles of France in particular. La Boétie's treatise thus became a specific critique of French monarchy and the *Discourse* was transformed into a seditious pamphlet serving the Protestant cause. Montaigne, who asserts throughout the *Essays* that he and his book are one, describes this misuse of his friend's work as a destruction of his body, which might have been torn into "a thousand different faces" (my trans; cf. Frame 752; 3.9) had he not come to its defense.

Before we begin our study of the *Essays*, my students and I spend a class session on La Boétie's text, which, because of its relative brevity (40 pages or so of very clear prose), offers a perfect mediation between the larger issues, raised above, involving political and moral philosophy and the specific rhetorical strategies of the essay form that Montaigne develops so brilliantly. For the sad fate of La Boétie not only illustrates the newly important role of propaganda in the early years of print culture but also offers an important rhetorical lesson as well. It suggests the risk run by any "objective" treatise, by any attempt to set forth a systematic argument about public life during a period of political trouble. Like Montaigne, La Boétie was a moderate Catholic. His treatise, which Montaigne calls a "scholastic exercise," makes the simple argument that one of the great mysteries of history is why many people allow themselves to be ruled by a single person. Were subjects simply to stop serving their rulers, says La Boétie, there would be no more tyranny. Yet it is the very abstraction of La Boétie's text that makes it so easy to appropriate. His *Discourse* is devoid of markers that might root it in history or in a particular context. It has, in a sense, no easily discernible background and thus can be made to take on significance contrary to the intentions of its author.

Against La Boétie's systematic treatise, one can set the images of both human activity and language presented by the *Essays*. Whereas La Boétie's text is separated from the person of its author, Montaigne insists on the rootedness of his book in his own experience. Furthermore, La Boétie's closely argued statements about life in the world contrast sharply with Montaigne's own digressive ramblings. By comparing their discussions of the relation between custom and innovation, one may begin to understand Montaigne's appropriation of the discourse of public action.

One claim of La Boétie's treatise is that human beings continue to allow themselves to be ruled by tyrants because custom has blinded them to the absurdity of the fact that one person rules over many. "Let us say then," says La Boétie, "that men take as natural those things to which they have become accustomed and which have nourished them. But only that is natural to which a simple and unperverted nature calls men. Thus the first reason for voluntary servitude is custom" (150). He goes on to compare the subjects of tyranny to dray horses, who first bite the bit and resist being tamed but later actually enjoy their harness. Thus custom makes political domination possible by clouding our relation to the world.

This concern for custom is a central issue throughout Montaigne's *Essays*, from his famous discussions of the new world cannibals to his analyses of judgment. It is first addressed comprehensively in "Of Custom and Not Easily Changing an Accepted Law" (1.23). In the first half of this essay Montaigne claims that custom is a "violent prejudice" whose only authority lies in the "hoary beard and the wrinkles of the usage that goes with it" (85; 1.23). This face is then described as a mask that, once torn off, restores the subject to "a much surer status." Custom is described by La Boétie as an epistemological problem with a political dimension. Montaigne follows La Boétie's claim that custom blinds human beings, but he is careful to excise from his argument anything that might seem to advocate the throwing off of customary or traditional political structures. For Montaigne, the problem is not how custom enslaves subjects to tyrants but how it keeps human beings from seeing the face of things (Starobinski, *Montaigne et mouvement* 87–111).

Yet Montaigne continues to use the very terms posited by La Boétie when his discussion of custom touches on the enslavement of peoples. His concern, however, is with laws instead of tyrants, with language and lawyers instead of deeds. "What can be stranger," he asks, "than to see a people obliged to obey laws that they never understood" (85)? And he goes on to condemn a legal system in which laws are incomprehensible to those they control because they are written in Latin and require the interpretation of lawyers. Tyranny here is the custom of the judiciary, which intimidates people through useless erudition in languages other than French. Given both La Boétie's precedent and the political context within which Montaigne writes, one might at this point expect a criticism of political power, which thrives on mystification—as Montaigne notes at several other points in the *Essays*. Yet Montaigne concludes the discussion of custom a paragraph later by arguing that, though he criticizes the way that custom dominates its victims, he is only talking about private life, "for it is the rule of rules, and the universal law of laws, that each man should observe those of the place he is in" (86). An epistemological critique of custom concludes with a conservative affirmation that makes "voluntary servitude" the duty of everyone in times of political trouble.

This reference to a "law of laws" is striking. It not only concludes Montaigne's discussion of the tyranny of the judiciary with a gesture of political submission but, by its very abstraction, it also defines the question of public and private in discursive terms. It raises again the issue with which I opened this discussion, the question of the relation between the personal knowledge of the essayist and the generalized, perceptual discourse of politics, law, and moral philosophy. Montaigne lays down the law of political conformity by invoking a universal statement applicable to all people at all times and beyond the whim of personal caprice. Yet at the very moment that he evokes a universal precept, Montaigne engages in his own ironic mystification. After recommending the "universal law of laws," he cites it word for word: "It is a fine thing to obey your country's laws" (86). The universal law says that we should obey the law. The citation he offers is a Greek proverb culled from a widely circulated anthology of ancient sayings. Montaigne cites this law, however, not in French, but in the original Greek—a language that neither he nor many of his readers have mastered. The very readers of the *Essays* thus find themselves in the position of those peoples, mentioned a moment earlier by the lawyer Montaigne, who are subject to laws they cannot understand. Domination through "foreign" laws gives way to the ironic affirmation of political conformity as the "law of laws." Yet in this new strategy of domination, it is Montaigne himself, through his processes of citation, who becomes both tyrant and liberator, since he first cites the law in a foreign language and then translates it.

By playfully turning the citation of a Greek proverb into a game of "domination" and mystification played with his readers, Montaigne leaves his imprint on the language of the public world. The proverb evokes the troubled background of the French wars of religion and the injustice done to his friend La Boétie. Indeed, Montaigne also mentions the phrase in "Of Friendship" (1.28), where he points out that it was his unfortunate friend's first precept (thereby making explicit the connection between La Boétie and this "law of laws" that "Of Custom" makes tacitly). Yet Montaigne's use of this fragment of "public" discourse within the textual play of "Of Custom" affirms the particularity of private sensibility and the power of the individual to recast the language of politics. The space that makes this new sensibility possible is the space of the essay itself, in which elements from different textual and historical backgrounds (the reference to "foreign" laws, the Greek proverb) can be given new meaning by being juxtaposed. Moreover, in the very specific context of the essay on custom, the juxtaposition is accompanied by a bracketing of questions of political domination, as Montaigne splits the question of custom (presented by La Boétie as a foundation of tyranny) into two parts. His claim in the first part of the essay that custom is a problem of epistemology is followed, in the second half of the essay, by the assertion that laws once established should not be easily changed. Montaigne may liken custom to a mask that hides the world, but he says of political life, "I am disgusted with innovation, no matter what face it may wear . . . for I have seen the very harmful effects of it" (86). The final pages of the essay assert the absolute split between public conformity and private liberty. The hinge in this structure, the foreign phrase that divides the essay exactly in two, is the proverb discussed a moment ago, with its claim, in Greek, that submission to the laws of one's country is a fine thing.

The chapter on custom offers a useful port of entry to a discussion of the *Essays*. It raises a number of issues that can be taken in various directions by both teacher and students. First, in terms of the teaching of the rest of the essays, the essay on custom, with its bipartite form, presents a somewhat schematic working-out of the problem of public and private. Later essays will address the same issue in much more complex ways. By beginning with this early essay, one can elucidate a problem that will appear throughout the book with (to recall Montaigne's description of La Boétie) "a thousand different faces." Moreover, in historical terms, Montaigne's clear anxiety about the world of politics opens the question of how political thought in the late sixteenth century attempted to rethink the relation between public action and private action. In my upper division courses on the Renaissance, I follow Montaigne's text with Corneille's *Le Cid*, which offers a dramatic treatment of the confrontation between private virtue and political centralization. In terms of the history of political thought, Montaigne's playful transformation of discourse about public life exemplifies a particular combination of intellectual skepticism and political conservatism that may be traced from Montaigne to later thinkers such as Emerson, Nietzsche, and Ortega y Gasset. The role of the essay form in this tradition is crucial, and Montaigne's text offers a good starting point.

Thus the historical problem of the collapse of civic order in late sixteenth-century France, what Montaigne calls "our troubles," may be taken as a fundamental background to the *Essays*. Since this historical context raises the general political question of the relation between private subjects and the public sphere, it also poses the problem of how private subjectivity defines itself at a moment of public disarray—a problem crucial to the rhetoric of Montaigne and to the development of the essay form. Moreover, Montaigne's insistence on the private world of skeptical reflection, as opposed to the riotous public world evoked by such contemporaries as Ronsard, d'Aubigné, and (though unintentionally) La Boétie, raises issues about the ways in which we as readers of the *Essays* define our own relations between the private experience of reading and the public world of action, between textual play and political trouble.

The Rhetoric of the *Essays*

Barbara C. Bowen

Renaissance Rhetoric

Let us suppose that you are an American undergraduate reading Montaigne's *Essays* for the first time. You know that this is a sixteenth-century book, and you have a few general notions about the European Renaissance—discovery of the New World, invention of printing and double-entry bookkeeping, flowering of art and architecture all over Europe, realization that the sun, not the earth, is the center of the universe—but few of these notions will help you to understand why Montaigne wrote the kind of book he wrote. Your intellectual luggage, as the French nicely put it, is deficient in two ways: you know neither what Montaigne and his readers had read nor how they thought about writing and reading. When you open a book for the first time, you have attitudes and expectations quite different from those of a Renaissance reader.

What can teachers do about this problem? About students' lack of familiarity with Montaigne's predecessors, very little. I can hardly stipulate, as the prerequisite for my Montaigne seminar, familiarity with the works of Plato, Cicero, Seneca, Plutarch, Diogenes Laertius, Augustine, Erasmus, and several dozen others whom students have never heard of, let alone read. I can, and will, ask them to read in translation a dialogue by Cicero and a few of Seneca's letters, Plutarch's moral treatises and Erasmus's *Adages* and *Colloquies*, but that's just scratching the surface. Too often students will have to take my word, or the word of other Montaigne scholars, about the earlier writers with whom Montaigne is explicitly or implicitly conducting a dialogue.

More can be done about the problem of how Montaigne's readers read, because most students are quite well informed about Renaissance educational methods and the training of schoolchildren (those fortunate enough to attend school) in the study of literature. Paul Grendler's survey of Italian education is generally applicable to France, and those who can read French will find a storehouse of information in Paul Porteau's old but still invaluable book on Montaigne and sixteenth-century pedagogy. One of the most important aspects of this training, for an understanding of Montaigne's essays, is the study of rhetoric.

The word *rhetoric* has today two distinct meanings, neither of which is relevant to the Renaissance. In academic circles, it is used by some modern critics to designate their particular method of looking at literary texts (Genette, *Introduction*; Kritzman, *Destruction*; and others). Such critics may discuss the same rhetorical techniques that Montaigne used, but in very different contexts; their analysis of metaphor and metonymy is not integrated into any "classical" rhetorical system, and they see literary works as independent of their author, which a Renaissance reader would not have been able to do. "Modern" readings of Renaissance texts can be intellectually stimulating, but they often have little connection with the attitudes of Montaigne and his sixteenth-century readers. The second modern meaning of *rhetoric* is pejorative: That's mere rhetoric, we say, postulating a dichotomy, which the Renaissance would have thought eccentric, between substance and "mere" style.

From antiquity through the eighteenth century, the basis of general education was the program of seven liberal arts: the trivium (grammar, rhetoric, logic) and quadrivium (arithmetic, geometry, astronomy, music). The content and emphasis of this program varied widely, but all pupils began with grammar (i.e., the acquisition of enough Latin to read it, write it, and converse in it) and then advanced to rhetoric. An excellent outline of what training in rhetoric meant can be found in the first chapter of Peter France's book. To summarize as succinctly as possible: rhetoric teaches how to speak and write Latin that is clearly organized, stylistically pleasing, and persuasive. Cicero and his followers divide rhetoric into five basic subjects: invention (not "inventing" in the modern sense but "finding" the arguments we intend to use); disposition (arrangement of these arguments in a coherent and convincing order); elocution (style: use of all forms of literary embellishment); memory (often elaborate mnemonic techniques); and delivery (not just intonation but gesture, facial expression, and even dress). By the sixteenth century the last two were much less stressed, since the emphasis was now on training writers rather than orators, and in the course of the sixteenth century invention and disposition were transferred to logic, leaving style as the essential concern of rhetoric.

Other basic principles of rhetoric are relevant to Montaigne's essays. Oratory, and hence literature, is of three kinds: judicial, dealing with conjectural legal and juridical topics, usually in the past (Brutus's and Antony's speeches about the dead Caesar in act 3, scene 2, of *Julius Caesar*); demonstrative, expressing praise or blame, usually in the present (Eudemon's eulogy of the young prince in chapter 15 of *Gargantua*); and deliberative, that is, persuading, dissuading, or exhorting, usually in reference to the future (Rodrigue's *stances* in act 1, scene 6, of *Le Cid*). Nearly all Renaissance literature is addressed to an implied reader or listener (whereas modern authors are more likely to be talking to themselves).

There are three kinds of style: lofty, middle, and low, and each has its specific linguistic conventions. Racine's tragedies are exclusively in lofty style (abstract vocabulary, Ciceronian sentence structure, constant use of periphrasis and metonymy), whereas Molière's comedies are usually in middle style but can use low style for the conversation of peasants and servants. Every speech (text) should be neatly divided (disposition) into separate parts, most usually: entrance (exposition), narration (what we are talking about), proposition (brief summary of the argument), division (into A, B, Ai, Bi, and so on), confirmation (supporting examples), confutation (of adversary's arguments), and conclusion. Try this on Hamlet's "To be or not to be" (deliberative) monologue, where you will find a proposition (line 1), a division ("Whether . . . or . . . ,"), a confirmation (lines 6–8), a confutation (lines 10–14), and a conclusion ("Thus conscience doth make cowards of us all"). Literary works as well as speeches often began with a *captatio benevolentiae*, an attempt to secure the reader's or listener's good will at the outset, and this attempt might well consist of the so-called modesty topos ("Unaccustomed as I am to public speaking . . ."). The persons addressed will presumably be more in sympathy with an author with whom they can identify.

We should not think of rhetoric only as training in oratory. It covered subjects that today are quite separate from it. It was always closely associated with logic, but it also embraced what we call psychology (the orator must be able to arouse the passions of an audience and to that end must understand the passions), literary criticism (as late as 1565, the first three sections of Ronsard's *Abbregé de l'art poetique françois* are "De l'invention," "De la disposition," and "De l'élocution"), and, more surprisingly, ethics. The traditional definition of the orator was "a good man skilled in speaking," and moral content and moral betterment were inevitable concomitants of literature until the end of the eighteenth century.

School training in this rhetorical setting was radically different from school training today in terms of reading, writing, and speaking. While reading, students kept commonplace books in which they collected dramatic speeches, pithy moral tags, and other "gems" culled from a variety of authors, to use when needed in their own writing and speaking. Lavish quotation from classical authors, which today would be frowned on as lack of originality, was the mark both of learning and of respect for the wisdom of the ancients.

Renaissance writing owes a great deal to another basic principle of rhetoric, *amplificatio*, the expansion of a subject by means of examples (which can be quotations from classical authors) and assorted stylistic devices. Peter France gives a delightful example, unfortunately in Latin, of this technique (3). Hamlet adds to "the whips and scorns of time" an impressive series of six illustrations of this abstract concept to make his moral dilemma more moving (or, as the rhetorician would put it, make his argument more persuasive). Not surprisingly, some students of rhetoric grew up to become Renaissance humanists with a passion for collecting commonplaces of all kinds: proverbs (4.151 in Erasmus's *Adages*); emblems (212 in the 1612 edition of Alciati); even *facetiae*, or jokes (981 in the 1574 edition of Lodovico Domenichi's *Facetie, motti et burle*). These works are all good illustrations of the art of *copia*, or stylistically varying what one says in as many ways as possible. One of Erasmus's great best-sellers was his book on this topic, the *De copia*, in which he provides 146 variations on the Latin sentence "Your letter gave me great pleasure," and 200 on "As long as I live I will remember you."

Both writing and speaking, then, were thought of not as the expression of original thought but as the deployment, upon traditional topics, of rhetorical skills and devices. The standard speaking exercise, until well past the Renaissance, was the *disputatio*, or argument between the supporters and adversaries of a stated position (this exercise survives today in the debates of our speech departments). The speaker's personal opinion about the debate topic ("that the world is flat" or "that women are inferior to men") was irrelevant. The basic written exercise was the *chria*, or essay on a commonplace topic: virtue, friendship, prudence. The topic could also be a paradox ("That drunkenness is a virtue"), a dilemma, or a question ("Was it right for Brutus to kill Caesar?").

Montaigne's Essays

How can all this help us to read Montaigne? Look first at the titles of his chapters, and you will find many standard rhetorical subjects. Commonplaces: "Of Idleness" (is it good or bad?), "Of Constancy" (how to define it), "Of Friendship," and many more. Paradoxes: "By Diverse Means We Arrive at the Same End," "That to Philosophize Is to Learn to Die," "Of Evil Means Employed to a Good End." Apparently small traditional topics that Montaigne will amplify into large essays: presumption, coaches, vanity. You will also find, especially in the first book, essays discussing traditional rhetorical topics. "Of Liars" is about memory, the fourth topic of Ciceronian rhetoric, and "Of Prompt or Slow Speech" discusses the relative merits for orators of improvisation and careful preparation.

But the rhetoric of Montaigne's essays is not, in any traditional sense, obvious. His chapters do not resemble formal, structured orations; they are more like the apparently rambling discourse of Seneca's letters, Plutarch's *Moralia*, and Erasmus's longer adages. And if you have already dipped into them, you may well ask, But doesn't Montaigne despise and reject rhetoric? Does he not categorize it in, by no coincidence, a chapter on Cicero as "mere babble and talk" (183; 1.40) and elsewhere as "our borrowed incrustations" (108; 1.26) and by a variety of other pejorative terms? Does he not constantly claim that the best language is "a simple, natural speech, the same on paper as in the mouth," "soldierly," unaffected, natural, and negligent (127; 1.26)? Did he not compose an entire chapter, "Of the Vanity of Words," attacking the presumptuous artificiality of rhetoric, "the art of deceiving and flattering" and even "that poison" (222; 1.51)? The very structure of some essays seems deliberately to undermine rhetorical order; "Of Friendship" and "Of Repentance" partly treat traditional subdivisions of their topics, only to conclude that none of them is "true" friendship or "true" repentance. Edwin Duval sees the chapter on Cicero as a clever piece of demonstrative rhetoric that is actually attacking Ciceronian "disposition" while apparently fulminating about style.

Disapproval of rhetoric is as old as rhetoric itself; in every age intellectuals have berated it for its affinity with lying and its vaunted ability to make insignificant things sound important. Montaigne's disparaging comparison of rhetoric to make-up and cookery, in "Of the Vanity of Words," dates back to Plato and is echoed by other sixteenth-century authors. Montaigne's attacks on rhetoric are part of his constant insistence on *things* as opposed to *words*; this is the framework of his most famous essay, "Of the Education of Children." The student will "be asked for an account not merely of the words of his lesson, but of its sense and substance" (110; 1.26); "I want the substance to stand out, and so to fill the imagination of the listener that he will have no memory of the words" (127; 1.26).

This words-things dichotomy sounds very much like our modern dismissal of mere rhetoric, but there is a crucial difference. Montaigne can disparage not just rhetoric but writing and writers, including himself, as much as he likes; "we do nothing but write glosses about each other," he says sneeringly (818; 3.13), and "so many words for the sake of words alone" (721; 3.9)! But he cannot, like a modern author with no rhetorical training behind him, write without reference to rhetoric. Every chapter owes something, whether in subject, in structure, or in style, to the rhetorical background sketched out above, and the plain, simple speech that is the same on the paper as in the mouth is an unrealizable dream—or a deliberate attempt to mislead. Critics disagree about the genuineness of Montaigne's apparent rejection of rhetoric.

We have already seen that many essays treat traditional subjects with some elements of traditional organization. "Of Glory" begins with a standard proposition that is also a division: "There is the name and the thing. The name is a sound which designates and signifies the thing . . ." (468; 2.16). "Of Friendship" treats the four obvious kinds of *amicitia* that would occur to any schoolchild: love of children for fathers, of brothers for each other, of men for women, and of Greek men for boys. Certainly, Montaigne loves to subvert "disposition" by changing the subject; inserting digressions; writing on two topics at once ("Of Vanity" is about both vanity and travel); beginning a chapter with something that appears completely extraneous, like the disquisition on painting grotesques at the beginning of "Of Friendship"; inserting the conclusion several pages before the end of the chapter, as in "Of Liars" ("In truth lying is an accursed vice" [23; 1.9]); or even first mentioning the subject of the chapter in its final paragraph ("Of Giving the Lie"). His constant additions to each chapter are another way of subverting disposition. Try reading just the 1580 text of a short essay in books 1 or 2, and then read the final version; you will get a quite different impression.

So far I have barely mentioned style, *elocutio*, most commonly subdivided into figures of thought, figures that appeal to the emotions, two dozen or so tropes, and over a hundred figures of words and syntax, most of which are no longer in our critical vocabulary. Montaigne uses dozens of these figures, but let us consider only some of the most important and first of all the one that is perhaps his particular trademark as a writer: asyndeton. In Ramist rhetoric this is a "figure of words" defined as the omission of logical connectives; a common dictionary illustration today is "I came, [and then] I saw, [and then] I conquered." Now look at a few sentences in Montaigne's last and greatest chapter, "Of Experience," in a passage on his cherished subject of the inadequacy of language:

> I have observed in Germany [what happened in Germany] that Luther has left as many divisions and altercations over the uncertainty of his opinions, and more, as he raised about the Holy Scriptures.
> [This goes to show that] our disputes are purely verbal. [Suppose] I ask what is "nature," "pleasure," "circle," "substitution." The question is one of words, and is answered in the same way. [Let's take this definition:] "A stone is a body." But if you pressed on: [and asked further] "And what is a body?" [The answer would be:] "Substance." [If you then asked] "And what is substance?" and so on, you would finally drive the respondent to the end of his lexicon. [So that instead of words leading us to things] we exchange one word for another word, often more unknown. . . .   (818–19; 3.13)

Readers of Montaigne quickly learn to supply the missing logical links as they go, but some rhetorical devices in the *Essays* are so subtle as to be easily missed. Digression, today usually considered a vice of style, especially by the French, was a perfectly respectable figure of thought and often used by Montaigne. Sometimes he likes to draw attention to it with charmingly comic effect, as when at the end of a chapter titled "Of Coaches," which discusses seasickness, fear, travel, royal virtue, royal ostentation, and European cruelty in the New World, he begins the last paragraph with "Let us fall back to our coaches" (698; 3.6). Another venerable figure of thought is prosopopeia, imagined speech by real or fictional characters. In "That to Philosophize Is to Learn to Die," Montaigne imagines a long consolatory speech by Nature (64–67; 1.20) explaining that death is part of the order of the universe; the whole passage is an exemplary demonstrative oration.

It is easy enough to find examples in the *Essays* of nearly all Renaissance rhetorical figures, but the one requiring most emphasis is undoubtedly metaphor. It has often been said that Montaigne thinks in metaphors, and many of them are hoary old chestnuts of the rhetorical tradition: life as a journey, human emotion as wind and water, education as agriculture and as digestion, literary creations as offspring, writing as woven material ("contexture" [301; 1.10]). Certainly Montaigne often uses and develops these metaphors in an original way, but his sixteenth-century reader would have been sharply aware of the difference between these time-honored analogies and the genuinely new and striking ones, especially for his own writing: the essays as grotesques (135; 1.28), as an ill-fitted mosaic (736; 3.9); the translation has "patchwork," which is not quite right), as a fricassee (826; 3.13), or as excrement (721; 3.9); in a much-discussed passage (504; 2.18), he compares himself to a painter producing a self-portrait and states that his book is consubstantial with (has the same substance as) its author.

Not just articles but books have been written on Montaigne's metaphors. I want here simply to draw attention to his application of both the tried-and-true analogies he learned as a boy and daring "new" metaphors that contrast with them. A number of other aspects of rhetoric should be stressed: his use of the modesty topos in his "To the Reader" (2) and elsewhere, his claim, for instance, that his is "a humble and inglorious life" (611; 3.2), when in fact he was twice Mayor of Bordeaux and a negotiator with king and princes; his constant appeal to supporting arguments, quotations, and anecdotes taken either from classical literature or from his own experience; his use of "dissimulation," not a moral defect but a rhetorical variety of irony often used for humorous effect, as in the modesty topos. And we must not forget that one purpose of rhetoric was to create an impression of spontaneity and even carelessness. The ideal courtier portrayed in Castiglione's *Book of the Courtier*, one of the sixteenth century's most read books, as Montaigne well knew, is characterized by "grace," which includes the untranslatable Italian *sprezzatura*, a kind of careless brilliance achieved only by the use of rhetoric. The courtier must have "knowledge" (invention); must speak or write with "a good order" (disposition); his words must be "proper, select, lustrous, and well formed" (style); and his speaking requires "a good voice . . . with distinct enunciation and with fitting manner and gestures" (delivery) (54–55). Having mastered all this, he will be able to persuade his audience that he is speaking or writing easily, naturally, and without artifice—precisely the impression Montaigne wishes his writing to give us.

To recognize and appreciate the rhetorical elements in the essays is not to belittle their originality but to heighten it. Out of traditional ways of thinking about writing, in which originality was not stressed, Montaigne produced his own writing, which is both traditional and new, both highly conventional and highly personal. The essays can speak directly to the modern reader about permanent human concerns, but I believe that recognition of the rhetorical tradition out of which they grew is essential to understanding them in their Renaissance context.

GENERAL APPROACHES

The *Essays:* An Overall View

Gérard Defaux

> There may be some people of my temperament, I who
> learn better by contrast than by example, and by flight
> than by pursuit. . . .
> —Montaigne, "On the Art of Discussion"

How should we teach Montaigne to our graduate and undergraduate students, what should we teach them when we teach the *Essays*, and why? Since instruction, as Montaigne himself remarks, is sometimes much better done by "contrast" than by "example" and by "flight" than by "pursuit," my tentative answer to these difficult questions will first assume a totally negative form. I begin with a statement of what we should not do if we want to approach the text of the *Essays* in a truly critical way—I mean in a way that may be considered both effective and pertinent to its object.

I am convinced that, to be at least possible if not productive, any reading of the *Essays*, and any apprenticeship of it, must at all cost avoid three dangers. Long the cause of much straying and foundering, they are even less excusable today, not only because their existence has been manifest for some time now but also because the rather infelicitous experience of certain of our predecessors might have served as a warning to us. I am speaking of the obsession with the referent, the temptation to anthologize, and the confusion of the voices and levels of discourse.

I call obsession with the referent the preoccupation—if not exclusive, at least dangerously dominant—that Montaignian criticism, from its very beginnings, has exhibited in general, not for the text of the *Essays* as such but for the author, the flesh and blood person who expresses himself in the text and who declares that he is portrayed there. The only "reality" of this author today is quite obviously that which the text gives him, a reality that could not exist except on paper, in and through the text. However, our first spontaneous reaction to the *Essays* has always been the wish to reconstruct this reality as an independent entity existing not only outside the text but also, in the most unexpected way, against it, against the obvious, given facts that the text itself provides. It is true that nearly all our classics, from Villon to Proust, have suffered from this so-called reconstruction. Such an exercise is tempting and even, in a sense, inevitable. But no one, I feel, with the exception perhaps of Jean-Jacques Rousseau, has been more subjected to this approach than Montaigne, whose text, "consubstantial with its author" (504; 2.18), perpetually invites the reader to extrapolate in this direction. Indeed, as we shall soon see, seldom has a text authorized to such a degree this displacement toward its author or so clearly stated its mimetic vocation, its referential and descriptive aims, its irrepressible desire for representation. We all remember, for example, the famous declaration made by Montaigne in his chapter "Of Repentance": "In this case we go hand in hand and at the same pace, my book and I. In other cases one may commend or blame the work apart from the workman; not so here; he who touches the one, touches the other" (611; 3.2).

That this kind of unequivocal and clear-cut statement repeats itself ad nauseam in the *Essays* certainly helps us understand why great scholars like Donald Frame, Alexandre Micha, and Roger Trinquet or, even more recently, Géralde Nakam, could write the books they wrote. But it should not make us forget the evidence that the leap this form of biographical criticism makes outside the text leads critics themselves, methodologically speaking, into a cul-de-sac. It leads them to questions that must necessarily remain unanswered; it creates in them a stubborn desire to resolve problems obviously not open to any solution. Indeed, what kind of results can literary critics hope to achieve, who devote their time, efforts, and energy to an evaluation of the precision with which Montaigne "approaches," "grasps," and "renders" reality? Their entire activity ultimately consists in wondering if, as the painter claims, the portrayal truly resembles the original, if the "painting" does not betray the person, if, in a word, "the Self of the *Essays*" and that of "the man who wrote them" are the same or not (Sayce, Essays 68). Postulating what is impossible and from the start locking itself in aporia, a strategy of this kind necessarily condemns its author to the most radical impotence, to the endless repetition of the same groundless discourse; it presupposes a given that, decidedly, since it no longer exists, does not allow for any verification and that, forever gone with the wind, consequently no longer depends on the realm of being but on the hypothetical one, at best plausible or possible, of fiction. Montaigne, however, had warned us of this critical aporia; he had taken every possible precaution to remind his reader that his book was being written "for few men and for few years" (751; 3.9), especially for those neighbors, relatives, or friends who already knew him and would be perfectly capable of judging the veracity of the testimony he left them, who would take pleasure in "associating and conversing with [him] again" (503; 2.18), who, finally, would be able to "recover here some features of [his] habits and temperament," and thus, by means of his book, "keep the knowledge they have had of [him] more complete and alive" ("To the Reader" 2). Since the self—the referent—is no longer here today to guarantee the truth of its representation, we have no choice but to give up a practice that, in any case, supposes on the reader's part a direct, intimate knowledge of the subject described. We are forced to abandon any inclination we might have to compare the original with its copy and to fall back on the text alone, approaching it with questions and concerns that will necessarily differ from those of Montaigne's contemporaries. Since his death, there has not been, there is no longer, there will never be anything exterior to the text, any *hors-texte* appropriate to the *Essays*. As Jules Brody said in one of his "philological readings" of Montaigne, "The man is dead, only his words endure."

Named, for lack of a better expression, the "temptation to anthologize" 'la tentation du florilège,' our second danger creates what is perhaps for the interpreter an even more pernicious risk, one less easily skirted than the former for several reasons. First, because it necessarily participates in any hermeneutical enterprise, being located in the text itself, at its very level, at the intersection of the page and the critic's gaze. Second, because the very specificity of the text here in question, its peculiar structure—what Montaigne himself calls his "embrouillure" (995; 3.9), its "allongeails" (963; 3.9), and other spirited variations—its appearance as a formless amalgam—a "marqueterie mal jointe" (964; 3.9), an "amas" of "pieces" (32; 1.8) and "parements empruntez" (1055; 3.12)—all these "mouvements fortuites et impremeditez" (963; 3.9) dictate, according to him, the elaboration of the text. All these well-known characteristics that make the *Essays* a text forever in the making, a fragmented, unfinished, reflexive, and open text, bear this risk, this temptation, to its peak. Nothing is in fact more legitimate for literary critics confronted with a text of this nature than to act on the authority of the disorder, negligence, and fragmentation that they believe are there, in order to indulge in an undue *bricolage* with the text. After all, does not our own raison d'être, as professional critics, lie precisely in explicating texts, in rendering them more accessible and transparent, more *readable* than they are—in accounting for the difficulties raised in their interpretation by substituting everywhere causality for chance, clarity for obscurity, and order for disorder, by bringing to the surface systems and structures, intentions and reasons concealed in the profundity of the text? And, if we want to carry out successfully this project of mastery, this twofold task of uncovering and penetration, what then could be more expedient than to devote ourselves at first, impelled by Montaigne's own practice, to a "plundering" of the text's finest flowers, to a pious and sanctifying gathering of the most memorable and best-written maxims, with the obvious moral aim of compiling from these an annotated catalog and thus presenting the reader—always in search of instruction—not only with the text's "substantificque moelle" but also with the pith, essence, and even quintessence of all wisdom and happiness? And, since a first step is generally followed by a second, what then could be more logical and more necessary, widening our horizons, than to devote ourselves to a thematic reading of Montaigne's *Essays*, to the fabrication of one of those syntheses whose titles are only too familiar to us: "Montaigne and Death," "Montaigne and Religion," "Montaigne and the Portrayal of the Self," or even—such subtle variations!—"The Conservatism," "The Stoicism," or "The Skepticism" of Montaigne?

In this respect, there is perhaps nothing more revealing than Hugo Friedrich's monumental work *Montaigne* (1968). Both its archetypal value and the admiration it inspires lead me to use it here as an example. As Friedrich clearly indicates in his foreword, his ambitions are more historical in nature than literary. What he seeks to isolate and describe above all in Montaigne is a *thought* and the importance and significance of this thought in our historical becoming. This explains the vast thematic groupings that he abstracts from the individual essays, essays that he never considers as the end of his analysis but as his basic material, from which he constructs his own discourse. This also explains the methodological bias that is an entirely natural result of his procedure: that is, to deal with individual essays in themselves, to consider them as textual entities in "exceptional cases" only. The author justifies this parti pris in a few brief remarks, as if it needed no justification, alleging not only the inherent necessities of his project but also the unfortunate lack of an orderly and synthetic mind revealed within the text. Since, he proclaims, there are only "very few" essays that really constitute a "whole," since—alas!—Montaigne "never quite surveys what he has already said about a matter" and finally since "no single passage expresses the totality of his thought concerning it," a critic who, like himself, essentially proposes to divide Montaigne's text according to subject matter is consequently "*authorized* to regroup the scattered fragments in order to reconcile them with each other" (9; my emphasis).

If this kind of reasoning itself needs no commentary, this is not true of the principles on which it is based. For in the end nothing, except of course the requirements of his historian-of-ideas project, *authorizes* Friedrich to say that the essays, taken in themselves, form only rarely a "whole." The very arrangement of the subjects in "chapters," the relative self-sufficiency of these chapters in the book—what Montaigne himself calls the lack of "continuity"—the often repeated affirmation that each of them constitutes, properly speaking, an *essay*, a testing of the author's judgment, all of this persuades us that, on the contrary, the essay, or the "chapter," is the only significant textual unit in Montaigne's work. And if Friedrich had had a clearer notion of the literary object, he certainly would not have attempted, to quote Jean-Yves Pouilloux, "to organize the disorder of the *Essays*," to sum up, to "regroup" reflections that are scattered in different places; he would not have tried "to adopt a comprehensive view of such and such a subject," to impose, finally, on the work a treatment that its author, an avowed enemy of all systems, would never himself have conceived. Instead, he ought to have used his talent "to pose the question of this very disorder" (40–41).

This is an extremely pertinent and fertile question, which allows us not only to define a protocol of reading better suited to the text but also to avoid the third and last risk in our critical exploration, the danger that I referred to as the confusion of the voices and levels of discourse. By this, I mean the insensitivity on the part of critics, the lack of discernment that obscures the nuances, differences, and contradictions in Montaigne's work; that trans-forms a subtle exercise in writing, an analysis of the self by the self through the process of *écriture*, into a treatise of practical ethics; that pushes us into a simplification and reduction of the whole, into taking each word in the text literally, forgetful of the spirit that quickens the letter. It is not enough, for example, to act on the authority of Montaigne's authorship to say subse-quently that all the discourses that we find in the *Essays* belong to him absolutely and to the same degree, that they all have the same direct and immediate relation to him, that they are all of the same nature and perform the same function. Of course, they all are in a sense incontestably his, but certain ones are more so than others.

In this respect, the capital distinction that Montaigne himself establishes at the beginning of "Of Repentance" (3.2) should receive more attention than it has heretofore. The passage is well known, but has it ever really been understood? To be sure, Montaigne tells us, his soul is always, as in the past, "in apprenticeship and on trial." If it could finally "gain a firm footing," he goes on, "I would not make essays, I would make decisions" (611). He therefore continues, as before, to write "essays." But he is no longer writing them in exactly the same way, or for the same reasons: he is now giving them a different function. Before, in the past, if writing already constituted for him the means of portraying himself and of making himself known, it also was used by him "to form" himself. His project was therefore twofold: on the one hand, descriptive and directed toward others; on the other, normative and reflexive, turned in on itself. Today, however, he no longer has the ambition of making himself other, better than he is; he does not any more wish "to fashion and compose" himself to "bring [himself] out" (504; 2.18). He is now content with "telling," with "representing," with "narrating" himself such as he momentarily is, with offering the reader "a record of various and change-able occurrences, and of irresolute and, when it so befalls, contradictory ones" (611; 3.2). This project of representation, of portraying the "passing," motivates him entirely from now on. It is no longer his concern to "form man"—to form *himself*—it is to represent himself as already (and rather poorly) formed. For this reason, he defines his book not only in relation to other books but also, and especially, in relation to itself, to this other that it has been:

> Others form man; I tell of him, and portray a particular one, very ill-formed, whom I should really make very different from what he is if I had to fashion him over again. But now it is done.   (610)

From this, at least it seems to me, there follows first of all the obligation for readers not to encompass in a single glance, not to place on the same level the 1580 text of the *Essays* and the text added by Montaigne after this date. Secondly, there follows the necessity of our asking ourselves the significance of this intended difference, its implications and consequences.

I think that a first answer to this question consists in saying that Montaigne's voice is much more *directly* perceived after the publication of the *Essays* of 1580. Before this date, indeed, Montaigne's writing generally remains submissive to its models. What we call the play of intertextuality is there fully exercised. Like the good humanist he undoubtedly is, Montaigne cheerfully plunders his sources. And the result very often seems to be real "concoctions of commonplaces" (808; 3.12). This is the period when Montaigne "hides" his little thefts and "disguises" them (809; 3.12), when he makes "others say" what he himself, left to his own resources, could not "say so well" (296; 2.10). It is the time of apprenticeship when, by his own later admission, certain of his essays "smell a bit foreign" (667; 3.5). And the time when, in fact, others—Seneca, Plutarch, Virgil, Lucretius, or Cicero—speak to us through Montaigne.

After 1580, on the other hand, this "bookish and borrowed" self-complacency gradually yields to a greater independence of thought and writing. We are thus no longer dealing with essays that, as with the majority of those in the first two books, directly acknowledge their parasitic and derived status. Here Montaigne is no longer relying on the classical authors but narrating himself. The henceforth exclusive project of self-representation frees him to a great extent from his models and sources. This is the period—the great period—when Montaigne makes "honey which is all [his]" (111; 1.26), when what he borrows from others is used by him less for initiating and sustaining his remarks than for "enhancing" them (296; 2.10), when he feels himself sufficiently *exercised* and *formed* not only to speak alone and in his own name but also to question openly the authority of the ancients, to subvert and properly deconstruct their discourse, to unveil the precariousness of the foundations on which they rest, the inconsistencies, manipulations, and contradictions that they sometimes propound.

However necessary and fundamental it might be, this distinction between distance and involvement remains too vague in itself to allow for the elaboration of a protocol of reading. It becomes effective and properly operational

only when we double it with considerations that are synchronic, considerations centered no longer on the history of the text but on its very structures.
I am speaking of the "system of commentary," the "two-fold status" of Montaigne's text, the undeniable reflexivity that constitutes it and by which
means, constantly detaching itself from its subject—from its "theme"—
straying from it, leaving it "in order to see about the way to treat it" (706;
3.8), it finally takes itself for subject and theme. Pouilloux possesses the
special merit of having been the first to have pointed out these partic-
ularities. His conclusions have been recently taken up most convincingly by
André Tournon. We no longer have the right to ignore them.

These two scholars have thus essentially reminded us that the text
of Montaigne is the locus of both an *enunciation* and a *judgment*. The enunciation is apodictic: its function is the transmission of a truth. The argu-
mentation to which it has recourse is either of a dialectical (syllogism) or a
rhetorical (enthymeme) nature. It naturally uses, as a starting point, a pre-
existing discourse, a discourse that is already constituted, canonized, viewed
as an authority in the field: medieval scholasticism (Aristotle), classical philosophy (Stoicism, epicurism, skepticism), humanistic knowledge of the time
(history, cosmography, law, medicine, etc.). This discourse constitutes Montaigne's basic material, the starting point from which his own writing will
unfold. This practice explains why, in Montaigne's writing, several voices
make themselves heard.

Judgment defines the second level of Montaigne's writing. It naturally has
the enunciation as its object. It confronts this latter, defies it, draws it into a
duel, into a subtle and tense intellectual jousting, submits it to a critique in
which judgment itself not only tests and strengthens itself but also reveals
itself to the reader, takes shape in writing, records its activity, leaving on the
page the traces of its efforts, of its failures or advances. Judgment has therefore an analytical function. It is through it that we can explain what Pouilloux
very aptly calls "the double play of the discourse of the *Essays*," the transition from that first instance of writing, "when affirmations were piled up in
relation to a truth asserted," to this second, "when they are taken to pieces—
deconstructed—in order to reveal the lie which they hide to themselves"
(101). It is this exercise that, in the third book, will become the "art de
conferer" and that allows us to uncover here the double meaning of the word
essay in Montaigne's text: by testing, in his *Essays*, the discourse of others,
by seeing whether these discourses "can be maintained," Montaigne tests his
own judgment and that of his reader.

This double meaning, rather banal in itself, acquires major importance by
its implications. It suddenly becomes the locus where everything is drawn
and resolved, the very principle by means of which our reading will define
and justify itself. It allows us to account for two singularly modern characteristics of Montaigne's writing: namely, on the one hand, a studied devalor-
ization of all that has to do with the "message," the "ideological content" and,

on the other, the indubitable valorization, the promotion of all that has to do, within writing, not with the subject itself, the argument, the theme that is treated but with the act of judgment, with the intellectual performance for which this subject, transformed into an object, becomes the pretext. The best expression of this double characteristic can be found in "Of the Art of Discussion": "We are concerned with the manner, not the matter, of speaking" (708; 3.8). This "matiere du dire" matters little, indeed, since it is, at most, only an opportunity that Montaigne uses to test his judgment, since, as Tournon convincingly concludes, Montaigne's discourse never principally aims to illustrate the remarks chosen by chance but "to show forth and put to the test the attitude of the speaker" (8).

Hence our own conclusion: Why not listen to Montaigne? Why not define a protocol of reading on the basis of the coherent indications his text gives us? Let us first be careful not to yield unthinkingly to the call of the referent. We are studying a text not in order to go outside of it but in order to remain within. Let us then understand, once this first step is taken, that Montaigne's text is a reflexive one, a text ruled and structured by a "system of commentary," a text of many voices and levels. Let us not therefore ascribe to him a "message" that, more often than not, does not belong to him. Montaigne affirms absolutely nothing, except, perhaps, that it is extremely difficult to affirm anything. Like ours, his project is essentially *critical*. It consists of examining, representing, and criticizing himself in the very activity of his judgment. And his text is in no way the locus of any ideological coherence but, on the contrary, the locus of the liquidation of all ideologies. What makes itself heard in the *Essays* is not the successive adoption of a group of philosophical systems—the grand and inevitable trilogy of Stoicism, skepticism, and naturalism—but the mind's resistance to any form of indoctrination, its ability to question legitimately the authority of any discourse, including its own.

Accordingly, what in my opinion remains to be done with this text, either in an advanced undergraduate class or a graduate seminar—Montaigne is definitely not for "principians" (938; 3.8)!—is to question Montaigne's overall project in its very essence, at this focal point where the representation and the testing of the self meet and blend together. Montaigne certainly had something in mind when he decided to call his book *Les Essais*. And he also had his reasons for proclaiming everywhere in his book of essays his unending desire to "portray" and "describe" himself (273; 2.6), to "represent the course of [his] humors" (574; 2.37), his "haste" to "bring [himself] out and put [himself] forth" (288; 2.8), the fact that he is constantly "hungry to make [himself] known" (643; 3.5). What we should ultimately do therefore is study the *Essays* in the light of its own *problématique*, in the philosophical perspective of mimesis and representation, of speech and writing, presence and truth and ask ourselves if Montaigne is as fully *present* in his writing as he forcefully claims to be.

The Essays in the Context of the *Essays*

Marianne S. Meijer

"Easy does it" in the teaching of Montaigne. A slow textual reading, entailing constant backtracking, is the only way to follow Montaigne's train of thought. Undergraduate students are not used to such a slow reading; they are in the habit of skimming through texts to grasp as fast as possible the main thrust of the "story." Teaching Montaigne therefore implies teaching a new way of reading. It also implies assigning small quantities of reading in order to reach the desired quality of reading. Thus I ask students to read the 1580 text first (layer a), then to repeat the reading but include the b additions (1588 edition), and finally to read the last version (c layer). Once Montaigne's thinking and writing process is understood, contextuality may be brought up; but in undergraduate classes, there is not always enough time for such subtleties. It seems to me that contextuality within the *Essays* can be discussed in a substantial way only in advanced undergraduate seminars and graduate courses focusing on Montaigne where students are capable of and have time for independent study and research.

Contextuality cannot, however, be ignored by any teachers of Montaigne. The problem of the ordering of the essays does exist and must be considered: are the essays separate entities that can be read at random "without fear of losing the thread, for there is none" (Luthy 34)? Is the order of the essays within the three volumes indeed arbitrary? Or should we assume that since "Montaigne's work throughout the various strata of the *Essais* reveals self-consciousness, self-control, and definite planning" (Pertile 199), the author exercised the same care in 1580 when he handed his printer, Millanges, his ninety-four chapters? After all, he specified with precision how and where to insert between five hundred and six hundred additions to books 1 and 2 in 1588 (and some were already made in 1582), and about one thousand were carefully indicated in the *Exemplaire de Bordeaux*, his copy of the 1588 edition found at his death. They may be digressions, but something brought them about and their placement was not left to chance or whim. Would the placement of the chapters have been treated differently? Is the order of the chapters in fact meaningful?

The reason we do not know this with certainty is that Montaigne never refers to his chapters by number, only by title. But from the start, titles of the essays were followed by numbering—chapter 1, chapter 2, and so on—and Montaigne never changed this, nor did he change the ordering. In the posthumous 1595 edition, chapter 14 of book 1 became chapter 40 of the same book, but this decision was not Montaigne's, for although he altered chapter 14 in many ways in the *Exemplaire de Bordeaux*, he did not change its numbering. From 1580 till his death in 1592 the chapters were numbered and their ordering remained unchanged. Even when he scrapped all of La Boétie's sonnets in chapter 29, of book 1, he kept the dedication and left the chapter number unchanged. These facts could be ascribed to indifference on

Montaigne's part were it not for the *Exemplaire de Bordeaux*, which demonstrates the constant rereading of his work and the precision with which he indicated the smallest stylistic or punctuation changes, as well as the insertion of short or long digressions or developments. Indifferent Montaigne was not.

The ordering could be chronological. For the first edition approximate dates of composition have been established, more or less convincingly, by Pierre Villey and Donald Frame: 1572–74: forty essays; 1573–74: five; 1575–76: two; 1578–80: twenty-nine; 1579–80: two; 1572–80: two; 1572–78: one; and 1572–80: fifteen. Even if it is certain that forty essays were written between 1572 and 1574, their precise chronological order is not known. Raymond La Charité, for example, believes that the very first essay of book 1 was probably written in 1578 but was placed at the beginning of the book because it stresses the inconstancy, variety, and diversity of man, a main theme ("Essays"). Villey concludes from its dedication that chapter 26 of book 1, "Of the Education of Children," was written around 1579–80, and yet it is found approximately in the middle of the first book. Chronology is not therefore a convincing explanation of the ordering.

Some critics believe in a planned structure of the work. Again, La Charité believes chapter 29 of book 1, "Twenty-Nine Sonnets of Etienne de La Boétie," to be the centerpiece of that book, with twenty-eight chapters on each side and the thirty-seven left-over chapters forming book 2 ("Coherence"). For Michel Butor, chapter 19, "Of Freedom of Conscience," is the centerpiece of book 2. His view is supported by Daniel Martin who sees this chapter as a monument erected to the glory of Julian the Apostate within the "architecture" of the *Essays* (*Essais*). Martin continues his architecture in book 3 on the basis of a mnemonic theory, where he assigns each chapter to a mythological god because the author alludes to a particular part of the fables pertaining to that god.

In my opinion, however, the ordering of the essays should be viewed in the light of the *Exemplaire de Bordeaux*. This 1588 volume of the *Essays*, which Montaigne used to prepare a new edition, contains the author's manuscript additions written in the margins. The Bordeaux specimen contains numerous erasures, corrections of typos, spelling, and punctuation, replacements of words, often to improve the rhythm and sound of the sentence. On the first page is a long list of admonitions to the printer concerning spelling, capitalization, punctuation, insertion of foreign language prose and verse quotations within the French text, as well as a request to print the title and the author's name on the top of each page. The thousand or so additions are also full of erasures and changes. Their insertion is carefully marked in the text, allowing us to guess what brought them on. I agree with Richard Sayce ("L'ordre") that thought associations often produce new passages; they can be brought about by images, word plays or puns, quotations, readings, political or historical events, personal experiences or incidents, as the essayist says, "according to their timeliness" (736; 3.9). These manuscript corrections and additions reveal Montaigne's working method. The constant rereading, this "rumination of texts" (Dresden), is an old habit, like the reading and rereading of the breviary; what is new here is that Montaigne applies it to lay texts and to his own. It is my contention that the same method was used from scratch and that the chapters were composed in the same way. Something brought on additional thoughts, and a new chapter was inserted. The reason given by Montaigne to explain the longer chapters of book 3 also clarifies the structure of the first two books: "Because such frequent breaks into chapters as I used at the beginning seemed to me to disrupt and dissolve attention before it was aroused, making it disdain to settle and collect for so little, I have begun making them longer, requiring fixed purpose and assigned leisure. In such an occupation, if you will not give a man a single hour, you will not give him anything" (762; 3.9). On the one hand, this might justify the additions to the first two books and, on the other, it might indicate that the reader should refrain from reading isolated chapters. They should be read in context, just as the additions should not be read separately but within the context of the essay in which they are found.

Let me give a single example: "Of Freedom of Conscience." The apology of Julian the Apostate has been considered a daring statement and a proof of Montaigne's lukewarm religion. But Keith Cameron has shown that the title and the content of this essay are similar to other political tracts of the time, that Julian the Apostate had been rehabilitated by others at that time, and that Julian's name came up regularly in the context of persecution and tyrants. Cameron discovered that freedom of conscience was then used as a last resort when all else failed to bring peace. He also noted that the Huguenots, especially after the Saint Bartholomew's Day massacre, compared the kings of France with Julian the tyrant, while other writers had rehabilitated Julian as a man who had left good memories. For the contemporary reader, Montaigne's essay on freedom of conscience must have had a familiar ring. But does Montaigne treat this subject as expected? Although the apology of Julian was not new, Cameron has pointed out what was new, namely Montaigne's insistence that Julian was a fervent pagan: "In the matter of religion he was bad throughout. He was surnamed the Apostate for having abandoned ours; however, this theory seems to me more likely, that he had never had it at heart, but that, out of obedience to the laws, he had dissembled until he held the Empire in his hand. He was so superstitious in his own religion that . . ." (508; 2.19). Montaigne then proceeds to provide details to prove Julian's pagan beliefs. He insists that Julian had never been a Christian:

> [H]e had incubated paganism, says Marcellinus, for a long time in his heart; but because all his army was composed of Christians, he dared not reveal it. Finally, when he saw himself strong enough to dare to

proclaim his will, he had the temples of the gods opened and tried in every way to set up idolatry. (509; 2.19)

Julian had hidden his true feelings; he had only pretended. He established freedom of conscience only in the hope of dividing the Christians, of provoking disorders, so he could vanquish them more easily. This justifies the comparison with the kings of France: they too pretend. They pretend to establish freedom of conscience, but it is only in order to put an end to the civil disorders; they too hope to reestablish a single religion. Julian aimed for the restoration of paganism; the kings of France "have pretended to will what they could" (509; 2.19); they have pretended to endorse freedom of conscience because in reality they hoped to restore Catholicism. When Montaigne compares the kings of France with Julian, it is not as fellow tyrants but as fellow pretenders, pretending to endorse freedom of conscience. Dissimulation is what Julian and the kings of France have in common, but it is an honorable comparison since Julian was also a great emperor.

The last words of the essay are of prime importance: "having been unable to do what they would, they have pretended to will what they could" (509; 2.19). This is a variation on a saying from the ancients that Erasmus included in his *Adages*: "Ut possumus, quando ut volumus non licet" ("As best we can, since as we would we may not" [146; 1.8.4]). Erasmus quoted it again in his *Ciceronian*: "As the saying goes, we must do as we are able, when we can't do as we wish" (363). Philippe Du Plessis-Mornay used it in his *Remonstrance aux estats pour la paix*, as cited by Cameron: "il faut vouloir ce qu'on peut, si on ne peut tout ce qu'on veut" 'one must want what one can do, if one cannot do what one wants' (288; my trans.). The subtle variation introduced by Montaigne—"*they have pretended* to will what they could"—might easily go unnoticed if the essay is not placed within its proper literary and cultural context.

The fifteenth chapter of book 2, "That Our Desire Is Increased by Difficulty," develops the subject indicated in the title, which then leads to desire for glory, treated in the next chapter, "Of Glory." But virtue does not depend on the opinion of others; one must be virtuous for one's own sake. Others only see appearances; one's heart can only be judged by oneself. How others judge us and how we judge ourselves is further discussed in the following chapter, "Of Presumption." The introductory sentence connects it obviously to the preceding one on glory: "There is another kind of vainglory, which is an over-good opinion we form of our own worth" (478; 2.17). Montaigne tries to describe his own personality fairly, trying neither to overestimate nor underestimate himself. To speak of oneself could be considered presumptuous; he defends himself against this rhetorical accusation in the next chapter, "Of Giving the Lie." Montaigne does not speak about himself for love of glory but to show himself truly as he is, without any lies. He hates lying and dissimulation:

> Lying is an ugly vice, which an ancient paints in most shameful colors
> when he says that it is giving evidence of contempt for God and at the
> same time of fear of men. It is not possible to represent more vividly
> the horror, the vileness, and the profligacy of it. For what can you
> imagine uglier than being a coward toward men and bold toward God?
>
> (505; 2.18)

But alas it is more common than ever: "dissimulation is among the most
notable qualities of this century" (505; 2.18). One of the most obvious examples is given by the kings of France who pretend to endorse freedom of
conscience, as explained in "Of Freedom of Conscience." This chapter,
whose real subject is the dissimulation of kings, illustrates not only how
common dissimulation has become but also how useful it can be in the
political arena. This dilemma, that the public good sometimes demands of
kings to act unethically, had come up previously in "Of Custom," which
ended by praising a king who, "being born to command, . . . knew not only
how to command according to the laws, but how to command the laws
themselves, when the public necessity required" (90; 1.23). While in the
chapters that preceded "Of Freedom of Conscience," Montaigne insists on
his hatred of dissimulation—"Now for my part I would rather be trouble-
some and indiscreet than flattering and dissembling" (492; 2.17); "The first
stage in the corruption of morals is the banishment of truth" (505; 2.18);
"Lying is an ugly vice" (505; 2.18)—he now gives an example of dissimulation
of which he seems to approve. Indeed, "Of Freedom of Conscience" is not
about freedom of conscience; it is about the "recipe of freedom of conscience"
(509; 2.19), freedom of conscience as a political trick, a preplanned policy.
Since the kings failed to vanquish the Huguenots, it is better for Catholicism
in the long term that the kings pretend to accept the coexistence of both
religions: "Et si croy mieux, pour l'honneur de la devotion de nos rois, c'est
que, n'ayans peu ce qu'ils vouloient, ils ont fait semblant de vouloir ce qu'ils
pouvoient" (672; 2.19). Donald Frame translated *Et si* as "And yet." I would
like to suggest, "And thus": "And thus I prefer to think, for the reputation of
our kings' piety, that having been unable to do what they would, they have
pretended to will what they could" (509; 2.19). Rather than suppose that the
kings have abandoned the aim to maintain Catholicism as the sole religion in
France (and doubt their piety), Montaigne believes that they only pretended
to accept freedom of conscience. This example of dissimulation he accepts; it
is the exception to the rule. "Of Freedom of Conscience" is a parenthesis, a
particular case suggested at the same time by these preceding chapters and
by contemporary events. This essay is a gloss on the preceding text; it is a
digression, an addition. It explains that the dissimulation of the king of
France is acceptable: "utilitate publica rependitur" '[it] is compensated by
public utility' (511; 2.20), the last words in the 1580 edition of the following
chapter, "We Taste Nothing Pure." This very short chapter stresses the idea

that there is not a single good thing that "we do not buy at the price of some evil" (510; 2.20), a generalization of the particular case discussed in the preceding chapter (the use of dissimulation to bring about peace), an additional development. Because the many additions in later editions tripled the length of "We Taste Nothing Pure," its link with "Of Freedom of Conscience" has become less obvious.

Thus the meaning of the chapter "Of Freedom of Conscience" is clarified when it is read in the context of its surrounding chapters. This interpretation is reinforced when one considers the juxtaposition of the first two chapters of book 3. In "The Useful and the Honorable," Montaigne discusses once again the use of dissimulation and lying as political means. He states very forcefully, however, that while rulers might have to resort to vicious actions for the good of the state, he, Montaigne, would not do so under any circumstances. He would never "deviate from [his] conscience" (605; 3.1). This rule of conduct also prevents him from lying to God, that is to say, from repenting without sincerity, as discussed in the following chapter, "Of Repentance." If there is no contrition, no firm resolution never to repeat the offense, repentance is a lie. Since Montaigne lives according to his conscience and tries to do his very best, he knows that he cannot and will not change. Therefore Montaigne rarely repents (612; 3.2). These two chapters complement each other; reading them together elucidates Montaigne's train of thought.

I believe that chapters brought on additional chapters in exactly the same way passages in the essays brought on new additions. For research as well as teaching purposes, we should apply Montaigne's way of reading and rereading. We should "ruminate" his text and view the essays as *chapters* of a book rather than as independent units. Even when focusing on a single essay in the classroom, instructors must take into account the surrounding chapters if they want to do justice to Montaigne's intentions.

Montaigne's Style

Colin Dickson

Problems of Order and Pertinence

It is altogether too easy for the scholar who has enjoyed a long acquaintance with Montaigne's rich and rewarding book to underestimate the challenge that it presents to new readers. Montaigne's text is composite: an apparently discontinuous montage of analysis, anecdotal example, reminiscence, quotation, and later additions, which he himself termed an "ill-fitted patchwork" (736; 3.9). Moreover, textual order is elusive, especially in the absence of conjunctions and connectives that might otherwise helpfully mark transitions or signal new directions to the reader. That the omission of such *mots de liaison* is a deliberate stylistic choice is beyond doubt: Montaigne views them as mere "links and seams introduced for the benefit of weak or heedless ears" (761; 3.9). In fact, according to Mary McKinley, his "prose generally confronts the reader with a characteristic structure of obstacles and dislocations. Abrupt or nonexistent transitions, apparent contradictions, long ponderous sentences or short staccato ones—all these aspects contribute to the disruptive and often disorienting effect of the *Essais*" ("Montaigne's Reader" 72). She sees in their *embrouilleure* or "entanglement" the potential to "both frustrate and seduce the reader" (73).

If one teaches Montaigne to undergraduates (as I do in an upper-level course in Renaissance literature for French majors) and if one prefers studying several essays in their entirety, it is therefore important to address the structural issues of order and pertinence directly and to choose the initial reading with some care. Starting with the preface, "To the Reader," will focus attention on issues of authorial voice and intended audience and usefully alert students to Montaignian irony; beginning with "On Idleness" will offer perspective on these questions and on writing as the instrument of self-study.

My own preferred point of entry into Montaigne's book is "Of Practice": it is unusually clear, pertinent, and brief, as Craig Brush points out ("Montaigne" 23–24), and it compels attention by focusing on a topic of universal import, the problem of confronting one's own death. The initial task that I set for students is to read the first two pages of the essay and to note how they are constructed. Provided with a list of questions prompting them to view this beginning as a succession of textual blocks, students determine the content and status of each sentence and decide how it relates to its context. Subsequent class discussion confirms and refines their findings and equips them to complete this essay and to embark on others, expecting that the arrangement of topics will deviate from simple linearity and anticipating that any particular subject will be discussed more than once and from differing perspectives.

Such a deliberate start on the *Essays* slows students' reading pace and enables them to be fully engaged by a kind of writing whose meanings tend to elude "the inattentive reader" (761; 3.9), especially in the later essays, where the array of topics is complex and the sources of textual order multiple. In Montaigne's short masterpiece "Of Repentance," for example, order springs from several sources, including the systematic exploitation of the contrast between interior and exterior (Gray, *Style* 223) and the opposition between mobility and fixity (Glauser 146); it stems as well from recurrence of the polysemous key word "form" and its derivatives (Kritzman, *Destruction* 127–32; Brody, "Du repentir").

Sentence Structure

"Of Practice" also serves as a useful initial example of sentence structure and its variety, a constant source of surprise for Montaigne's reader. Turning to its unhurried beginning, we find a number of compound-complex sentences strongly coordinated by semicolons, in which relations between coordinate and subordinate clauses are marked by such signposts as "though . . . unless besides . . . otherwise" (267; 2.6). Such clear marking of subordination highlights the structure of the essay's opening sentences with its branching proliferation of dependent clauses, which I like to display using the diagrammatic technique suggested by Richard Sayce (*Style* 89–103). More often, though, Montaigne uses few linking words and phrases, as Erich Auerbach has pointed out in his masterful explication of the beginning of "Of Repentance." Such parataxis is but one of the textual strategies serving to implicate Montaigne's reader, who is forced to supply the missing connectives.

The Montaignian sentence tends to be ample, elaborated through accumulation, enumeration, and digression, as well as later additions. Even a sentence where Montaigne proposes an ideal of terse, "soldierly" self-expression reflects this tendency toward amplitude. He begins, "The speech I love is a simple, natural speech, the same on the paper as in the mouth; a speech succulent and sinewy, brief and compressed, not so much dainty and well-combed as vehement and brusque . . ." (127; 1.26), and continues, after quoting Lucan's epitaph, for forty-five more words. In the third volume of the *Essays* and in the additions to the first two, however, the proportion of short sentences increases, a fact that Floyd Gray (*Style* 29–32) relates to Montaigne's desire to paint a mobilistic self-portrait, an intention clearly stated in "Of Repentance": "I do not portray being. I portray passing" (611; 2.2). Some of these sentences, "brief and compressed" to the point of being maxims, bring into the fabric of the *Essays* a contrasting laconism and serve more to involve the reader than to present a distillate of normative wisdom. It is worth pointing out to students that the punctuation and paragraphing of modern editions often set them apart from the body of Montaigne's text—in which they were originally given no such prominence—and thereby encourage an exaggeratedly "ethical" reading of the *Essays*.

Word Choice

A glance at the beginning of "Of Practice" suggests one source of amplitude: the frequent use of quasi-synonymous word pairs or phrases like "exercise and form our soul," "inexperienced and new to the combat" (267; 2.6). A reflection, perhaps, of his legal background and experience in translation, this rather typical trait of Montaignian style slows the tempo of these lines, as does an occasional apposition ("too pleasant and easy" [267; 2.6]).

Frequently, word pairs present contrasting ideas, expressed perhaps by phonetically nearly identical words or etymologically related ones (Sayce, Essays 301–08; Winegrad). Among the instances well rendered in the Donald Frame translation, we find Montaigne's affirmation in "Of Cannibals" that we should judge things "by reason's way, not by popular say" (150; 1.31; cf. "la voye de la raison, non . . . la voix commune" [202; 1.31]). Referring to self-study in "Of Presumption," the essayist tells us, "blame my project if you will, but not my procedure" (495; 2.17; cf. "project" versus "progrez" [653; 2.17]). And in "Of Husbanding Your Will," he warns that we do not feel "the things that charm us compared with those that harm us" (782; 3.10). Montaigne's final essay, "Of Experience," which dwells on human pleasures, is rich in figures of sound and suggestive of the gratification of auditory sensuality when it speaks of accepting these pleasures "with more gusto and with better grace" (849; 3.13) and, when confronting pain and pleasure, of being "as anxious to extinguish the one as to extend the other" (853; 3.13). Sound and rhythm of words can, of course, be the motivation of longer word groups, as when Montaigne speaks of "an argument [where] there would always be matter for answers, rejoinders, replications, triplications, quadruplications, and [an] infinite web of disputes" (497; 2.17).

Enumeration

Longer accumulations of nouns, adjectives, or verbs give the Montaignian sentence an exploratory character, progressively adding new ideas rather than converging on exact ones. As Montaigne recognized (in a typically concrete image), only limited precision was achievable in a language that "slips out of our hands every day, and has halfway changed since I have been alive" (751; 3.9). Moreover, the vocabulary of the Essays shows deliberate semantic broadening, the polysemous word essay itself providing an excellent example (Telle).

Metaphor and Simile

Alerting students to the part played by metaphors and similes in the Essays is important, for they are a major means of expression of thought and feeling and are to be found on virtually every page (in fact twice as often as in

Rabelais and four times as often as in Proust). And imagery is an aspect of literature that undergraduates are able to explore and write about with some success, though thematic subjects are perhaps the safest ones to suggest to students searching for a topic.

Among the questions that I provide students starting to read "Of Practice," several focus attention on metaphorical expression; for example, one item reads, "The phrase 'new to the combat' is a military metaphor: are there others in this passage?" Class discussion points to the phrase "exercise and form our soul" (267; 2.6), which, taken by itself, is but weakly metaphoric. However, it acquires metaphorical force from its context, which includes the phrase "might relax and soften the firmness of their soul" (267; 2.6) at paragraph's end, together with the references to action and the related military images. This potential of context to endow Montaigne's fluid vocabulary with new implications and to renew worn or dead metaphors contributes significantly to our sense of continually discovering something striking and unexpected as we read the *Essays*.

Montaigne's originality in the use of metaphor is evident in the domain of mental phenomena, where sixteenth-century French (and even Latin) provided inadequate speculative instruments. Through "psychological imagery" (C. E. Clark 84–122), the essayist explores this new territory and reflects a keen interest in the workings of the unconscious mind. Speaking in "Of Practice" about his feelings after the accident, Montaigne says:

> It seemed to me that my life was hanging only by the tip of my lips; I closed my eyes in order, it seemed to me, to help push it out, and took pleasure in growing languid and letting myself go. It was an idea that was only floating on the surface of my soul, as delicate and feeble as all the rest, but in truth not only free from distress but mingled with that sweet feeling that people have who let themselves slide into sleep.
> (269–70; 2.6)

The essayist returns twice to this image, in which the soul is seen as a physical body endowed with a sensitive outer surface. He speaks of incipient sleep in which we "follow voices with a blurred and uncertain hearing which seems to touch on only the edges of the soul," and he cites "passions which touch only the rind of us" (271; 2.6).

However, it is in essays like "Of the Education of Children," "Of Repentance," "Of Husbanding Your Will," and "Of Experience" that students will discover how intensely metaphorical Montaigne's vision can be. In "Of the Education of Children," such a variety of alimentary images portray education as a form of nutrition that Gray describes them as composing a sort of "subterranean current" linking the different parts of the essay (*Style* 210–22). The profusion of images contrasting fixity and mobility in the beginning of "Of Repentance," and ramifying throughout the remainder, expresses in metaphorical terms the dichotomy between repentance (or change) and non-repentance central to the essay. In some essays, networks of recurring images can contribute significantly to short-range order and unity, even if they are not the most numerous. It is worth asking, for example, what "Of Husbanding Your Will" would be without the "transactional" images of commercial exchange (C. E. Clark 115–22) and the motifs of sea and storm studied by Jules Brody (*Lectures* 44–49). Would we read the final pages in "Of Experience" with as much interest without its alimentary imagery and triumphal banquet motif (Dickson) and without its concluding metaphorics of verticality, as in "on stilts we must still walk on our own legs. And on the loftiest throne in the world we are still sitting on our own rump" (857; 3.13)?

At the Collège de Guyenne, Montaigne accomplished a rite of passage admitting him, like other sons of the elite, to the Latin writing, speaking, and thinking world of the learned (Ong, *Rhetoric* 130). His education, like that of many men of affairs, provided him with the stock of similitudes and metaphors from classical sources that were "a mainstay of prose writing and oratory [and were] used to argue, to persuade, to influence the course of events," as Carol Clark points out, placing Montaigne's performance as a writer within the context of literary practice in his time (20). In the essay on education, as we have just mentioned, Montaigne draws on this stock, using images of eating and digestion and adding the equally familiar ones of the field under cultivation, of bees gathering pollen (C. E. Clark 44–46, 53–64). What sets him apart from other writers is the freedom with which these and even more conventional materials are drawn upon, transformed, and reinterpreted. This is perhaps not surprising in a book representing the synthesis of the interests and eclectic reading, the lifelong experience and reflection of such an independent-minded author. So compelling and at times so unusual is the metaphorical vision in Montaigne's later writings that Brody has suggested that metaphor is no longer a "simple style device, and even less the vehicle of a philosophy or an idea. It *is* that idea . . ." (*Lectures* 52; my trans.).

Montaignian Closure

Among the contributions of recent critical theory to Montaigne studies has been the application of the essentially rhetorical notion of closure to the *Essays*. It might seem a paradoxical undertaking to study endings in a book as subject to revision and expansion as Montaigne's, but both Marcel Tetel ("Les fins") and François Rigolot (*Les métamorphoses* 131–49) have done so, enumerating various types of ending. Tetel's four-fold typology is based on function and includes "recapitulating" (Ciceronian), "reorienting," "opening," and "auto-referential" endings; Rigolot examines the motivation of various endings and finds that they can be "rhetorical," "stylistic," "egocentric," or (again) "auto-referential." Both critics emphasize the "suggestive" quality of Montaignian endings: though a number are emphatic and memorable (as in "Of Cannibals," "All this is not too bad—but what's the use? They don't wear breeches" [159; 1.31], and in "Of Vanity," "you are the investigator without knowledge, the magistrate without jurisdiction, and all in all, the fool of the farce" [766; 3.9]), most endings are problematic. Not surprisingly, a look at the ending of "Of Practice" proves instructive and reveals that it exemplifies both closure and its undoing in the *Essays*.

In its original form, this essay signaled its imminent ending in the penultimate paragraph by making explicit the completion of the narrative of Montaigne's brush with death: "I do not want to forget this, that the last thing I was able to recover was the memory of this accident . . ." (272; 2.6). The original last paragraph secures closure in three ways. It offers a metatextual judgment of Montaigne's performance as a writer, offering the opinion that "[t]his account of so trivial an event would be rather pointless, were it not for the instruction . . . derived from it" (272; 2.6). It summarizes preceding discussion in categorical terms: "in truth, in order to get used to the idea of death, I find there is nothing like coming close to it" (272; 2.6). And it enlarges the perspective, relating this essay to Montaigne's enterprise of self-study: "What I write here is not my teaching, but my study; it is not a lesson for others, but for me" (272; 2.6).

Since every word in the *Essays* is the potential point of attachment of a new development, such a closure, however satisfyingly conclusive, can be "reopened." Montaigne appends in final revision, "And yet it should not be held against me if I publish what I write" (272; 2.6) and expands the essay by fully half its original length. Thus the essay mimes in its textual elaboration the revival of its author, once taken himself for "finished."

Can we say that the new ending is more effective? The new penultimate paragraph challenges the reader—"If anyone gets intoxicated with his knowledge when he looks beneath him, let him turn his eyes upward toward past ages" (275; 2.6)—and contains a number of additional "closural allusions" (B. H. Smith 172–82) that evoke retrospection ("remember the lives of the two Scipios" and "so far behind him" [275; 2.6]) and finality ("in the end" [275; 2.6]).

The final paragraph moves from the many admirable figures of the preceding one to the single one of Socrates, the exemplar of probing self-study carried to its lucid conclusion and "hero" of the final essays (Frame, *Essais* 50–51). The monitory final sentence is a concentrate of the challenges issued earlier and refers directly to self-expression and, by implication, to Montaigne's writing (as did the earlier ending of the essay): "Whoever knows himself thus, let him boldly make himself known by his own mouth" (275; 2.6).

The later addition defers "terminal" closure, refocusing the essay on the process of self-study and its result, a self-portrait (Brush, "Montaigne" 30–34). The narrative of the accident now becomes one instance, among others, of self-study. Thus, the motivation of this lengthy coda is "auto-referential" (to use Rigolot's term), and its effect (or "function," as Tetel would say) is "reorienting," for it utterly transforms our reading of the original essay.

Exemplifying the *Essays'* "anticlosural" tendency (B. H. Smith 234–60), this ending is more suspensive than conclusive. Students will see closure secured more convincingly in "Of Cannibals," "Of Repentance," and the finale of "Of Experience," but their early encounter with the problematics of closure in "Of Practice" will help to impress upon them the uniqueness of the *Essays*, by definition a book never finished and one forever inviting the complicity of the reader.

INTERDISCIPLINARY APPROACHES

Montaigne and Politics

David Lewis Schaefer

I am a political scientist who has taught seminars entirely devoted to Montaigne as a political philosopher. These seminars, in which the whole text of the *Essays* was assigned (Donald Frame's translation), were offered both at a large public university and at the liberal arts college where I now teach. Students were required to write two ten-to-fifteen-page analytic papers on different chapters or groups of chapters of their own choosing from the *Essays*; each class began with a student reading a fifteen-minute oral summary of his or her paper aloud, as an initial basis for discussion. Most class members had already taken my introductory survey course in the history of political philosophy, from which they acquired not only experience in the close reading of texts but also a basic familiarity with the thought of such philosophers as Plato, Aristotle, and Machiavelli, with which Montaigne's teaching must be compared if it is to be understood.

Because I believe that understanding a work like the *Essays* requires that the student focus as much attention as possible on the text itself, I avoid assigning secondary works, with the exception of two articles. The first of these, "Montaigne's Intention and His Rhetoric" (Schaefer, ch. 1), assigned during the first week, discusses Montaigne's manner of writing, challenges the "evolutionary" interpretation of his thought, and highlights the political intent underlying the *Essays*. The second, Hans Jonas's "The Practical Uses of Theory," is assigned in conjunction with the "Apology for Raymond Sebond" because of its lucid elaboration of the philosophic presuppositions of the transformation of natural science undertaken by Bacon and Descartes, a transformation that is foreshadowed in the "Apology." The only other text I recommend to students is Jacob Zeitlin's three-volume 1935 translation of the *Essays*, useful for its notes (the most comprehensive available in English) and commentary. Although I often differ with Zeitlin's interpretations, they furnish a good starting point for discussion, since they summarize a broad consensus of scholarly opinion. Finally, I provide the class with a fifteen-page list of corrections to Frame's translation in places where he is insufficiently literal.

Although Montaigne is not usually thought of as a political philosopher, his interest in political affairs is undeniable. Not only does he expressly devote numerous chapters of the *Essays* to the consideration of political and military issues but his book as a whole is strewn with references to and judgments of prominent political figures and events of his time and those of antiquity. It also includes accounts of his own policies as mayor and as negotiator among the conflicting parties in the civil wars that continued through most of his adult lifetime. The more fundamental questions concern the centrality of politics in Montaigne's understanding of human affairs, the profundity of his political reflections, and the extent to which he intended to promote political change through his book.

Scholarship on the *Essays* during the early decades of the twentieth century exhibited a radical disagreement on the last-mentioned issue. Such prominent Montaignists as Pierre Villey and Fortunat Strowski attributed to the essayist an extreme dichotomy between the realms of private reflection and public action: while Montaigne sought to exercise the widest possible liberty of judgment, they contended, he opposed all efforts at public "reformation" and displayed a most scrupulous regard for all established law. By contrast, Arthur Armaingaud viewed Montaigne as a pioneer political liberal and champion of religious toleration, who aimed to overcome the theological disputation that provided the occasion for the civil wars by a skeptical attack on Christianity and by promulgating an Epicurean ethic that would supplant it ("Etude"). Armaingaud even contended that Montaigne was responsible for conveying to the Protestants the antimonarchical *Discourse on Voluntary Servitude* authored by his late friend Etienne de La Boétie and that he emended the text prior to its publication so as to make its depiction of the tyrant unmistakably applicable to Henry III, the reigning monarch at the time the discourse was published (*Montaigne*).

The predominant scholarly view of the *Essays* today favors Villey's "conservative" interpretation over Armaingaud's "liberal" one. Representative of this consensus are the works of Frieda Brown (*Conservatism*), Starobinski, and Keohane ("Individualism"). Yet fundamental difficulties in the conservative reading remain unresolved. In the first place, as Richard Sayce (Essays, 259) points out, however conservative Montaigne's political *intentions* may seem, the overall influence and *effect* of his book were far more revolutionary than conservative (see too Fleuret). Given Montaigne's acknowledged mastery of literary style, how can such an enormous disparity between authorial intent and effect have occurred? Furthermore, the conservative interpretation attributes to Montaigne such a radical separation between the spheres of thought and action that even partisans of this interpretation concede it may reflect an erroneous or shallow judgment on his part (Brown, *Conservatism* 83). The structure and policies of the French monarchy in Montaigne's era were hardly conducive to widespread enjoyment of the intellectual independence that Montaigne recommends. Neither Catholic nor Protestant partisans acknowledged the legitimacy of a sphere of private conscience and judgment that government was bound to respect as a matter of principle. Nor was it likely that the practice of speaking one's thoughts openly, as Montaigne recommends, would support an automatic obedience to established authority. In fact, Montaigne expressly acknowledges the tension or incompatibility between liberty of judgment and practical subordination to authority: "Obedience is not pure or tranquil in a man who reasons and argues" (498; 2.17). Elsewhere he indicates that he intends the "license" that characterizes his self-portrait in the *Essays* as a model to be emulated by others (642; 3.5). Given Montaigne's express recognition of the obstacle posed to such liberation by the laws and customs of his time (e.g., 32; 1.13; 83–85; 1.23; 166; 1.36), he could hardly have believed that it could be accomplished while maintaining, in Brown's words, "strict adherence to authority and the complete unity of Church and State" (*Conservatism* 83).

The essay that provides the most obvious and extensive evidence to support the conventional interpretation of Montaigne's political attitudes is "Of Custom, and Not Easily Changing an Accepted Law." Here Montaigne indeed combines an account of his own radical independence of judgment and a denunciation of the injustice and irrationality of French laws with an apparent profession of hostility to all forms of political innovation and an assertion that the wise person, while exercising unlimited freedom of private judgment, should behave entirely in accordance with established law. Yet viewing these remarks within their context of the essay as a whole, relating them to relevant remarks elsewhere in the *Essays*, and comparing some of the remarks with the classical source from which they appear to be derived sheds a different light on Montaigne's intent.

The argument of "Of Custom" may be divided into three parts: an opening section in which Montaigne describes the power of custom to shape and distort our judgment, elaborating this theme with a lengthy account of the curious customs practiced by various foreign peoples, who would find European ways no less strange than the Europeans judge theirs; a middle section that contains the remarks cited above; and a concluding section, generally neglected by commentators, in which Montaigne elaborates the circumstances that justify or necessitate political innovation, going beyond or even against established laws.

The passage in the middle of the chapter wherein Montaigne expresses "disgust" with all forms of political innovation refers directly to the civil wars. Montaigne condemns not only the Protestants but also their "imitators," the militant Catholic defenders of the established religious order, for so esteeming their theological "opinions" as to "overthrow the public peace and introduce so many inevitable evils . . . . as civil wars and political changes bring with them," thereby "encourag[ing] so many certain and known vices in order to combat contested and debatable errors" (86–87; 1.23). While this passage makes clear Montaigne's opposition to the innovation of civil war, it leaves unresolved whether he thought a purely conservative posture offered an adequate remedy. It is noteworthy that his profession of disgust with innovation is succeeded by an acknowledgment of the need to adapt laws, on occasion, to the "urgent necessity" engendered by "Fortune" (89; 1.23). Elsewhere, Montaigne suggests that the present state of France is one of those occasions. In "Of Presumption," he denounces the corruption of French morals and the barbarity of many of his country's laws and customs but avows that "because of the difficulty in improving our state and the danger of everything collapsing, if I could put a spoke in our wheel and stop it ["l'arrester"] at this point, I would do so with all my heart." In the sequel, however, he indicates that France's situation does not allow such a remedy: "The worst thing I find in our state is instability, and the fact that our laws cannot, any more than our clothes, take any settled ["arrestée"] form" (497– 98; 2.17). He implies that the true alternative to such ill-advised "reformations" as the Protestant one is not a die-hard conservatism doomed to failure but a wisely guided change that would remedy both France's instability and its corruption.

Montaigne resumes the theme of political change and preservation in "Of Vanity." After reiterating his opposition to "the present morals of our state" and its "unruly . . . form of government," he argues anew against innovation, asserting that "the best and most excellent government for each nation is the one under which it has preserved its existence" (723, 729–31; 3.9). But once again, his conservative posture proves misleading. In view of his repeated observation of the instability of the French state, it is doubtful that Montaigne regards the existing regime as capable of maintaining the nation. After denouncing the "monstrous" morals of his time, he praises prudent reformers who aim to restore things to their "natural" condition (730–31; 3.9).

Despite Montaigne's prudent professions of conservatism, the treatments of political change in other essays suggest that the author regards the contemporary situation of France as corresponding to those discussed in the last part of "Of Custom": a condition sufficiently dire to require a supralegal remedy, rather than being soluble through adherence to tradition. To reconcile this inference with Montaigne's seeming denunciation of all political innovations earlier in that chapter, one must compare the passage in "Of

Custom" where Montaigne questions the desirability of ever changing the laws with the classical source on which it is based. In introducing this passage, Montaigne remarks, "Here is something from another vat" (86; 1.23). The "vat" is Aristotle's *Politics*, from which both Montaigne's central argument in this passage and the second part of the chapter title appear to have been borrowed. In *Politics* 2.8, Aristotle warns against changing the laws for the sake of only minor benefits, since all such changes tend to reveal the artificiality of law and hence to weaken citizens' reverence for it, on which the habit of law-abidingness depends.

When one compares Aristotle's argument against encouraging political change with Montaigne's adaptation of it in "Of Custom," several significant differences emerge. In the first place, Montaigne has so rigidified Aristotle's argument as to make a travesty of it: whereas Aristotle merely warns against excessive changes, Montaigne expresses doubt that the laws should *ever* be changed. And rather than supporting the doubt with reasoning like Aristotle's, Montaigne limits himself to citing three examples of the ancients' hostility to change—as if an appeal to custom could settle the issue of the authority of custom. At least one of these examples, that of an ephor "who so rudely cut out the two strings that Phrynis had added to music" without regard to the possible improvement they may have represented, is presented in such a manner as to make this posture appear wholly unreasonable (86; 1.23). At the same time that Montaigne weakens the rhetorical force of Aristotle's argument, he overtly violates its spirit: whereas Aristotle demonstrates the periodic need for legal change by criticizing "barbaric" laws and customs of the remote past, Montaigne, earlier in "Of Custom," provides an extensive critique of many *currently existing* French laws for their irrationality and injustice (85; 1.23). These remarks can hardly have been intended to encourage Montaigne's audience to hold the existing order in greater reverence.

I infer that by acknowledging that his warning against changing laws came from "another vat," Montaigne meant that it does not come from his own "vat" of thought, and that he does not agree with it. The insincerity of Montaigne's criticism of changing the laws is further suggested by the fact that in other essays, he contradicts some of the remarks concerning the absoluteness of one's obligation to obey the laws that had led up to it. In "Of Solitude," he contradicts the claim in "Of Custom" that each man owes himself to the public (174, 178; 1.39; cf. 769; 3.10). In the "Apology for Raymond Sebond," he disputes the principle that every man should obey the laws of his country, protesting that he cannot have his "judgment so flexible" as to conform to the ever-shifting opinions of the ruling classes who enact them (437; 2.12). And, contrary to his praise of Socrates's extreme law-abidingness in "Of Custom" (85–86; 1.23), Montaigne later criticizes that posture and explicitly states his unwillingness to emulate it (743; 3.9; 821; 3.13).

In contrast to Montaigne's denunciation of the Protestant Reformation in "Of Custom," an early hint regarding the desirability of another kind of "reformation" is supplied in the third chapter of the *Essays*, "Our Feelings Reach Out Beyond Us." There Montaigne describes as "an easy reformation and a cheap one" that men "avoid expense and pleasure the use and knowledge of which are imperceptible to us" (12; 1.3). The immediate context of this seemingly ironic remark—a discussion of funeral customs—might obscure its significance; but the same theme is picked up in "Of Custom," where Montaigne suggests the need to restore "indifferent things such as clothes . . . to their true purpose, which is the service and comfort of the body" (85; 1.23). The examples of "indifferent things" that follow this statement are indeed concerned only with fashions in dress. But the previous argument of the chapter suggested that many things more significant than clothing are in essence indifferent, since nature dictates no particular way in which they should be arranged. By illustrating the great variety of rules in different nations governing such matters as sex, the family, property, religion, and marks of nobility, Montaigne aimed to show that the way in which one orders these things is an indifferent affair, since any one way may be considered as inherently reasonable or "natural" as any other.

If such matters are inherently indifferent, then—as another essay suggests—an enormous range of freedom is opened up to one who would tear the "mask" from things, as proposed in "Of Custom," and refer them to "truth and reason." At the beginning of "That the Taste of Good and Evil Depends in Large Part on the Opinion We Have of Them," Montaigne argues that if people "are tormented by the opinions they have of things, not by the things themselves," it "would be a great point gained for the relief of our miserable human condition. . . . For if evils have no entry into us but by our judgment, it seems to be in our power to disdain them or turn them to our good" (33; 1.14). As the argument of this quasi-Stoical essay proceeds, it becomes doubtful that Montaigne can succeed (or intends to succeed) in demonstrating that such miseries as pain, disease, and poverty are not in fact evils. But he nonetheless reports being barely touched by some "common causes of affliction" that trouble others, citing his near indifference to the death of his children (42; 1.14). The reason for his tranquility, he later explains, is that he finds it easy enough to "bear misfortunes that do not affect [him] personally" (800; 3.12). More specifically, he distinguishes between "[t]he sufferings that affect us simply through the soul . . . which are almost indifferent to [him]," and "the really essential and bodily sufferings," which he abhors as much as anyone (575; 2.37).

The essayist encourages his readers to emulate his attitude. Since the soul is far more malleable than the body, he urges people to adapt their souls to their bodies' needs, in a manner "conducive to our repose and preservation" (39; 1.14). This remark harmonizes with the recommendation in "Of Custom" that "indifferent things" be arranged to serve our bodily needs. It also elaborates the ground on which Montaigne denounced the conduct of both parties in the civil wars: the "contested and debatable" things over which they fight are *opinions about the good of the soul*. The vice both of the Reformation and of the Catholic response to it is that they produce evils that are undeniably wrong (because of their perceptibly and unavoidably harmful effect on the body), such as torture and bloodshed, in the name of opinions that are indemonstrable (because they concern things that have no tangible reality). Herein lies the true meaning of the "reformation" Montaigne proposes in "Our Feelings Reach Out beyond Us": to forego "imperceptible" expenses and pleasures is to abandon concern with the divine or transcendent, things of which we can have no true knowledge. Our moral and religious opinions, being concerned with essentially indifferent matters (since there is no natural standard, accessible to reason, by which their validity could be tested), should be revised to accord with our bodily needs, which are not at all matters of indifference.

The radical implications of Montaigne's proposed reformation emerge later in the same essay, when he describes himself as "almost" ready to vow "irreconcilable hatred" against popular government, despite regarding it as "most natural and equitable," on account of the "inhuman injustice" the Athenian demos displayed in executing their generals for having failed "to gather up and bury their dead" after the battle of Arginusae (12; 1.3). Although this statement is customarily read as embodying an antidemocratic bias (Guizot 33–34), such a reading overlooks the truly remarkable fact that Montaigne is describing popular rather than monarchic government as in principle the most natural and equitable form.

To understand this passage, we must recall why the sailors' burial concerned the demos: their belief that it was an obligation of piety, reflecting the concern with intangible goods that Montaigne has deprecated. He calls the Athenians' belief an "importunate superstition" (13; 1.3). In his view, the chief defect of popular government, which would otherwise be the justest form of rule, is the people's proneness to religious superstition, which disposes them to commit acts of gross injustice. It follows that, if the people's proneness to superstition could somehow be overcome, popular rule would be unqualifiedly the best form of government.

The preceding survey is intended both to suggest the kind of political project that the *Essays* as a whole embodies and to illustrate the degree of care in reading that must be exercised if that project is to be comprehended. Montaigne conceives his book, I believe, as the means of fulfilling a dual role for which he describes himself well fitted in the last essay, "Of Experience": serving as an "adviser" to kings, while helping to alleviate the lot of the common people (825–26, 844; 3.13; cf. 291; 2.8). By launching a skeptical attack on the religious beliefs and transcendent moral aspirations with which the people have been inculcated by lawgivers and clerics (389; 2.12; 414–15; 2.12; 477; 2.16; 769; 3.10), Montaigne diverges from the practice of previous philosophers, who outwardly deferred to such doctrines, despite their unbelief in them (29; 1.11; 440–41; 2.12; 757; 3.9). His intent is to promote civic peace and individual tranquility by liberating humanity from excessively "elevated" aspirations and from superfluous legal restrictions that interfere with their enjoyment of harmless bodily pleasures. By "rationalizing" the moral foundation of politics, Montaigne also aspires to obliterate the tension between politics and philosophy that compelled previous philosophers to conceal their thoughts (379–80; 2.12). By uncovering the flimsy foundations of conventional political hierarchies—in such essays as "Of Cannibals," "Of the Inequality That is Between Us," "Of Sumptuary Laws," and "Of the Disadvantage of Greatness"—he prepares the ground for a new form of government dedicated to securing the equal rights of all individuals, possibly through the mechanism of a revived republicanism (see, in this respect, "Of Friendship" [144; 1.28]; "On Some Verses of Virgil" [646–47; 3.5]; "Of Vanity" [738, 764–66; 3.9]; Schaefer, chs. 5, 12). Montaigne is one of the earliest philosophic architects of modern liberal politics.

Distinguishing the serious political project that the *Essays* embodies from the protective rhetorical surface that conceals it requires a particularly attentive and reflective kind of reading, as the author himself indicates (751; 3.9). In view of Montaigne's denial of ever "erring" unintentionally (496; 2.17), the reader must be wary of assuming that seeming contradictions in the text reflect their author's carelessness, rather than rhetorical subterfuge. Considering Montaigne's insistence that his thought has remained consistent throughout the *Essays* (616; 3.2; 736; 3.9), one must similarly be skeptical of interpretative schemes that claim to explain the evolution of his thought. While the overall text of the book does exhibit an evolution in style (and partially in substance), it is likely that this evolution reflects a rhetorical strategy rather than a change in Montaigne's real position. The "earlier," imitative, quasi-Stoical essays convey a protective appearance of conservative traditionalism. Having won his readers' trust by means of this posture, Montaigne proceeds to subject the premises of the traditionalist position to a withering critique, notably in the "Apology for Raymond Sebond," and to supplant it with a libertarian, egalitarian, and hedonistic ethic that is set forth most fully in book 3.

Despite the engaging character of Montaigne's ostensible self-portrait in the *Essays*, it would be misleading to take that self-portrait literally (Ballaguy; Marcu). Authors who lived under less tolerant regimes than our own had good reason to obscure their heterodox views (Strauss). In general, the student must learn to pay attention to what Montaigne is doing, not merely what he says he is doing: for instance, when he professes near the end of "Of Glory" to be willing to uphold the "false opinion" that favors glory if that opinion has political utility (477; 2.16), the reader cannot afford to overlook the fact that Montaigne has devoted the bulk of the chapter to undermining that opinion. Similarly, his profession of utter subservience to the Church at the outset of "Of Prayers" should not obscure the heretical content of the remainder of the chapter. And when Montaigne seems to express diametrically opposed views on a controversial subject, it is reasonable, as Armaingaud suggested, to be more suspicious of the sincerity of the more conventional statement ("Etude" 190–91; see also Strauss). Students should be encouraged to compare Montaigne's quotations and paraphrases of other sources with the originals (using Zeitlin's notes as a guide); as in "Of Custom," interesting discoveries often result. No particular remark in the *Essays* can be understood without regard to the context of argument in which it occurs and its relation to the book as a whole. If a given argument seems foolish, it is far more likely that we have missed Montaigne's point than that he was a victim of the superstitions of his time. Given the many weaknesses of Villey's "evolutionary" schema (Schaefer, ch. 1), it is unwise to rely on the distinction among successive textual "strata" to explain apparent contradictions in Montaigne's argument.

Montaigne's wit and style constitute an ever-present inducement to study the *Essays*. But he himself deprecated these qualities of his book by comparison with the virtues of *substance* it embodies (184–85; 1.40). These virtues include the profundity of its author's thought, the delineation and exemplification Montaigne provides of what it means to be a philosopher, the articulation of alternative "role models" (Cato, Alexander, Socrates, and Montaigne himself) among whom the reader is supplied with grounds for choosing, and an account of the tension among the various goods we seek (beauty, honor, virtue, health, pleasure, freedom, utility, understanding), which compels us to choose. In my experience, once students have been persuaded and assisted to read the *Essays* with sufficient diligence to discover these things, they find it (as I do) no less relevant to the fundamental human issues today than it was when Montaigne composed it.

Although instructors may find it difficult to cover the whole of the *Essays* in a course, selections must at least be made with Montaigne's admonition in mind that any abridgment of a good book is a bad abridgment (718; 3.8). In selecting chapters for assignment, one must try to include essays that express the various strands of Montaigne's thought, so that apparent "contradictions" may be confronted and studied rather than avoided. Finally, one must be aware that even essays ostensibly devoted to trivial subjects like thumbs and sleep may prove, on careful study, to embody points of fundamental importance, covertly expressed.[1]

NOTE

[1]Portions of this essay are reprinted from David Lewis Schaefer, *The Political Philosophy of Montaigne*. © 1990 Cornell University. Used by permission of the publisher, Cornell University Press.

Just Say No: Montaigne's Negative Ethics

T. A. Perry

A debate has raged over the importance of Montaigne's ethics. In contrast to Jacob Zeitlin's view (cited in Schwartz, "Conscience" 245) of the *Essays* as "a landmark in the history of ethical thought in Europe," Gustave Lanson's reading sees in Montaigne almost no ethical system whatever. The problem lies in part with Montaigne's rambling method, for the essayist was the most unsystematic of writers, and such words as *doctrine* and even *ethics* seem inappropriate. I support Zeitlin's view but first try to understand how the impression of an amoral Montaigne is even possible. Note well that I make no attempt at a full and comprehensive treatment of Montaigne's ethics; I wish, rather, to highlight one of its most interesting and neglected features. My presentation follows two pedagogical steps: description and evaluation.

We may approach the problem of perceiving Montaigne's ethics by considering two favorite topics of generations of readers: Montaigne's *self* and his *wisdom*. Many readers see a close correlation between the two, namely, that Montaigne's *sagesse* consists precisely in what he has to say not about the world or about other selves—ethics—but about his own *moi*, notably its discovery and cultivation. Working from this perspective, we often lose sight of the moral argument because of Montaigne's attentive involvement with his own self and the subsequent confusion between *conscience* or "consciousness" and moral *conscience*, forgetting that, morally speaking, Montaigne views his *moi* as merely the most available of many others. He reports on this particular one because it is the one he knows best and the one for which he is responsible.

My focus here is not on Montaigne's self, not on the understandable absorption of others' selves into his own, but rather on what he considers the proper kind of action toward other selves. We cannot leave the *moi*, however, without noticing that Montaigne's most explicit discussion of the topic has a curious emphasis, offers a precious hint on how to behave toward selves (others or one's own): "Authors communicate with the people by some extrinsic mark; I am the first to do so by my entire being, as Michel de Montaigne, not as a grammarian or a poet or a jurist" (611; 3.2). Only the name can point to the entire being, and Michel de Montaigne can begin to be grasped only by rejecting all qualifications, by saying what he is not. Roland Barthes's understanding of this approach is a necessary and sufficient commentary:

> In Morocco they obviously had no image of me; the typically western effort I made to be *this* or *that* evoked no response: neither *this* nor *that* was returned to me in the form of a nice adjective, they had no inclination to comment upon me, they unknowingly refused to feed and to flatter my imagination. At first this dullness of human relations

was exhausting, but slowly it appeared to me as a civilized value, as the truly dialectical form of a lovers' dialogue.   (*Roland Barthes* 47)

To qualify someone, even with an innocent gesture of praise, is an act of violence against that person, so that the only loving approach to the other requires the constantly defensive position of saying what he or she is not. "I may be the person who wrote this book," Montaigne would admit, "but this book is *not me*" (in a much-quoted saying Montaigne speaks of his book as "consubstantial with its author" [504; 2.18]; he does not speak of himself as consubstantial with his book). This approach is hardly "negative"; quite the contrary: it is a refusal to reduce or disperse, by qualification or any type of specification, a perceived richness. But its presentation as original and wise ("I am the first to do so") refers to its negative method.

Turning to ethical action, we again fail to recognize Montaigne's ethical teachings because of a modern confusion about what constitutes action. This point is usually clarified for my students by a simple example. I answer a knock at the door and am greeted with a punch in the face. How should I respond? "Punch the person back" is the usual answer. But who is this assailant? Is my attacker demented? Perhaps the person mistook me for someone else? We agree that simply to hit back before these issues are clarified would be wicked and that striking back would be rather a reaction than an action. Inevitably we come to the conclusion that the true action would be to hold back my reacting hand and, at least for the moment, *do nothing*. Quite different from cowardice or indifference (which, of course, might also be possible motivations), my inaction requires considerable efforts of mind and will. There is thus a crucial distinction between external activity, such as a reactive punch, and action proper, which may of course lead to activity but which is located in the mind and will. Let us then call *action* the efforts of mind and will when directed to external activities, and let us call the opposite a *reaction* or, etymologically speaking, a *passion*. In our example, a lack of restraint on my part would have been motivated by a passion for revenge and would have brought me suffering (Latin *passio*), not necessarily the physical suffering of reprisal but suffering at a much more crucial level of my humanity, since I was out of control. My intent here is not to save what Philip Hallie terms the "Inward Government" theory of ethics (158) but rather to establish that inaction toward others can be a very humane and difficult action. In short, in our search for how Montaigne would have us behave, we expect recommended actions and fail to note the paradox of active inaction.

Montaigne's approach to ethics through negative definition, through non-saying and nondoing, is part of a more pervasive mind-set. In Montaigne the concept of negative ethics has three distinct but interrelated focal points. Let us call them logical, social and moral.

1. The first phase of definition in Montaigne often consists in saying what a

thing is not. In friendship, to give an example that parallels the one above on self-definition, he can only say, positively speaking, that it is a certain "je ne sais quoi," but he does know that it is not erotic love, not cohabitation, and so on. Montaigne may have learned this from the love theorists—it is the dominant approach of Antoine Héroët's "La Parfaite Amye" (1544), for example—as well as from the theologians' *via negativa*, asserting only what God is not. But it is more probable that in his habit of negative definition he leaned heavily upon the skeptics' refusal to assert anything positive and also Stoics such as Epictetus, who divided the entire universe, in order to define moral humanity, between what is within my power and all the rest, what is *not* within my power.

2. In the social sphere, Montaigne frequently views the good as the simple negation and avoidance of evil. The point was commonplace in the aphoristic tradition of medieval Spain and can be summarized by the following Sephardic proverb: Better the absence of evil than the presence of good. Or, more dramatically: Better the death of ten righteous people than the life of one wicked person. In other words, it is better to remove the wicked than even retain the righteous.

Here are Montaigne's formulations: "Princes . . . do me enough good when they do me no harm" (739; 3.9). Or, referring to the troubles of his day: "I know well what I am fleeing from, but not what I am looking for" (743; 3.9). Again, it is incorrect to view this as negative, any more than it is negative to view health as the absence or avoidance of disease. On the contrary, it supposes that health is the good and normal state of a human being but that it can be maintained only by removing all obstructions. Thus, referring to Plato's notion of a person's highest occupation, Montaigne recommends not the pursuit of justice but rather the simple avoidance of injustice.

3. It would appear that Montaigne takes a negative view of those who sit on their hands: "for justice has cognizance and corrective power also over those who are on holiday" (721; 3.9). But it is quite possible that justice will favorably judge those who do nothing, since "abstention from doing is often as noble as doing, but it is less open to the light" (783; 3.10). He then adds a telling apology: "and the little that I am worth is almost all on that side." We can now see Montaigne's constant self-abasement in a different and more positive light. Indeed, his harsh self-criticism, his contemptuous self-identification with "vagabonds and idlers" (721; 3.9), his complaint at being "unsuited for doing good or doing evil" (724; 3.9) are all familiar tricks. Observe how in the very opening essay he registers his distaste for cruelty and revenge by declaring himself "wonderfully lax in the direction of mercy and gentleness" and then goes on to associate this trait with "weaker natures, such as those of women, children and the common herd" (4; 1.1). His habit of negative self-definition comes to a head in his surprising list of qualifications for public office: "without memory, without vigilance, without experience,

and without vigor" (768; 3.10). But we have learned from Montaigne that negation works best against negation, so that he continues his list by setting off these four absences of positive qualities against four absences of negatives: "also without hate, without ambition, without avarice, and without violence" (768; 3.10). In brief, Montaigne defines himself through what he is not; or, as another Sephardic proverb put it, A thing's goodness is known through its opposite. An even more clear and decisive example, pushed to the point of paradox, is Montaigne's discussion of virginity, where he concludes that "there is no action more thorny, or more active, than this inaction" (655; 3.5). Again, action has nothing to do with activity, and restraint can be a high form of human action.

Pedagogically, we have now completed the first step, the description of a telling tendency of Montaigne's thinking: negative definition, avoidance of danger, refusal to state the positive. To reach this stage students are presented with a complete essay, notably "Of Vanity," as well as a listing of explicit examples of negative thinking from other essays, and our class discussion focuses on similarities and differences. My students are especially fond of discussions based on their own experiences: How important are negative characteristics for getting a job (e.g., I don't smoke, don't steal, etc.)? Students in the humanities are interested in connections with the semiotic square and are eager to explore A. J. Greimas's applications to literature. For example, in dealing with any term we must first notice its simple opposition. Thus, the opposite of *true* would be *not true*, whereas the contradiction would be *falsehood*. These possibilities alone supply a rich conceptual apparatus for exploring Montaigne's text.

We now proceed to the second pedagogical step, considered by many students the more intriguing: the obligation to evaluate what we used to call the argument's relevance. Once the descriptive phase has been completed, simply ask your students, What is the value of all this, how does this strike you? One interesting reaction is a feeling of pessimism, for students sense that there is something suspect in the tactic of always considering the ills one does not have or would like to avoid. To show the positive side, point out that related to negative ethics is a kind of philosophical consolation which consists in always imagining that things can be worse; thus, "let us measure ourselves with what is below: there is no one so ill-starred that he may not find a thousand examples to console him" (733; 3.9). An important corollary in the physical and political-social world would be "[a]ll that totters does not fall" (733; 3.9). I offer quotations from E. M. Cioran as a good modern comparison, except that he never says yes to anything and, indeed, in order to avoid disappointment is always on the lookout for new forms of unhappiness.

Another area of concern is the passivity involved in negative ethics, for Montaigne was not a doer, not only because he often recommended not doing as the better course but also because he distrusted enthusiasts and do-gooders (have students read the beginning of the essay "Of Solitude"). His refusal to be a partisan seems an archetype of what was to become a certain type of European intellectual, a type satirized by Sartre in *The Flies*. But even before the religious wars, Rabelais had had similar reservations toward active types, people in constant need of *occupations*, read as *au cul passions* or "passions up the arse." However, those of us who grew up in the fifties are perhaps more aware of the tragedy of the opposite course, those gifted dropouts who took to the woods and refused to bring babies into this corrupt world and still imagine that theirs is the more virtuous way, as if going down the river in a canoe or combing the expanses on a Harley Davidson were as noble as doing homework with a fifth grader. Ah, the bliss of Thoreau, the spiritual profundities of Zen, as against the pedestrian car pools . . .

It seems to me that one of Montaigne's messages to our students is Nancy Reagan's Just Say No, and its modern use can help us understand what Montaigne was up to. Few of us have any illusions that such tactics will root out drugs among our youth, any more than Montaigne thought that his withdrawal would be totally effective against the ills of his day. Personal appeals are only that, but they do presuppose givens without which ethics is not even conceivable: personal responsibility and conscience. Such appeals emerge especially when we become conscious of being under siege, when it seems vital for at least a few to keep a clear head and remember where we should be headed, or at least what we should be avoiding. Negative ethics is a response not to an existential crisis but to a historical one; it attempts to say, when things are this bad, how one should act—by not simply reacting and joining the crowd. Highly aware that actions and values are contextual, Montaigne seems to be addressing us directly: "In a time when it is so common to do evil, it is practically praiseworthy to do what is merely use-less" (722; 3.9).

Albert Thibaudet would have it that the ancients' *neminem laedere* 'harm no one' is a simple matter, hardly worthy of Montaigne's noble strivings (268). But is it? Did Montaigne write only for bookworms and recluses or also and even especially for active people? Consider once more the very first exemplum of the book, dealing with how to avoid those infuriated warriors who have "vengeance in hand." And harming others can also occur inno-cently, so to speak, as Barthes discovered in Morocco; to avoid this com-pletely during normal living with others would be, according to Montaigne's ethics, a remarkable achievement. Today's students are receptive to the suggestion that the highest form of medicine may very well be the preven-tion of disease, a point well understood by all traditional moralities: "To depart from evil is understanding" (Job 28.28); "The highway of the upright turns aside from evil" (Prov. 16.17 [RSV]). Or consider how negatively the Book of Psalms goes about defining human goodness (and many of our stu-dents are passionately curious about religious texts):

> Blessed is the man
> who walks not in the counsel of the wicked,
> nor stands in the way of sinners,
> nor sits in the seat of scoffers. . . .
>
> (Ps. 1.1)

None but the naive would imagine that these constitute complete ethical programs, but they are good places to begin and necessary steps to any moral progress. And without being able to say no, we could never engage in what are now normal obsessions: mundane activities like dieting, balancing a budget, staying sober.

The common image of Montaigne as an amoral relativist is most pernicious and must be openly discussed with our students, for can this possibly describe the very person whose sensitivity to other creatures extended even to the plant world and whose hatred of cruelty and deceit and dishonesty was as absolute as one could imagine? In truth, the real relativist was Machiavelli, who was ready to maneuver and deceive and compromise every value when circumstance required. The surprise is that such a supposedly comprehensive study as Hugo Friedrich's *Montaigne* could totally fail to notice and discuss his subject's ethical presence. But maybe the main contribution of the *Essays* has been to sensitize us boisterous moderns to another negative quality that was Montaigne's by education and temperament and that we are invited to discover: the quality of being *sans bruit*, noiseless. For the grandest representation of this quality in world literature, I direct students' attention to Goethe's dazzling display of the tumultuous churning of the heavenly spheres at the start of *Faust* 2: "Yet your appointed, Lord, venerate the quiet motion of Your day." We too, in reading Montaigne, must learn to look for what is barely there and yet maintains the entire structure with its quiet presence.

The *Essays* and the Visual Arts

Tom Conley

The three books that constitute Montaigne's *Essays* are a watershed of sixteenth-century French culture. For historians and critics alike, Montaigne sums up a century that grew painfully from humanism into the strife of civil war. The essays are also a mix of chronicle, autobiography, and compilation. Their indeterminate form offers a prismatic and comprehensive picture of a person and of the practices of early modern France. The visual arts make their complexity accessible to readers of every condition. The essays often refer to aesthetic objects with admiration and, more tellingly, they deploy them in the arcane and evasive strategies of their composition. Students of any background can therefore approach the *Essays* through the common idiom of the visual arts. If cultural historians are correct in remarking that the Renaissance did not make distinctions among painting, architecture, and literature as we do (McGowan, *Forms* 247), it follows that reading affords the pleasure of learning about the artistic temper of the time, of grasping how Montaigne writes in and through the plastic arts and how the work in fact accounts for them at the same time it distorts them in its printed form.

Placed at the end of a century no less "corrupt" (505; 2.18) than his, we can observe that a comparison of essays to visual media provides clues about style and composition that would be less accessible through exclusively discursive or linguistic approaches. In fact, the splendor of the *Essays* becomes especially attractive for those beginning the task of reading Montaigne's complex, sedimented, and multilingual diction. The arts inform the composition of the essays in at least four ways. First, Montaigne relies on portraiture to convey the character of his nascent autobiography. Second, Montaigne inherits the art of perspective from Italian artists (residing at Fontainebleau since the reign of Francis I, in the first third of the century), which is applied to the verbal form of his work. The same rules of perspective are bent in order to distort, by way of architecture and techniques of painting, the lines of Montaigne's self-portrait. Third, the essays develop a tactic of association clearly linked to practices of framing and of relations of center and circumference in mannerist painting and etching. Finally, many essays are written in tandem with iconic representations of themes contemporary to the author. Juxtaposition of art and text allows readers to see how Montaigne writes in dialogue with what he sees or draws from specific works, common icons, or architectural sites.

A figure crucial to the pictorial design of the three books is the author's self-portrait. Its development corresponds to the self-conscious pose of the author as he presents himself through the fabric of the *Essays*. Pierre Villey and later scholars (e.g., Beaujour) have shown that Montaigne's project evolves from commentary and chronicle into a project of self-representation. As the essayist becomes conscious of the act and process of reading and writing, he likens himself to what would soon become a great and sustaining genre in baroque painting. Since the fine arts and literature do not develop in identical ways or at the same speeds, it can be said that no single painter or sculptor quite resembles Montaigne. Yet, only thirty years later, Rembrandt would begin a similar enterprise, in which his many self-portraits, executed from the 1630s up through the 1660s, record myriad changes depicted on the artist's face and in his many theatrical guises. The early self-portraits are crisp, dramatic, and almost prepossessing; the later, great paintings (e.g., the great self-portrait of 1665, in the Prado) show the artist in his studio, consubstantial with the layers of pigments that make up the figure and ground. Yet, where Rembrandt displays a life of self-representation that evolves over forty years, Montaigne's picture covers only twenty. Deeper affinities, however, are clear: when we read the *Essays* from beginning to end—an adventure that we all should undertake at least once in our lives— the text of Montaigne's self-description evinces duration in the movement and layerings of language written at different intervals and in changing contexts. The self-portrait is necessarily unfinished. It arches back over itself and retouches its earlier impressions in ways unavailable to a painter of portraits. Montaigne's textual autobiography develops in distinctly plastic ways. As in the blurred and tonal lines of Rembrandt's paintings, in which, on close inspection, figure and ground are confused, the shift in Montaigne's chronicle or quotation from observation to self-depiction is indistinguishable even to the most alert reader.

A sense of the evolution can be gleaned when we trace the patterns of Montaigne's pictural metaphors. In "Of Idleness," the birth of the monstrous project of self-reflection brings "chimeras and fantastic monsters, one after another, without order or purpose" (21; 1.8). Comparison of the writing to grotesques or to fanciful decorative borders of frontispieces (of the post-1580 edition of the *Essays*) links the author's imagination to the painter's practice of framing (Zerner; Reed and Wallace 28, 34, 36). Monstrous shapes appear absorbed into the shape of the printed writing in "Of Practice," when Montaigne avows, "[W]hat I chiefly portray is my cogitations, a shapeless subject that does not lend itself to expression in actions" (274; 2.6). Writing becomes tantamount to drawing and painting the unpredictable movements of the self as it pursues its own description (Conley, *Unconscious*). The essayist traces the meanders of the mind in ways comparable to the etcher's art. Yet the self-portrait is always grounded in the paradox of writing that *paints* the self with words. In the famous passage on the relation of the reader and the writer of the *Essays*, in "Of Giving the Lie," Montaigne again uses a metaphor of art to show how the picture of the self emerges from a dialogue of speech and sight shared between the autobiographer and his interlocutors: "Painting myself for others, I have painted my inward self with colors clearer than my original ones. I have no more made my book than my book has made me—a book consubstantial with its author" (504; 2.18). This remark, which appears in the

1595 edition, reflects what the author confesses at the outset of "Of Repen-tance": "Now the lines of my painting do not go astray, though they change and vary. I do not portray being: I portray passing" (610–11; 3.2).

For the first time in Western literature a work of writing puts forward a relation of rivalry with painting. The author shows how the discursive por-trait is developed through a montage of images and words; how a painting cannot express change in the fashion of his own verbal portrait. Even though Montaigne ended the 1580 edition with the image of the book as "this mute and dead portrait" (596; 2.37), painting and writing are of clearly different orders but also in and of each other. Writing is and is not painting (Derrida, *La vérité*). The analogy dissolves into an identity that paradoxically respects the autonomy of picture and writing. By devoting much of his own career to self-portraiture, Rembrandt seems to be one of very few painters whose work corresponds to what Montaigne undertakes in the temporal and pic-tural dimensions of the *Essays*.

Now if the self-portrait emerges from our experience of the discourse of the *Essays*, we must ask if Montaigne uses the comparison of writer and painter in a technical as well as a metaphorical sense. The tabular composi-tion of the *Essays* clearly uses scenographic practices inherited from the art of perspective developed since Brunelleschi and Alberti (Edgerton 124–32). Their innovation involved the construction of optical illusion by means of one- and two-point perspective. Before an appropriately gridded painting, the eye of a viewer is drawn to a vanishing point designed according to geometrical procedure. In the visual arts, development of a perspectival method marked a discovery of an order with effects as vast as those caused by the invention of printing or the conquest of the New World. Armed with perspective, an artist could deploy artificial means to produce scenes that draw the viewer into an illusory depth and toward a point that could be equated with the sign of God. The vanishing point, the axis toward which lines of the painting converge, was allegorized as a juncture of the physical and ideal worlds. Since Dante's time, the arts of rhetoric have known similar techniques (Rigolot, *Le texte* 90–92). Modes of discursive framing located "plot points" in writing or speech, so that authors could direct their words toward and away from an axis or enigma placed at a strategic site—usually near the center—of their verbal compositions.

At the virtual axis of the first volume of the *Essays* (1580), Montaigne appeals to the painter's craft in order to identify how his book is designed in the style of a perspectival painting:

> As I was considering the way a painter I employ went about his work, I had a mind to imitate him. He chooses the best spot, the middle of each wall, to put a picture labored over with all his skill, and the empty space all around it he fills with grotesques, which are fantastic paint-ings whose only charm lies in their variety and strangeness. And what

> are these things of mine, in truth, but grotesques and monstrous bod-
> ies, pieced together of divers members, without definite shape, having
> no order, sequence, or proportion other than accidental.   (135; 1.28)

The grotesque recalls what he mentions in "Of Idleness," but now the author
implies that he maps out the essays according to one-point perspective. In
each volume a vanishing point, or a hidden, axial spot, is denoted at a chosen
center. Thus, each book comprises an odd number of essays that place a sum
of even units about a single, central text or portrait. In the 1580 and 1588
editions, the twenty-nine sonnets of Etienne de La Boétie make up the
"portrait" around which the essay-grotesques are elaborated. The site
matches the number of sonnets with that of the chapter (29), the cipher and
setting designating where Montaigne and his friend vanish into each other.
In 1595, the text states that "these verses may be *seen* elsewhere" (145; 1.29;
my emphasis). Once set, the center is displaced. Yet with an ambivalent or
arcane figure placed at the center, each volume obeys the same compositional practice and leads to the same effect: a visual coordinate entices the
reader to use optical means to seek the center from any given textual point.

Since he is an often demonic and unreliable narrator, Montaigne twists
the same techniques of centering. No sooner is a perspective fixed than the
author appeals to an anamorphic or oblique means to distort what would
otherwise be an obvious or overly didactic visual scheme. "My ideas follow
one another, but sometimes it is from a distance, and look at each other, but
with a sidelong glance ["veuë oblique"]" (761; 3.9). Here and elsewhere
Montaigne adopts the mannerists' love of extended and contorted forms
(Dubois 122–31) that essay the limits of perception and representation of
human anatomy. In these areas the author appears to make direct appeal to
painting, sculpture, and architecture for the sake of blurring and bending
the otherwise "fixing" effects of language and image.

An elegant example is "Of Three Kinds of Association." There Montaigne
sets forth a comparative and visual centering of three of his keenest pleasures: books, women, and friends. The deliberative exercise entails weighing
their various virtues but also choosing the visual placement of two of the
terms on either side of the central one that would—given the perspectival
method—be a vanishing or transcending term. The symmetry announced in
the congruence of the volume (3), chapter (3), and number of associations (3)
seems maniacal. It is immediately twisted by the play of fixing and bending
of the first sentence: "We must not nail ourselves down so firmly to our
humors and dispositions" (621; 3.3). The text alludes to *four* humors under a
chapter about secular trinities, suggesting that what is so "firm" ("ci-fort") is
also what divides into two (in the Latin *furca* behind *fort*).

The uncanny ciphering of the beginning is matched at the end of the essay
by Montaigne's strange description of his library. His room is "on the third
floor of a tower" (629; 3.3). There, when at ease, he will "turn aside a little

more often" (628; 3.3) to catch a sweeping perspective of the area. Montaigne gains a panoptic view of the environs by twisting all around the central core that is his observing and writing body. In detailing the levels of his tower (chapel, bedroom, and library), the account turns up and down the space in a fashion that appeals to the effect of a spiral staircase. The text translates the optical effect of torsion that mobilizes the otherwise stable, perspectival view when a spectator looks down a straight (or Italianate) stairway based on a rectilinear plan. In sketching a curvilinear view of his world, Montaigne describes a vision that recalls the great experiments of the chateaus of the Renaissance (such as the Francis I stairway at Blois, shown in fig. 1). His vision summed up a medieval tradition at the same time that it invested motion and torsion into open space (Guillaume 30). Montaigne's verbal art incorporates the same principles. Thus, when he utters with false modesty, "I live from day to day, and, without wishing to be disrespectful, I live only for myself; my purposes go no further" (629; 3.3), the present indicative, "I live" ("je vis") equivocates on *vis*, which conflates seeing and turning. "I twist" is inscribed in the same statement. In the context we associate the panoptic description with a dizzying and bending view that, like the effect of an *escalier à vis*, turns up and down and around Montaigne's tower. As Marie-Madeleine Fontaine suggests, the writer of the Renaissance, like the architect, "builds" his or her text from geometry and numbers and to the very degree that the spiral staircase corresponds to the "the most profound tendencies of the literary imagination" (115).

Fig. 1. The Francis I stairway at Blois. Photograph by the author

The teacher who assigns the *Essays* to undergraduate and graduate students often encounters perplexed responses. When the text is compared to analogous representations in painting and architecture, however, readers quickly obtain a sense of the iconography of Montaigne's world. As the *Journal de voyage* shows, Montaigne has a highly developed ocular sense. His eye roves everywhere and catches detail (Schapiro 146). Students are thus well advised to look at the essays as mottled or composite shapes inspired by conventional themes seen in contemporary paintings. "On Some Verses of Virgil," a beautifully complex treatment of love, melancholy, sexual difference, the sublime, and old age, is wrought with painting and sculpture. Delayed citation of Virgil's *Aeneid* (645; 3.5), subsequent to what is announced in the title, offers more than an art of amorous delay: a pictural and textual depth is gained when the mannerists' conventions of depicting Mars or Vulcan in embrace with Venus is brought into view (Chastel 151–52). Montaigne refers not only to texts of Virgil or Lucretius but also to entire conventions of painting: "This painting is the result not so much of manual dexterity as of having the object more vividly imprinted in the soul" (665; 3.5). Verbal and pictural icons are compared; when plastic representations of the myth accompany the reading of the text, we discover how the essay constitutes a reflection on the taste and a general style of an epoch. Further, when Montaigne begins the same chapter with the exhortation to have us instruct our souls to follow stiff and solemn rules of behavior, he infuses the stoical tone of his words with pictural figures that belong to sixteenth-century stereotypes. The common person is advised to approach conduct "with some respite and with moderation; it goes mad if it is too continually tense" (638; 3.5). "Tense" translates "bandée," a participle that denotes being blindfolded (and erotically charged) by allusion to "blind Cupid," the putto who is the topic of vision and desire in many pictural treatments of love and Platonism (Panofsky). Reference to the icon in the verbal play twists the stern counsel into comedy and also initiates an ambivalent and multifaceted treatment of the topic. Inscription of the sign of Cupid through the band over his eyes tells the reader that the text will weave its discussion from shards of scenes common to French and Italian schools of painting.

Teaching the *Essays* from the standpoint of the visual arts can lead students into the textures of the period, the evolution of its iconographies, and especially toward a language that shares much with prevailing aesthetic programs. Rembrandt's self-portraits, for example, can be shown in chronological montage as a foil to the temporal composition of the *Essays* and the textual evolution of the self-portrait. Titian's and Tintoretto's studies of space, torsion, and historical subjects can accompany Montaigne's diction and readings of similar themes. The still life and "vanitas," dear to the baroque imagination, can be shown adjacent to "Of Vanity" or "Of Experience" to illustrate different ways of representing the same reflections. These images become sites and memory aids from which extensive textual analysis can be developed but always within the tensions that comparative analysis brings to language.

For a Sociology of the *Essays*

Philippe Desan

Sociology focuses primarily on groups, not on individuals. Although individual case studies do interest the sociologist, it is only to the extent that individual cases reveal attitudes and behaviors that can be generalized. Literary critics have often resisted adopting a sociological approach to literary texts because of the difficulty of developing a theory that encompasses the interrelations of the text, the author, and society. The case of Montaigne and the *Essays* is not an exception. In a sociological study of the *Essays*, one of the essential aims is to move fluidly, and dialectically, from the author to the text and to society in order to demonstrate how these three components overlap. When teaching the *Essays* to undergraduate students, one must be able to establish a relation among the author, the text, and Renaissance society at large. To do this, however, one must first situate these three components in relation to the crucial notions of infrastructure and superstructure, notions that are now a subject of debate within the field of the sociology of literature.

In *The Protestant Ethic and the Spirit of Capitalism*, Max Weber situated this debate in the Renaissance. Sociological determinism and causality remain the major stakes in our perception of the Renaissance as a historical period. A moment of massive economic, social, political, religious, and cosmological transformation and upheaval, the late Renaissance poses the problem of the "social" in relation to the "literary" perhaps better than any other era. The emphasis has normally been placed on a few historical individuals—Copernicus, Luther, Calvin—whose ideas and writings are said to have opened the door to modernity. Proponents of this neo-Hegelian view maintain that a new moral and historical vision, unique to the Renaissance, inspired new forms of economic and scientific behavior. In short, simple qualitative changes occurring within the superstructure (particularly in the spiritual domain) gave rise to a redefinition and reorganization of the existing economic order. The availability of interest-bearing loans in societies adopting the Protestant ethic is often cited as evidence of this view. Were one to read the *Essays* from such a perspective, one could attribute to the individual alone the means of effecting qualitative social change. Montaigne himself might then be considered one of the principal figures who made it possible to define modernity. The values represented in his *Essays*—the good savage, cultural relativism, moral permissiveness, and so on—would be taken as evidence of a change in the "social." In contrast, the Marxist position reverses the Weberian relation between these two structural poles, taking what it posits as the cause to be a mere effect. From a Marxist viewpoint, the Renaissance represents a transitional period between the feudal order and the modern capitalist economy. The rise of the bourgeoisie and the centralization of capital are believed to have led to a redefinition of social relations.

According to this view, the spiritual and the social orders merely reflect the economic order.

When I teach the *Essays*, I address these divergent approaches to understanding a literary text, devoting the first two or three class meetings to posing the theoretical problem of the relation between a text and society. While I evoke the dangers of a theory that asserts that literature reflects society, I also consider the danger inherent in the belief that literature can be viewed as offering a resistance to political, economic, and social phenomena and that literature therefore helps shape society. It is important for students to understand that these two interpretations represent conflicting poles. Ultimately, students have to decide for themselves and take a theoretical stand on the issue. Reading and interpreting a text demand that we make important theoretical decisions. The particular interpretation we give to the *Essays* reveals an ideological choice. In any event, it is necessary to refer to the text itself in order to determine how the literary, the social, and the economic are expressed in relation to one another. In my teaching I emphasize that only an analysis of discourse permits us to see just how these three components interact. My experience has shown that students prefer a positivistic approach to a text, if only as a way of starting to speak about Montaigne and his time. Concrete examples, at least for undergraduate students, are always more rewarding than abstract theoretical ideas.

The language of an era emerges through its individual verbal performances. Because discourse is the primary vehicle for conveying the dominant ideology of a period, discursive tensions provide evidence of various social phenomena. Analyzing discourse is the sole empirical means we have for determining ideology. Although all discourse forms an integral part of the social, I point out to my students the presence of economic preoccupations in the social discourse of the *Essays*. Examining social discourse allows us to comprehend the everyday organization and superstructural functioning of society. Moreover, such discourse "speaks" of its own relation with the infrastructure. Therefore, the infrastructure-superstructure dichotomy is no longer pertinent when we are dealing with discursive analysis; the two poles merge to form a single ideological discourse.

During the late Renaissance (1570–90), a very specific period of which Montaigne can be considered representative, social discourse can be conceived of and expressed only through the nascent economic discourse. From the end of the sixteenth century onward, this new economic discourse— produced, formulated, and diffused daily by the merchants and shopkeepers in the marketplace or on the public square—penetrates social discourse. Economic discourse, then, does not precede, or cause, social discourse; it redefines it.

The unit of analysis that I employ in the classroom is therefore the "utterance." More specifically, I am concerned with utterances that reappear in a systematic fashion and whose terms are organized around various semantic axes, themselves in transition. I call these discursive axes the "axes of socioeconomic utterances." I accept V. N. Volochinov's presentation of the utterance as an analytical unit and its placement within the following order: (1) the economic organization of the society, (2) social communication, (3) verbal interaction, (4) utterances, (5) grammatical forms of the language ("La structure"). While I set aside the issue of the directional aspect of this schema, I retain the structural relation between these five units of analysis.

Before demonstrating the influence of the new axes of socioeconomic utterances on the ideology of the late Renaissance as witnessed in Montaigne, it is necessary to situate these utterances within their extraverbal context. Not only did the late French Renaissance experience political, religious, and cosmological crises, but the period underwent a linguistic crisis as well. Mikhail Bakhtin speaks of a new "linguistic consciousness" awakened during the Renaissance that put an end to the ideological centralization of the Middle Ages (*Esthétique de la création*). The feudal language that survived in the vernacular literature of the early Renaissance, which foregrounded such terms as *virtue, ideal, glory,* and *honor,* in the late Renaissance was confronted with a new type of economic discourse that made abundant use of commercial expressions. These accounting, banking, mercantile, and commercial terms literally invade late sixteenth-century utterances. The predominance of utterances containing economic metaphors and expressions is not a phenomenon that emerges suddenly. For a long period of time, noble and commercial discourses vied with each other for dominance. In the late Renaissance, language becomes the scene of a struggle between two value systems, two opposing ideologies.

It is precisely the displacement and transformation of common sense that draws our attention in the *Essays*. A new discourse breaks down the barriers that before the end of the sixteenth century had separated the idealistic and atemporal values of the nobility from the economic materialism of everyday bourgeois life. A common language now combines the discourse of the social and economic spheres within a single utterance, thereby modifying the semantic and grammatical scope of language. I will go so far as to say that, from this time on, social discourse is conveyed through economic discourse and the two become identical. All social matters are understood through economic discourse, and conversely, all economic matters are conceived as social relations. The economic and the social overlap to comprise what will hereafter be a single language, the basis for "socioeconomic discourse."

Montaigne expresses better than anyone else this struggle taking place within language. He develops a hybrid discourse, a particular style and semantic range where the noble and commercial discourses meet and intermingle. This discursive hybridization demonstrates an ambivalence, a profound hesitancy in the face of nobiliary and mercantile values. Montaigne's socioeconomic utterances thus form a heteroglossia, as Bakhtin has conceived it; that is to say, his discourse accounts for the ideological contradictions of an era. The new discursive horizon we discover in Montaigne's *Essays* incorporates some elements that at first appear contradictory but are soon assimilated into a new type of discourse, a discourse that eventually will surmount the heteroglossia to found a new semantic and ideological terrain of common sense ("le sens commun").

One could easily compile from Roy Leake's concordance to the *Essays* a complete list of Montaigne's numerous economic utterances. The famous Montaignian "self," for example, has often been seen as an object of exchange and commercial interaction, as innumerable passages in the *Essays* show. I point out to my students how Montaigne uses the term *commerce* to describe all human relations. This semantic shift is typical of Montaigne's unconscious attempt to collapse the social and the economic. I take a series of economic terms such as *price, value, cost, give account, market,* and so on and ask students to analyze the context in which Montaigne uses these terms. To facilitate their research I always photocopy the page of Leake's concordance where these words are listed. Each student is responsible for an "axis" of economic discourse, and part of the oral assignment is precisely to connect the stylistic peculiarities of the *Essays* with the economic and the social ones contained not only in these words but also in their larger literary context.

Another example is Montaigne's definition of *value* in the *Essays*. It has often been stated that during the Renaissance exchange value comes to dominate use value and that all fabricated objects come to be considered only in terms of their exchangeability. Montaigne confirms this fact. He tends to place himself within a system of production, such as the composition of the *Essays*, and to consider his relations to others as a form of commerce where value can be acquired. The exchange with the ancients (through reading) often also produces new value for Montaigne. Once more, a close analysis of this type of socioeconomic utterance reveals how Montaigne generates value through his literary interactions. Exchange and commerce become the basic categories for a discourse that cannot escape the logic of an increasingly economic mode of thinking.

All human relationships accrue a market value when placed on the market. Montaigne's *Essays* can be seen as the forum where such an exchange occurs. Value reveals itself at the time of exchange; ideas are submitted for judgment, weighing, and evaluation, as Montaigne affirms: "after having well weighed and considered their qualities" (226; 1.54). The qualitative aspect of nobiliary values, as they have hitherto appeared in ordinary language, is unconsciously replaced in the *Essays* by what might be called a quantification of human relations and exchánges. Like mere merchandise, human "goods" are governed by the implacable laws of the market and assume a qualitative value. It is perhaps the realization that reducing human relationships to quantifiable economic exchanges is inevitable that incites Montaigne to abandon this particular form of commerce. While he abandons "men's commerces," however, there remain still other forms of commerce for him to explore.

Like human relationships, social institutions acquire their true meaning when they are considered as marketplaces. Marriage, for example, can fully be understood from an economic standpoint: "As for marriage, for one thing it is a bargain to which only the entrance is free . . . and a bargain ordinarily made for other ends" (137; 1.28). Montaigne later states: "[Good women] don't come by the dozen, as everyone knows, and especially in the duties ["marché"] of marriage; for that is a bargain full of so many thorny circumstances that it is hard for a woman's will to maintain itself whole in it for long. Men, though they are in it on a little better conditions ["affaire"], have a hard time to do so" (563; 2.35). As a place of exchange between men and women, marriage is expressed through the image of the marketplace, and cultural tradition thereafter develops in economic terms. Montaigne extends his conception of the marketplace even further when he broadens to the extreme the semantic possibilities of the word *market*, declaring on a number of occasions that life itself is a trade: "How easy fortune makes it for me to trade in my life" (753; 3.9).

At the undergraduate level the most pedagogically sound approach for helping students understand the juxtaposition of the economic and the honorable in the *Essays* is to focus on the chapter that opens Montaigne's third book, "Of the Useful and the Honorable" (3.1). Here a close textual analysis of the author's vocabulary highlights the problems in question. First of all, I point out to the students that the topos of the useful and the honorable was one of the most heavily discussed themes during the last decades of the sixteenth century. More specifically, "Of the Useful and the Honorable" provides evidence of a deeper ideological problem that manifested itself clearly after 1572 (the year of the Saint Bartholomew massacre), after the period during which Montaigne wrote the *Essays*. The ideology of this era reflects a profound historical hesitancy between the defense of a chivalric ideal, Ciceronian ethics, and nobiliary values on the one hand and of a pragmatic, commercial, "bourgeois" conception of society on the other. The useful supplants the honorable on a daily basis, on the political and social planes as well as on the economic one. To counterbalance this invasion by the "useful," Montaigne undertakes a defense of the "honorable."

However, Montaigne accepts the inevitability of a pragmatic society, especially in the realm of politics. He clearly states that lying and betraying do exist, but this is a world in which he will not participate: "The public welfare requires that a man betray and lie and massacre, let us resign this commission to more obedient and suppler people" (600). What is interesting in this essay, and what I point out to the students, is the opening paragraph. To reinforce the dichotomy between two types of discourses and ideals, it is essential to use the French text as the English translation loses the "economic" components of Montaigne's discourse.

I start with a close analysis of the first few sentences. Speaking of his "fantasies" (the matter of his book), Montaigne notes, "Mine escape me as nonchalantly as they deserve ["qu'elles le valent"]. All the better for them ["D'où bien leur prend"]. I would part with them promptly for the little they are *worth*. And I neither *buy* nor *sell* them except for what they *weigh*" (599; my emphasis). I have the students discuss this passage, which clearly sets a commercial and economic tone to Montaigne's activity. However, once the students have compiled a list of the economic language in the first three paragraphs (*worth, cost, to buy, to sell, to weigh, to trade, to negotiate* ["négoce"]), I have them analyze the following passage: "The way of truth is one and simple; that of private *profit* and the advantage of one's *business* is double, uneven, and random" (603; my emphasis). I then move on to the nobiliary discourse as it is represented in this essay. I underline how Montaigne speaks about the world of deceit in which he lives and how he contrasts this world with an ideal "man of honor" (605) who never "deviates from his word" (607). At this point I ask the students to draw up a list of the words that directly or indirectly refer to the nobiliary ideal in this essay: *glory, promise, honor, honesty, justice, duty, obligations, gentleness, courtesy,* "greatness of heart," and so on. All these qualities enable Montaigne to speak of "a soul of rich composition" (609).

These two lists of words provide a good basis for the way I approach this essay. I then argue that, in the third book of the *Essays*, Montaigne raises one of the most important questions of the late Renaissance: Can the useful and the honorable coexist in the late Renaissance? Montaigne indicates in the first lines of the essay that the "useful" belongs neither to the public sphere nor to culture. Rather, it belongs to nature: "there is nothing useless in nature, not even uselessness itself" (599). The concept of the useful undergoes redefinition during the late Renaissance: it is no longer applied solely to nature but begins to infiltrate social discourse as well. Montaigne is constantly aware of this passage of the useful into social discourse. His inner conflict over the useful/honorable dichotomy is evidenced by the way his language hesitates between these two discursive poles. Throughout the third book, the idea of conflict is inherent to such a lexical opposition.

Montaigne conceives of all discourse as a form of exchange. Where the useful is concerned, however, the verbal exchange can lead only to deceit and disappointment for the two parties involved: "there is no reason of utility for which I would permit myself to lie to them" (602). Thus, the useful is associated explicitly with deceit, which is defined as a distortion of speech. Montaigne employs the expression "deviate from his word" (607) to describe this discursive perversion. Whereas use and custom harken back to a set of fixed and honorable values anchored in an irrecoverable past, the useful is concerned with the means rather than the ends of the exchange. The distortions begin to surface once the process of exchange and communication is underway. Despite the exchange's useful character, it is nonetheless deformed by the opposing parties and consequently rendered dishonest. One no longer finds here the direct, monologic communication of honorable discourse. Rather, the single voice is replaced by the multiple-voiced dialogism of useful discourse, where the communication act is of greater consequence than the end of the communication.

Deceit and bargaining prevail and thereafter denote the useful character of the epoch's new social, political, and commercial practices: "Innocence itself could neither negotiate among us without dissimulation nor bargain without lying" (603). For this reason, the first chapter of the third book establishes an explicit lexical correspondence between notions of bargaining and negotiation and the distortion of discourse. The role that economics plays here is perhaps more important than either politics or religion to our understanding of the essay. Montaigne includes in his category of the useful the notion of a gain: a profit will be made in the course of the dishonest exchange by at least one of the parties involved. Useful communication, as opposed to honorable communication, produces a winner and a loser.

It is precisely this gap separating "deceitful words" (604) and action, honesty and utility that Montaigne finds so objectionable. One can no longer establish a direct correspondence between the word and its referent. Frank and open conversation is disappearing; a game of linguistic subtleties, on which human action is based, is being created in its stead. We enter into a new political (as the late sixteenth century understood the term) and economic era where speech and subsequent action no longer bear a necessary relation to each other. The inflation and corruption of words are phenomena unknown before this period. These linguistic upheavals also mark an important ideological turning point, characterized by a veritable crisis in discourse. Just as the development of a merchant economy rendered a return to a feudal economy impossible, the new social and political rules made a return to Ciceronian ethics equally unfeasible. The increasing abundance and complexity of linguistic, political, and economic exchanges irremediably diminished and perverted the category of the honorable to the benefit of the useful.

In the midst of such ideological changes, the subject finds himself in an unstable position. Montaigne's dilemma is to secure his own position between these two competing ideologies. He resolves the difficulty raised for the subject by injecting his personal experience into the space between the useful and the honorable. Montaigne's experience, and more specifically the writing of that experience, provides the basis for establishing a correct balance between the two models.

When teaching the *Essays* to undergraduates one must also address the issue of whether Montaigne's economic discourse is merely idiosyncratic or symptomatic of larger linguistic and ideological phenomena. To do so, one must turn to other texts and study this type of discourse as it occurs both synchronically and diachronically. I have found it useful to bring to the classroom several other examples that enable me to claim that Montaigne is not an isolated case. I distribute two or three short odes by Ronsard to show how the poet sees his art as a remunerable labor, and I point out how expressions like "laboring hand" and "labor of my fingers" recur frequently in Ronsard's *Odes*. Ronsard considered his poetic activity as a "trade" (or a *trafic* in French): "I am the trader of the Muses," he liked to explain to his friends (ode to "Bertran Berger de Poitiers"). As revealed in the utterances I have discussed, Montaigne's discursive habits point to a qualitative change occurring in the linguistic practice of the period. Because the *Essays* may be regarded as verbal relations and exchanges with others, the text is essential for the analysis of social discourse during the late Renaissance.

The discursive heterology present in the *Essays*, reflected in the opposition between merchant and nobiliary discourse, coincides with the social and political crises of the late Renaissance. The economic success and social mobility of the merchant bourgeoisie are accompanied by a profound transformation at the linguistic level: the "common sense" of language is redefined, adapting itself to the new worldview and to merchant discourse. The manner in which social relations, as well as all human activity, including literary and artistic activity, are apprehended and described seems to coincide with the mode of economic organization that prevails from the end of the sixteenth century onward. The literary text thereafter is approached and organized as a commercial object and is conceived purely as a commodity. It is thus natural that not only the content, the utterances, but also the structure of the literary work, the form of the essay, can be approached as an accounting book, closely tied to the economic sphere. The late Renaissance marks a decisive moment both linguistically and ideologically. A battle of and for language erupts between two divergent systems of values from which the economic discourse of the marketplace will emerge victorious.

CONTEMPORARY CRITICAL APPROACHES

The *Essays:* Autobiography and Self-Portraiture

Richard L. Regosin

Montaigne's *Essays* should appeal to college-age students grappling with questions of personal identity and facing the daunting task of defining their personal relation to their studies because these are fundamental issues for the essayist himself. The upper-division French and comparative literature students in my seminars on the *Essays*, on autobiography, and on self- and social identity in sixteenth-century literature discover their own concerns in Montaigne's preoccupation with articulating or forming a self and in his effort to determine what is his own and what is foreign to him. Montaigne, of course, is always himself a student, as his essay "Of the Education of Children" indicates, and he finds himself, like most students, pressured by the authority of traditional learning and by the weight of conventional ideas and values. And again like the college-age student, he reveals a psychological and intellectual insecurity that makes him susceptible to social pressures, to fads of all kinds, to flattery. In spite of the enormous differences that separate our American students from Montaigne—differences of time, place, culture, language, learning, and age—they can find the concerns of a kindred spirit in his desire to be something as an individual and in his effort to avoid being totally absorbed by the outside world.

Montaigne indicates from the very outset of the *Essays* that this is a book about himself: "I am myself the matter of my book," he says in his preface, "To the Reader" (2). But students familiar with the autobiographical genre from their high school and college freshman literature courses will be perplexed by what follows, for it will not coincide with what they already know about traditional forms of self-presentation. The knowledge the students have can still serve them, however, and this is a particularly important lesson at this point in their education. They can begin their discussion by exploring the ways in which the text frustrates their expectations; they can approach the question of what the essays are by determining what they are not. Our students will recognize that the essays are not the chronological narrative of a life, a retrospective account of the historical and psychological events that comprise that life and explain or justify what it has amounted to over time and at the present moment of the writing. Montaigne does not say, with the autobiographer, "Here is what has made me what I am, here is the past life I have lived that has brought me to where I am today."

As students should begin to see, serious reading starts with simple questions that allow us to observe and to describe. The work of analysis and interpretation requires that we determine the language appropriate to speak about the text before us. Since the traditional terms—*narrative, chronology, retrospective, account, life as fully formed*—are inappropriate, how should we describe the *Essays?* We can begin with the seminal word *essay* that Montaigne chooses as his title, for among other things this word helps us overcome an initial stumbling block, the problem of understanding how this book in which Montaigne claims to speak only about himself can also be about many other things. I begin with etymology to derive the figure of the scale and to connect weighing with thinking since in Montaigne's languages (both Latin and French) these connections reside within language itself. R. E. Leake's *Concordance des* Essais *de Montaigne* identifies over 150 noun and verb forms of essay, and an analysis of selected uses in context is an important interpretive exercise that turns up the necessary relation between "essaying" as trying out thought and judgment and as writing. A close reading of the essay "Of Democritus and Heraclitus" shows Montaigne explicitly essaying the subject of "essaying" itself. If, as he says there, "Every movement reveals us" (219; 1.50), especially the movement of thought itself, we begin to understand that the essays really are always about Montaigne and that the term "auto-bio-graphy" is in some sense appropriate after all, that the elements of self-reflexivity, life, and writing are central to our understanding of the *Essays.*

We are still (or perhaps always) concerned with lexical problems, with questions of definition: What is this "life" that is being written in the *Essays?* We could, of course, gather the scattered personal references and organize them in a coherent sequence to tell the "story" of Montaigne's life. Some readers have done this. Or we might draw out the essayist's ideas and compile what we could consider his intellectual biography, the "life" of Montaigne's "mind." Others have done this as well. But just as Montaigne's life is not the story of a self already formed before the writing and narrated or represented in the text, so it is not a life that can be fully formed and totalized after the writing. A reading of "Of Idleness," a particularly "autobiographical" essay, suggests that what we might call the textual persona of

Montaigne is a self unformed, in process, and that the writing itself is the very process of formation; it is its life. A reading of "Of Vanity," which begins with the richly suggestive "Who does not see that I have taken a road along which I shall go, without stopping and without effort, as along as there is ink and paper in the world?" (721; 3.9), indicates that the forming of that self, that life, like the writing, is *always* in process, always, like Montaigne's text, under revision. Showing students a copy of a page from the famous "Bordeaux exemplar," the 1588 edition of the *Essays* with its modifications, deletions, and marginal additions in Montaigne's own hand, provides them with tangible evidence of the open-ended way in which the writing, and the life, proceed.

This "life," then, is lived reflexively, in the present, by continually testing thought and judgment, taking stock, reforming, retesting, and so on in infinite regress, just as the writing endlessly reflects upon itself, reads itself, rewrites, rereads. In this activity Montaigne composes and recomposes his persona through the matter and form of his thought and in that matter and form, gaining insight into his own diversity and mutability through the multiple and often contradictory perspectives from which he applies his judgment to the subjects of his essays and to himself. This means that we as readers discover Montaigne in his language as well as in his ideas. We find him not only in his personal references and anecdotes but in his rhetorical figures, not only in his opinions about friendship or about education but in his syntactical structures, not only in his quotations and classical allusions but in the semantic richness of his lexicon and its patterns of repetition, association, and opposition. Thus, in "Of Vanity," for example, Montaigne's life will comprise the literal events of managing the household and travel; it will be composed by assaying the feelings and attitudes that both produce his activity and are its products; and it will be formed by the composition of lexical and semantic relations that make traveling and writing figures of the self and of its life through the concept of *vanitas*. Vanity, the essay demonstrates thematically, structurally, and rhetorically, resides not only outside the self but within; it is in every sense of the word an "in-forming" principle: "Get rid of it I cannot without getting rid of myself" (766; 3.9), Montaigne says as he concludes.

I want to come back to our starting point and to the ways that Montaigne articulates his concern that his reading and his study contribute to his self-formation but not overwhelm it. Even a cursory look at any of the essays gives our undergraduates a feel for the extent of Montaigne's erudition and the prominent place of quotation, paraphrase, and learned allusions in his writing. We can also point to those capital moments when the essayist himself reflects on this practice and disparages it: in "Of Vanity," for example, where he refers to the "ill-fitted patchwork" quality of his text (736; 3.9), or in "Of Physiognomy," where he recognizes that his borrowings might appear as "a bunch of other people's flowers" (808; 3.12). This disparity between

Montaigne's condemnation of citation and his apparent persistence in its use—which students often see as hypocritical—suggests that much more may be at stake here than simple consistency. The essays are inconceivable without Montaigne's extraordinary learning and his intimate knowledge of the Latin and Greek classics (either in the original or in translation) and of contemporary Italian and French literature and culture. At the same time, the powerful opposition that operates in the text between self and other, between what is native or inside and that which is alien and outside, makes all learning problematical. From the outset, in the liminary "To the Reader," what is domestic, private, simple, natural, and ordinary is valued over what is artificial, ornamented, studied, or acquired (2). By examining Montaigne's use of the single word "borrowed" 'emprunté' in essays as diverse as "Of the Power of the Imagination," "Of Solitude," "Of Books," "Of the Art of Discussion," "Of Vanity," and "Of Physiognomy," we can appreciate both the ubiquity of the issue and the essayist's concerns. Both "Of Pedantry" and "Of the Education of Children" are important, and accessible, expressions of Montaigne's pedagogical ideal that acquired knowledge be personalized and made one's own.

A much more difficult essay, but one to which I return often with my students, is "Of Physiognomy." The students find the prose particularly dense and the structure perplexing, especially since Montaigne does not seem to get to the issue of physiognomy until the last few pages of his text. It is worth grappling with the essay's language and with the problem of coherence or unity because of the central role played by the seminal figure of Socrates. Especially in the later essays, Socrates becomes a sort of alter ego for Montaigne, a figure in whom he sees himself as he would be, or perhaps into whom he projects qualities and attitudes he seeks for himself. Socrates's language becomes for the essayist the ideal language, his attitude toward death the essential human attitude, his skepticism and acceptance of ignorance the highest form of wisdom, his humanity and generosity the perfection of our nature. Montaigne's portrait of Socrates is his own ideal self-portrait.

In the context of the *Essays*, Socrates's supreme gesture is to have brought back the human gaze from objects unknowable, from the cosmos, from things metaphysical, from all that is "outside," to the only important object of knowledge, the self: "It is he who brought human wisdom back down from heaven, where she was wasting her time, and restored her to man, with whom lies her most proper and laborious and useful business" (793; 3.12). Time and again, Montaigne reproaches himself for his presumptuous talk about himself (in "Of Giving the Lie," for example), but Socrates is always the guarantee that the self is the only thing worth talking about; he is the ultimate guarantee of Montaigne's autobiographical project. In "Of Physiognomy" the essayist makes the claim, again in Socrates's name, that we hardly need anything outside ourselves to live at ease: "Socrates teaches us that it [learning] is in us, and the way to find it and help ourselves with it. All this ability of ours that is beyond the natural is as good as vain and superfluous" (794; 3.12). But the irony of this claim is particularly striking given the impressive book learning that Montaigne displays in the *Essays* in general, and which he specifically admits in this essay (808), and it is heightened by the opening lines: "Almost all the opinions we have are taken on authority and on credit" (792). Even what we know of Socrates, Montaigne adds, is secondhand. How then are we to understand the relation between what is natural and what is foreign to us? Of what is the *bios* of autobiography composed and how are we to compose it?

The problem of the life or the self is for Montaigne ultimately a problem of composition, a problem of writing about oneself, or of "writing" oneself (autography). The material with which one works is always borrowed and the challenge is to appropriate it, to transform it or to deform it to make it one's own. Thus the essayist seeks to rewrite Socrates as the model of nature, to cast him as his own first-person discourse, to reenact his speech, as he does in the long paraphrase of Socrates's address to his judges from the *Apology*, and to recuperate his ethical postures. In the process Montaigne replaces Socrates as the emblem of nature—both because he has not had to reform his inward nature and because his physiognomy is a guarantee of his soul, as the concluding narratives confirm. And even though an "outside," a "surface," his text participates in nature itself, because his writing, like his face, is the place of nature's presence.

While the strategy of self-composition is laid out and practiced in "Of Physiognomy," and impressive logical and rhetorical resources are brought into play to fashion a coherent and natural self, the issue itself is not resolved, as the paradox of Plutarch's presentation of the two faces of things, "variously and contrastingly," in the concluding lines of the essay reveals (814; 3.12). The self can never entirely naturalize the foreign—and borrowed—material out of which it must compose itself, and it can never entirely overcome the artifice of attempting to make it its own through reading and writing. At the same time, only the effort to domesticate learning, knowledge, and opinion can create the sense of a self; only the artifice that is learning and writing itself can provide access to the natural at all. Montaigne's "life" is lived, and written, within these bounds, between the competing pull of world and self, of outside and inside, of artifice and nature. In the double dynamic of "essaying," of testing his judgment and writing, Montaigne gives ongoing expression and substance to the change and variety that he finds at the very heart of being.

My own preference in teaching Montaigne is to emphasize the dynamic and problematical "autobiography" over the more traditional, and admittedly more accessible, portrait of the settled and serenely wise Renaissance humanist. I believe that this reading can allow students to glimpse how learning must become an active process, how it is always a personal process, and how it is inevitably an endless process. The text opens before us a life that is constantly monitored, and accordingly revised and recomposed, although it can never be totally controlled or mastered. And this last point is an important one, for it is a measure of Montaigne's humanity that even as he concentrates his gaze intently upon himself, there are qualities, attitudes, and postures that escape him. A close reading of "Of Presumption" reveals that the essayist falls into the very trap he would avoid, that in his humility and self-depreciation, and in his exclusive concern with himself, he exhibits the most scandalous presumption. This essay is often cited as one of the most autobiographical because Montaigne includes a wealth of personal detail and appears to reveal his most intimate thoughts. I would claim that it is autobiographical precisely because it reveals more than it intends, and perhaps more than the writer actually knows, and because in and through the writing the life of the writer is inscribed in all its complexity, its multiple and paradoxical aspects. This is where we and our students can enter as readers to bring the text to life.

A Reader-Oriented Approach to Teaching Montaigne

Cathleen M. Bauschatz

When students begin to read Montaigne for the first time, they are often struck by different features of the text than is the *suffisant lecteur* who has read and studied the *Essays* many times. Rather than look at the text as an artifact, students tend to want to read the *Essays* to find out what Montaigne was like. As Peter Rabinowitz has shown, most "real" readers (as opposed to academic readers) embark on a quest for authorial intention when they begin a book, which no amount of New Critical or poststructuralist briefing can dislodge. In teaching Montaigne in French to a mixed group of advanced undergraduate and first-year graduate students at the University of Maine, I found that students approached the reading of the *Essays* first as a personal quest to get to know Montaigne and then as a way to find out differences and similarities between the essayist and themselves.

Naturally language, vocabulary, style, and structure are all problems for students reading sixteenth-century French for the first time. But compared with Rabelais, whom we had spent the first half of the semester studying, Montaigne appeared much easier. More important, students with no previous knowledge of the French Renaissance now had a framework or schema in which to place some of the new information that they received on Montaigne and his times (Anderson and Pearson). Finally, reading Rabelais had already prepared them to be skeptical of the dictionary as a tool for reading sixteenth-century French. Rather, they were prepared to plunge in and "just do it"—to decipher the text on their own. This strategy heightened their sense of personal encounter with the *Essays* and with Montaigne himself.

However, one particular difficulty, for which the reading of Rabelais had only partially prepared the class, was Montaigne's use of Latin quotations. My students, as foreign language majors, were intrigued with Montaigne's facility in Latin and often commented on it in their papers, even going so far as to include their own Latin citations. As they struggled to translate sixteenth-century French, some found it comforting to realize that Montaigne had mastered an even more ancient and difficult language and that he had used methods similar to those of the modern "total immersion" school. One student commented, "I am beginning to review Latin, in order to read Montaigne's ancient influences better." For most, however, the Latin quotations in the *Essays* represented an obstacle to be bypassed, not a source of illumination.

Like the early humanists described by Thomas Greene, students were generally overwhelmed with the discovery, through Montaigne, of an ancient world they knew almost nothing about. "There are so few young people who know a word of the ancient philosophers—everyone is ignorant of classical works," writes another of my students. Reading Montaigne sometimes gives beginners the unsettling feeling that they inhabit a new Dark Age.

Student evaluations from the course included one comment on the combined satisfaction and frustration of studying the Renaissance: "I feel that I have learned a great deal about this literary period, but the more I learn, the more I realize that there is so much more to learn." Reading the *Essays*, or any humanist text for that matter, can initially erode students' confidence in their knowledge and their ability as readers.

Closely related to the students' reluctant discovery of antiquity is another discovery: that of the conflict between youth and age. For readers in their early twenties, many views in Montaigne, particularly his ideas on love, are impenetrable. For example, students cannot accept the preferability of friendship to love described in "Of Friendship," which is, paradoxically, one of the first chapters in the book to engage them personally. One young man wrote a marvelous dialogue between Montaigne and himself, in which he returned from a tragic love affair to admit defeat: "Alas, good old Montaigne! You were right! However you will appreciate that I not only put one finger into the electric socket, I even put in a second one, to feel the effects." This student had disregarded Montaigne's advice on love but, with his "electric socket" metaphor, showed that he had internalized the idea of learning from experience, found in "Of Experience."

A third difficulty described by students concerns a difference in values: Montaigne's perceived "elitism," in particular his attitude toward women and "le vulgaire." One young woman commented, "Another thing which strikes me is that Montaigne writes for a very elite group of individuals." This perception sometimes led to claims that Montaigne would not be the same if he were writing now: "Would he have the same psychology today that he had at his own time? I don't think so." This sort of conflict represents a refusal to accept as real the Montaigne of the past—who is unlike us in many ways—and an attempt to force him to be more like the modern reader.

Most readers, rightly or wrongly, do come to see Montaigne as like themselves and feel able to bridge the gaps of age, gender, geography, language, values, and historical context that separate them from him. One student, after making an analogy between the insights in "Of Cannibals" and her observations on soldiers returning to Bangor, Maine, from the Persian Gulf, commented, "After having read several essays . . . we begin to think about our own time and the questions which are being asked now. If we arrive at that stage, the linking of the ideas of Montaigne to ourselves . . . is created. At this moment, the essay is not four hundred years old, but contemporary."

This perception of similarity—and sometimes of false similarity—contains its own dangers. As William Kerrigan and Gordon Braden point out in *The Idea of the Renaissance*, the traditional response of the "rhetoric of professorial power" would be to answer, in a chilling tone, "Interesting, Miss Hull. But in the Renaissance . . . " (x). We all struggle daily with students' discoveries that Montaigne is "just like" Nietzsche or Andy Warhol, that he prefigures "Bill the Cat" or that his ideas on education or the environment are "really modern." Finding a proper response to these discoveries requires us to tread a fine line between indulgence of error and repression of creativity. But ultimately it is worthwhile to pursue, despite the many linguistic and temporal difficulties posed by the *Essays*, students' discoveries of similarities between Montaigne and themselves, even, at times, if they are wrong. Despite the fact that students perform what they believe to be an author-centered reading of the *Essays*, we must be reader-centered enough as teachers to realize that students do learn many things from reading Montaigne and that not all of these things are directly about the essayist.

The Montaigne section of this course required students to keep a journal in which to note their reactions to the *Essays* as well as random thoughts that occurred to them along the way. While writing in their journals, many commented on the affinity they felt with the essayist, who was also alone and sitting in a room writing, possibly looking out a window, as they were. Earlier in the semester, we had seen on video the Kenneth Clark episode that treats Montaigne—the trip with Clark through the rooms of the château and into Montaigne's study, with a pause to look at the view from his window, had obviously touched them.

Student comments on the theme of solitude were often moving and deeply felt: "There is something of myself which I can only touch when I am alone. . . . Everyone needs a place just for himself to find peace." A second student commented that, to understand Montaigne, we should follow his example: "It seems to me that, in order to read an author for whom the principal pleasure and work is to observe himself thinking, we can do no better than to imitate him in his working conditions." She goes on to say, "Since much of Montaigne's thought has to do with the position of man in nature, a window which permits us to observe natural phenomena would be profitable."

Closely related to the theme of physical solitude, or that of being alone in "a room of one's own," was the frequently stated awareness of the act of writing, of watching oneself write, and of the *rapprochement* with Montaigne achieved through this process. On journal writing, one student commented, "Keeping a journal is a good idea, even though it takes a lot of time. At any rate, it is very interesting to see my own thoughts on a piece of paper. This is also a good idea because Montaigne contradicts himself many times and even if I contradict myself, I can tell myself the truth for myself, and not for Montaigne. And even though 'according to Montaigne' is worth more for others than 'according to me,' still 'according to me' is the most important to me." A better formulation of Montaigne's commitment to authenticity would be hard to find in our critical literature. Moreover, this reflection also indicates that the initial lowering of self-confidence caused by the difficulties in reading Montaigne can be gradually reversed once students begin to respond to the epistemology of self-study in the *Essays*.

Another reader also commented on the use of journals: "To profit from reading Montaigne, then, one must keep a journal where are mingled notes on reading, summaries of the thoughts of the author, and personal reactions, those thoughts provoked by reading: the transformation which constitutes the development of our judgment." Finally, a student wrote about the process of artistic creation, with a parallel to the way in which Montaigne continually adds to the *Essays*: "I always want to change something in 'finished' works. For me nothing is finished unless it is taken or rather snatched away from me. I am never satisfied that a work expresses me as well as I wish to be understood. The problem is that I change every day."

The dilemma of contradiction and change, despite the unchanging nature of the written word, provides a transition to the most universal theme, expressed by virtually all readers, whatever their age, in responding to Montaigne. This, of course, is the motif of search for self, for identity, which represents the strongest personal theme for traditional and nontraditional students alike. On the need to develop self-knowledge and self-appreciation in relationships with others, one student reflected, "I see better now that appreciation of oneself engenders necessarily appreciation of oneself through and across others . . . the more I think about it, the more I see that the road which leads to romantic as well as personal satisfaction is only blocked by a gate whose key is confidence engendered by self-knowledge."

Two other writers compared Montaigne's self-discovery with their own. One wrote, "He is in the process of discovering himself, as I am, by thought put in writing. To read Montaigne, then, is to listen to one's own thoughts. . . . Reading Montaigne is hard, but it is an experience of discovery—discovery of Montaigne in reading him, and of oneself in following his example." A second reflection is the following: "Finally, to read Montaigne is at the same time an encounter with another mind and an encounter with oneself, with our own thoughts and opinions. In this sense, reading Montaigne is a continuous task, and the work of Montaigne is an open work. It is not a form of reading which one can perform without participating in it."

The last sentence shows clearly the value of using a reader-oriented approach in teaching Montaigne. For in allowing readers to react on their own level to the *Essays*, we teach them much more than the historical and biographical circumstances of the book, its ancient sources, philosophical alignments, and stylistic devices. Students also learn important truths about reading, writing, the relation of both to judgment or self-knowledge, and which truths must be learned for themselves—not just "for Montaigne."

But, paradoxically, readers actually do learn valuable ideas on education through those offered by Montaigne himself in "Of the Education of Children" and elsewhere. Like him, they learn a valuable lesson: "I do not speak the minds of others except to speak my own mind better" (108; 1.26). In reading about the bee-honey analogy for the learning process, the student inevitably does "transform and blend [ideas from elsewhere] to make a work that is all his own, to wit, his judgment" (111; 1.26). This discovery that what students learn is actually found in the text itself brings us back to the author-centered perspective on reading Montaigne noted at the beginning of this essay. We are left with the circular realization that students may learn how to read Montaigne from Montaigne, often without being completely aware of it.

In reading Montaigne to discover what he was like, students follow the desire he expressed in "On Some Verses of Virgil": "I am hungry to make myself known, and I care not to how many, provided it be truly" (643; 3.5). When readers move from perceiving Montaigne as different from themselves to seeing him as more like themselves, they are making the same transition that Montaigne did when he moved from the statement "Their most universal quality is diversity" (598; 2.37) to the statement "Each man bears the entire form of man's estate" (611; 3.2). When they successfully eliminate the distinction between "according to Montaigne" and "according to me," they are only echoing Montaigne's discovery in "Of the Education of Children": "It is no more according to Plato than according to me, since he and I understand and see it in the same way" (111; 1.26). Finally, when students realize that they understand themselves, at least fairly well, they are making the same discovery that Montaigne made in "Of Repentance": "At least I have one thing according to the rules: that no man ever treated a subject he knew and understood better than I do the subject I have undertaken: and that in this I am the most learned man alive" (611; 3.2).

In the course of reading and studying Montaigne, students inevitably read and study themselves—and in the process we, as teachers, must be prepared for the eventuality that they may leave us behind. This possibility too is found in Montaigne, who has no great love for teachers, as we learn in "Of Pedantry." Not only does he point out that "a teacher [is] always the butt in Italian comedies" (97; 1.25), but, more seriously, he sees the teaching profession as one that may do more harm than good: "These schoolmasters, as Plato says of their cousins the Sophists, are of all men those who promise to be the most useful to men, and who, alone of all men, not only do not improve what is committed to them, as does a carpenter or a mason, but make it worse, and take pay for having made it worse" (101–02; 1.25). This criticism may seem an extreme statement of Montaigne's antagonism toward the teaching profession, but it does bring us back to the realization that, up to a point, students do learn from reading Montaigne on their own, almost at times in spite of us.

One final example of this troubling phenomenon appears in a student paper, in theory an essay on Montaigne, in the style of Montaigne: "Without a guide, without a master, without a professor I can let my thoughts go. Sometimes I don't have any: this is the moment of my greatest pleasure, when it seems that I am happy. Happiness is found at the moment when one has no thought at all. People often say that we are hedonists—we seek pleasure. Pleasure, happiness, that is the goal whatever the method used to find it. Pleasure is what I seek."

What has this student learned about Montaigne and the Renaissance? Obviously his response shows some of the limits of a solely reader-oriented approach to the study of earlier texts. While as a scholar I may lament the shortcuts the student has taken to cull from Montaigne values that seem to appeal to him, still as a reader-teacher I must applaud the audacity that allows him to state that his best ideas—or nonideas—are reached in the absence of a professor. In fact, this is a theme he may have found in Montaigne! The dilemma described here is one of the surprising—and often frustrating—mixed blessings of teaching Montaigne to undergraduates. At its best, however, this sort of personal, idiosyncratic reading reaches some of the goals of "interactive" rather than "extractive" approaches to texts:

> Rather, [interactive reading] is one [process] in which the reading activates a range of knowledge in the reader's mind that he or she uses, and that, in turn, may be refined and extended by the new information supplied by the text. Reading is thus viewed as a kind of dialogue between the reader and the text. (Grabe 56)

This insight about reading is also found in the *Essays*, in Montaigne's well-known tennis metaphor for the reading process:

> Speech belongs half to the speaker, half to the listener. The latter must prepare to receive it according to the motion it takes. As among tennis players, the receiver moves and makes ready according to the motion of the striker and the nature of the stroke. (834; 3.13)

At times, as in the student example quoted above, this dialogue is in danger of becoming a monologue and one that could be elicited by almost any text, or no text at all. Occasionally, we must admit that the reader can miss the ball completely. There is, after all, a limit to reader-oriented pedagogy. As teachers, we need to help students prepare to receive a serve, retrieve the ball when it goes outside the court, and determine what the rules are for who "wins" at the end of the game.

Montaigne, of course, also recognizes the need for a teacher, even if he objects to the pedagogical analogy of "pouring water into a funnel" (110; 1.26). While the tutor lets the student "clear his own way," listens to him "speaking in his turn," and asks "his pupil [to] trot before him," still the tutor must be there for these things to take place. Finally, Montaigne's best-known contrast on education, that between the "well-made" and the "well-filled" head, is actually found in a sentence describing the teacher, not the student: "I would also urge that care be taken to choose a guide with a well-made rather than a well-filled head . . ." (110; 1.26). This exhortation is a formulation of Montaigne's often repeated preference for judgment over knowledge. Rather than letting our knowledge interfere with the contact between students and the text of the *Essays*, we must instead work to facilitate that contact, using our judgment to help serve as referee to the dialogue or tennis game that does take place, ultimately, between the reader and Montaigne.

Montaigne and Psychoanalysis

Lawrence D. Kritzman

Psychoanalysis and literature have traditionally been in an agonistic relation in which the former has been granted special privileges in the heuristic encounter with verbal art. Accordingly literature's function was one of passivity before the imperialist authority of psychoanalytic theory. More often than not the literary text succumbed to the positivist application of the analytic fantasy of Freudian domination so that literature became a mere reflection and reification of the *already known*.

Yet one may still read literary texts from a psychoanalytic perspective and transcend the traditional master-slave relationship that constrains the analytical discourse figured in verbal art. Among others, Shoshana Felman has discussed the necessity of generating implications between literature and psychoanalysis by exploring the ways in which psychoanalysis constitutes a "fiction" and literature puts forth an analytic discourse that enables us to come to terms with the workings of the unconscious (8–9). In no other place can this encounter be more fruitful than in the pedagogical situation where the analysis of the "literarity" of literature can fill the gaps that a student might encounter with a specific psychoanalytic theory.

In teaching Montaigne's *Essays* in a course on psychoanalysis and literature at Dartmouth College, I often have my students read a particular analytic text along with a specific essay. My intention is to show how, on the one hand, psychoanalytic theory can help to elucidate the dynamics of the Montaignian writing project and how the essay, on the other hand, represents a self that dramatizes a conceptual framework for the workings of the mind.

For the purposes of this essay I would like to implicate Jacques Lacan's article "The Mirror Stage as Formative of the Function of the I" and Montaigne's essay "On Friendship" in a conceptual dialogue. In both the Lacan text and the Montaigne essay we are dealing with the question of ego formation and the psychical condition that is the result of a certain form of narcissistic development. If Lacan's text theorizes the genesis of the human subject due to the reflection of the self found in the visual perception of the mirror, the Montaignian essay figurally represents the undoing of the self through the shattering of an ideal union.

In principle, Lacan's article gives the student certain basic theoretical concepts to consider. It deals with two key topoi that are worked out in "On Friendship": the relationship between self and other and the edenic illusion of unity associated with symbiotic bliss. I have selected the Lacan essay on the mirror stage as the point of departure for my pedagogical strategy because it puts forth its own "fiction" of ego formation based on an illusion that mixes image with reality. In Lacan's metaphoric model of ego development children of six to eighteen months of age experience a formative event when they recognize themselves in the mirror, and they believe that the reflection is part of a whole self. Underdeveloped and as yet biologically inadequate, a mirror-bemused infant engages in a quixotic form of ego building by introjecting the self's other—the reflection in the mirror—and accepting it as an ideal unity.

> The *mirror stage* is a drama whose internal thrust is precipitated from insufficiency to anticipation—and which manufactures for the subject, caught up in the lure of spatial identification, the succession of phantasies that extends from a fragmented body-image to a form of its totality. (4)

This narcissistic metaphor enables the child to overcome its feeling of inadequacy—its anatomical incompleteness—by accepting the blissful pleasure associated with seeing two as one. According to Lacan the mirror stage provides an anticipated sense of self-mastery derived from the illusory unity the child believes to have found in the visual perception of the mirror.

What is striking about Lacan's theory of ego formation is the hypothesis that the sense of self begins with a narcissistic investment in an image that creates a false sense of autonomy. The child's perception of the shift from fragmentation to the illusion of unity reveals the unquestionable alienation underlying the process of ego building:

> This *Gestalt* symbolizes the mental permanence of the I, at the same time as it prefigures its alienating destination; it is still pregnant with the correspondences that unite the I with the statue in which man projects himself, with the phantoms that dominate him, or with the automation in which, in an ambiguous relation, the world of his own making tends to find completion. (2–3)

For Lacan, then, the ego is the product of an imaginary relationship, the spatial identification with the reflection of a human form. What motivates this relationship is the recognition stemming from the absence of the (m)other. The perception of this ontological void propels the child, unconsciously driven by a sense of nostalgia, to seek out its "other" and to compensate for the feeling of deprivation in the pure plenitude of an imaginary identification. The subject's specular re-cognition of a totalized self-image is, in fact, a misrecognition of the self; its identification is with the image of another.

Lacan's theory of ego formation provides students with certain key themes that are implicated in the reading of Montaigne's essay "On Friendship." Lacan's reading of the mirror stage not only depicts the model of an ego ideal but also dramatizes the difficulty of representing oneself to oneself. As we will discover in Montaigne's text, subjectivity can only be constituted through a mirror image, a two-person structure in which the subject is dependent on nondifferentiated images for its sense of being. The other, who is ostensibly one's double, must be perceived as the same and engaged in a consubstantial relationship.

It is indeed tempting to find thematic parallels between Lacan's "fiction" of ego formation and Montaigne's "theory" of lost friendship. By now it is a critical commonplace to view the death in 1563 of Montaigne's best friend, the humanist writer Etienne de La Boétie, as having motivated the essayist to compose the *Essays* in order to overcome mourning, to memorialize the friend, and to create a surrogate object of communication with which the essayist could dialogue. In the solitude of real life, the text becomes a substitute for the absence of the "real" friend and a compensation for what Montaigne can no longer have.

To be sure, La Boétie's demise is described as having produced a feeling of inconsolable loss: "The loss would be mine, for I would lose the company of so great, so wise, and so sure a friend, such a friend that I would be certain never to find another like him" (*Complete Works* 1048). If Lacan's theory of the imaginary anticipation of corporeal unity is a proleptic gesture based on an illusory act of totalization that can never authentically be realized, then the undoing of the euphoria of wholeness depicted in Montaigne's text can only be described retrospectively as a sense of loss that can never fully be recaptured. The alienation intrinsic to the metaphor of ego formation in the first example is an ontological given while that of the second is a result of death.

In drawing on additional evidence found in texts such as Montaigne's letter to his father describing La Boétie's death as a "human calamity," the student will realize the extent to which this relationship was idealized and the effect produced by the dissolution of the magical union. The absence of the friend, however, gives Montaigne a literary vocation of sorts. The narrative recounting the death scene contains La Boétie's appeal for the essayist to become the executor of his friend's literary "will." In the chapter "On Friendship," La Boétie is represented as a man who, through his example, can be associated with the glory of antiquity: "In the matter of natural gifts, I know no one who can be compared with him" (135; 1.28). Not only does Montaigne inherit his friend's literary estate as a sign of affection, but he "acts out" the intellectual legacy of this friendship in the writing of the *Essays*. As I have attempted to demonstrate elsewhere, language gives form to the voice of bereavement and functions as a symbolic reenactment of La Boétie's will ("Romance" 75). Montaigne transforms the text into a memory place, a tomb on which is inscribed the literary praxis inherited from the friend.

Indeed, loss sets the writerly act in motion, and the essay "On Friendship" particularly represents affect as the symptomatic mark of separation: "I only drag on a weary life. And the very pleasures that come my way, instead of consoling me, redouble my grief for this loss" (143). The signs of bereavement in this text are translated through images of emptiness and transience (the repetition of the verb *perdre* 'to lose') that depict the feeling of loss reflected in the text. Taking on a quasi-mystical tone, Montaigne envisions his life as "nothing but smoke, nothing but dark and dreary night" (143). The truly unrepresentable nature of this deep mourning transforms the memory of friendship into a web of signifiers that no signified can ever fully recover in the writing of the *Essays.*

For Montaigne, the death of the friend represents the death of part of the self; it reinscribes the thematics of transience into a theory of human development: "I was already so formed and accustomed to being a second self everywhere that only half of me seems to be alive now" (143). The fragmented ego is thus the result of a break with an edenic past—the idealized friendship—that is transcribed as an evacuation of plenitude. If the image in the mirror is perceived as constituting the self's oneness in Lacan's essay, the disappearance of the ground for the ego ideal in Montaigne becomes part of the lack that loss establishes. To speak of fragmentation, then, is to evoke an unchanging absence that undermines the presence of being.

To intensify the singularity of his friendship with La Boétie, Montaigne compares it with other relations from which it is excluded. In the rapport between fathers and children it is respect that creates inequalities and renders the communication necessary for friendship impossible. Victims of inevitable rivalry, brothers are incapable of the harmony that must exist between two friends. The relation between husbands and wives also precludes the establishment of friendship since it is essentially a contractual one. Furthermore, carnal love, according to Montaigne, forecloses on the possibility of friendship because it is constantly attuned to the vicissitudes of desire. And the classical notion of homosexual association, that "licentious Greek love" (138) based on the disparity of age and physical attributes, is excluded because it prevents the harmonious union of friendship and transgresses the rules of Christian morality.

Clearly, the friendship that Montaigne envisages is derived from the reinterpretation of ancient models. From Cicero, the essayist borrows the theme of perfection that is intrinsic to true friendship: "so the union of such friends, being truly perfect, makes them lose the sense of such duties, and hate and banish between them these words of separation and distinction: benefit, obligation, gratitude, request, thanks, and the like" (141). In rewriting this topos Montaigne discovers a zone where differences are replaced by a kind of transcendental idealism in which value is mirrored in the friend that one incarnates.

In drawing on an Aristotelian topos Montaigne describes the friend as another self. Rooted in a relation of perfect communication and mutual reflection, this idealized friendship realizes the singularity of an objectless self-absorption that assimilates two into one:

> For this perfect friendship I speak of is indivisible: each one gives himself so wholly to his friend that he has nothing left to distribute elsewhere. . . . The secret I have sworn to reveal to no other man, I

can impart without perjury to the one who is not another man: he is myself.   (141–2)

Montaigne fixes himself on an image that draws him even closer to his "real" self. If the communication with the other is simply a dialogue with the self, it is because object-choice for the desiring subject is not for the other per se but for the self within the other. The essayist's narcissistic merging with La Boétie creates a situation whereby the friend becomes so fused and identified with his own being that to see the other is to see oneself: "In the friendship I speak of, our souls mingle and blend with each other so completely that they efface the seam that joined them . . . " (139). Unlike the Lacanian model in which the double is a fictional extension of the self, the fusion of the souls described here highlights the fuller relation that life will ultimately efface. This undivided oneness with the other thus represents a spiritual plenitude that constitutes an ideal self, "the most singular and unified of all things, of which even a single one is the rarest thing in the world to find" (142).

Robbed of his friend's gaze, Montaigne has, in effect, lost his self-image: "He alone enjoyed my true image, and carried it away. That is why I myself decipher myself so painstakingly" (752 n14; 3.9). On the verge of ontological blindness resulting from the dissolution of the undifferentiated "sacred bond" (138) of friendship, the essayist, having assimilated the "nothing" of the friend's death, expresses the feeling of nothing itself (the "dark and dreary night" [143]). If emptiness becomes significant for Montaigne, it is because of the exceptional quality of what can no longer be: the friendship that is the very model of itself.

What becomes interesting now is to redirect the student's attention to the essay's exordium and to examine the metaphor inscribed there in terms of the text's rhetorical structure. Montaigne compares his writing to "grotesques" surrounding the "rich, polished picture, formed according to art" that he initially tells us will occupy the center of the chapter and stand as a monument to his friendship: La Boétie's *La servitude volontaire*. But the rhetorical coda to the essay undoes, in a way, Montaigne's gesture of filling the "empty space" with La Boétie's "letters." By claiming he composed it "by way of an exercise" (144) Montaigne finds ample justification for its excision from the text. The absence at the center of the essay is replaced by Montaigne's essay on friendship, what may be termed the essayist's very own "friendship with writing" (Kritzman, *Destruction* 70). This enables him to transform the text into an epistemological mirror functioning as a simulacrum of the dialogic rapport with La Boétie. The recovery of the lost friend is therefore only possible in the self-creation constituting the fiction of the essay; the corpus of the mourner becomes the embodiment of the corpse.

If, as Anthony Wilden claims, "the self . . . is the correlative of the other upon whom it was more or less unconsciously modeled" (595), the act of self-portraiture realized here enables the writer to approximate a sense of being that, without this textual performance, would have totally disappeared. The essays are constructed around a void constituting "the hidden face of Narcissus" (Kristeva, *Black Sun* 5) that functions as an emblem of the fragmented ego. This gesture is meant to inaugurate a mode of reflexivity incorporating a mimesis of communication with the "other" but one whose self-reference falls back upon itself without being able to rejoin itself: "Whatever I may be, I want to be elsewhere than on paper" (596; 2.37). Whereas Lacan's mirror stage constructs the imaginary from the dual symmetry of reflexivity, Montaigne's exercise in self-study represents a textual mirror always already beyond its ontological source. The consubstantiality Montaigne endlessly poses as an ideal—the attempted return to the symbiotic bliss found in the perfect communication with La Boétie—is subverted by a writing process that shatters the potential symmetry between self and other. This substitute form of reflexivity constructs a subject whose fate is to search for its other and in the process engages in the futile quest for a unified sense of self: "Who does not see that I have taken a road along which I shall go, without stopping and without effort, as long as there is ink and paper in the world?" (721; 3.9). Writing after the fall from the perfect communication of friendship therefore has a dynamics of its own, generating a multiplicity of textual "subjects" produced by the lacerating syntax of ever-renewed self-images.

By their very nature, then, psychoanalytic readings are dialogic, based as they are on the interplay between self and other. This exercise in reading psychoanalytically enables students to become more familiar with the rhetorical structures that translate how the writing of the *Essays* figures the dynamics of desire and how it represents the effects of these fictions.

The *Essays* as Intertext

Mary B. McKinley

> Books have served me not so much for instruction
> as for exercise.
>
> —Montaigne, *Essays*

Intertextualité emerged as a literary term in the French intellectual discourse of the sixties. Credit for coining it generally goes to Julia Kristeva, who, acknowledging her debt to Mikhail Bakhtin, argues that intertextuality was central to all writing: "Any text is constructed as a mosaic of quotations; any text is the absorption and transformation of another. The notion of intertextuality replaces that of intersubjectivity" (*Reader* 37). For a simple working definition of intertextuality, we can borrow Jonathan Culler's "the relation of a particular text to other texts" (139) or Gérard Genette's "literal presence of one text within another" (87). The emphasis on the word *text* in these cases, as well as Kristeva's opposition of intertextuality and intersubjectivity, places that relation at the level of process, focusing on writing (*écriture*) rather than on the author and the referential content of the works. Most discussions of intertextuality, like Kristeva's, challenge traditional notions of subjectivity and redefine the author.

How can the concept of intertextuality enlighten us—teachers and students—about the *Essays*? Although my answer shows an endorsement of that approach to teaching Montaigne, I would like at the outset to raise two flags of caution about using any modern literary theory to teach Renaissance works. First, we must avoid anachronism in attributing to Montaigne concepts and ways of thinking that have emerged in late twentieth-century culture. It can be stimulating to point out similarities between aspects of the *Essays* and qualities associated with modernism and postmodernism: focus on the self, the artist as protagonist, dislocation and fragmentation, the unstable self, a work that reflects on its own production, and so on (Wilde). Indeed, one thing that often attracts students to Montaigne is that he seems so modern, so like us. But we can best understand those similarities when we view him as historically other. We need to approach Renaissance writers as the humanist philologists taught them to approach the ancients, by respecting the temporal and cultural distance that separates them from us. The second word of caution is that the theory should not overshadow the *Essays*. Our primary goal is not that our students master recent theoretical discourse—although fluency in that discourse is certainly an asset for graduate students. We want to help them to appreciate an endlessly fascinating book written some four hundred years ago. Following Montaigne's advice, we should let theory serve us not so much for instruction as for exercise.

Theories of intertextuality can stimulate our thinking about how Montaigne composed the *Essays*. To any seasoned reader, Kristeva's phrase "a mosaic of quotations" evokes most pages of that book. Yet, on first reading, students are more likely to notice the "intersubjective" aspects of Montaigne's endeavor. Indeed, the opening address, "To the Reader," seems to invite just such a reaction, because Montaigne presents his book as a self-portrait: "it is myself that I portray" and "I am myself the matter of my book" (2). Many of the pages that evoke the most spirited reactions in students convey an urgent yearning for a fusion of the self with the other: on the one hand, the poignant nostalgia for the lost union with his deceased friend La Boétie, "the one who is not another man: he is myself" (142; 1.28), and on the other, the driving desire to be known by others: "I am hungry to make myself known, and I care not to how many, provided it be truly" (643; 3.5). A prominent message in the *Essays* is Montaigne's expressed desire that the essays represent the subject—himself—to his readers. I have found it effective to let students follow the quest for intersubjectivity as one of several threads weaving through the first few chapters that we read, slowly and carefully. Here I should emphasize that it is essential for students, even undergraduates discovering Montaigne for the first time, to read complete chapters and discuss in each case, if only briefly, what holds the chapter together, how it develops, and how those aspects of Montaigne's style might relate to what the essay says.

In these early readings I point out to students how frequently Montaigne associates intersubjectivity and books. Montaigne first knew La Boétie by reading his *Discours de la servitude volontaire*: "I am particularly obliged to this work, since it served as the medium of our first acquaintance" (136; 1.28). In "On the Education of Children," he argues that "mixing with men is wonderfully useful, and visiting foreign countries . . . to bring back knowledge of the characters and ways of those nations, and to rub and polish our brains by contact with those of others" (112; 1.26). Yet, shortly after, he specifies, "In this association with men I mean to include, and foremost, those who live only in the memory of books" (115). Books mediate Montaigne's efforts to know the other. And they do so, he tells us, not primarily by their referential content, their "matter," but by their more "textual" qualities, their style: "[E]very day I amuse myself reading authors without any care for their learning, looking for their style, not their subject. Just as I seek the company of some famous mind, not to have him teach me, but to come to know him" (708; 3.8). At first it may seem paradoxical that the reader work toward knowledge of authors, not through what they say but how they say it. Yet this is exactly what Montaigne asks of his own reader, for example, in the opening of his chapter "Of Books": "These are my fancies, by which I try to give knowledge not of things, but of myself. . . . Let attention be paid not to the matter, but to the shape I give it" (296; 2.10). Montaigne emphasizes, in his own book as in the books of others, the process of textual production, the shaping and styling of language that we might call *écriture*. Furthermore, he makes it very clear that his activity of reading and his process of writing are intricately related. One grows from the other. The essays were produced through the "absorption and transformation" of other texts. I like to let students discover how Montaigne created his book by responding to and evoking literary precursors. This discussion naturally leads us to examine the Renaissance term for that process: imitation or *imitatio*, as Latin rhetorical treatises called it.

In introductory Renaissance literature courses, it is necessary to point out that privileging originality among a writer's talents is a fairly recent notion. Students are usually surprised to learn that the word *plagiarism* did not exist in the sixteenth-century—the *OED*'s first attestation is 1621. Several of Montaigne's comments on writers, in "On the Education of Children," seem to describe what we would call plagiarism (see, e.g., 107; 1.26). Although he disparages those writers, their crime is not so much a moral failing—having passed off another's work as their own—as it is a lack of skill. They did it badly, without covering their tracks. They failed as practitioners of *imitatio*. To appreciate Renaissance writing, our students have to set aside the pejorative connotation that our culture has given to imitation. We need to show them that, in the sixteenth century, the adjective *mere* was not an appropriate modifier for words like *imitation* and *rhetoric*. Several excellent studies of *imitatio* (Castor; Cave; Compagnon; Greene; Quint; among others) can introduce advanced undergraduates and graduate students to this Renaissance approach to *écriture*. If they come to Montaigne at the end of a course on Renaissance literature, they will probably already have encountered *imitatio*. It may have been stated theoretically, as in Joachim du Bellay's *Défense et illustration de la langue française* (1549), a work that is itself, in part, an imitation of an Italian treatise on poetic language. Or, they may have seen a rewriting of one work by a single dominant precursor; for example, Ronsard's "A la fontaine bellerie," a wonderful imitation of Horace's ode "O fons Bandusiae." Examples can become increasingly complex when one work—even one passage—yields evidence of several model authors. Renaissance writers show their originality and skill by how well they absorb and transform the works of their predecessors.

Montaigne is a master of *imitatio*. He incorporates seemingly countless model authors into his book, and he does so in several different ways. Most obvious among them are the Latin quotations. Numbering more than thirteen hundred, they are set in italics in most modern French editions, following the example of the editions published in Montaigne's lifetime. Fragments of prose are inserted within Montaigne's own prose, while lines of poetry are set apart, creating a more obvious rupture in the flow of his discourse. Students using an English translation should note that Montaigne did not identify the authors of the quotations, as Donald Frame so thoughtfully does. Generally, students find the quotations frustrating, impeding their progress through what is already very challenging prose. Even graduate students usually experience difficulty in their initial reading of the *Essays*. To compensate, they tend to skip over—in effect, to banish—the quotations from their reception of Montaigne's text. It is important to acknowledge that their experience of difficulty is nearly universal, that the *Essays* is a challenging work, but that their diligence will be rewarded. As a general principle of reading literature, I like to urge students to question the obstacles, to examine the words that frustrate their movement through a passage. Montaigne's Latin quotations reward the reader's questioning scrutiny. In a utopian classroom, students would have read, or would have time to read, the works that Montaigne read. But even in our own real-world classrooms we can illustrate Montaigne's *imitatio* by having students read him along with a few manageable segments of his precursors' texts.

Students first encounter a quotation of poetry in the second chapter of book 1, "On Sadness." Montaigne evokes from Ovid's *Metamorphoses* (bk. 6) the figure of Niobe, overwhelmed by grief at the death of all her children and changed into a rock. Montaigne stops to insert the line "[p]etrified by her woes" (7; 1.2). The line reinforces the metaphor of petrification to convey the stunning force of grief. Moreover, close scrutiny of both Ovid's and Montaigne's passages shows additional echoes of Niobe's story. In a post- 1588 addition to that place in the chapter, Montaigne tells the story of a German captain, Raisciac, who, on discovering that a fallen soldier is his son, is in effect petrified: "the impact of sorrow, freezing his vital spirits, dropped him in this condition stone dead on the ground" (7). To shape his description of Raisciac's death, Montaigne calls on Ovid's language in describing Niobe. In this case, Montaigne refers obliquely not only to Ovid but to himself, to his own earlier introduction of Niobe into his chapter. His text becomes a mosaic of quotations (McKinley 16–20).

By their Latin words and their italicized presentation on the pages of the *Essays*, the quotations draw attention to their status as other, as foreign immigrants invited by Montaigne into his book. Less obvious are the other forms of *imitatio* that he practices. It may come as a surprise that the final pages of the "Apology for Raymond Sebond" (455–57; 2.12) reproduce almost exactly part of Jacques Amyot's translation of Plutarch's *Moral Essays*. Montaigne only obliquely acknowledges his borrowing by mentioning "this most religious conclusion of a pagan" at the end of the essay (457). Often, the shape of Montaigne's prose seems to have been determined in part by the books he was reading, as in his description of Raisciac's death. Even more subtly, he sometimes presents as arising from his personal experience an anecdote that, on investigation, appears to be a fabrication based on his reading. For example, the story about his experimentation with goat's blood as a cure for kidney stones, recounted in "Of the Resemblance of Children to Fathers," proves to owe more to his reading of Renaissance scientific treatises than to any firsthand dealings with goats (Cottrell 66–78). At times when Montaigne is giving what seem to be the most direct accounts of intimately personal experiences, the ghosts of precursor texts hover behind his prose. In his essay "On Friendship," for example, to communicate the relationship with La Boétie that he calls "so entire and so perfect that certainly you will hardly read of the like" (136; 1.28), he calls on his readings of Cicero, Horace, Catullus, Plutarch, Virgil, and Terence, among others. The essay can be read as one of Montaigne's most autobiographical revelations or as his contribution to the humanist tradition of writings on friendship, an exercise of *imitatio*. The most fruitful readings of "On Friendship" probe the relation between self-representation and literary imitation in that essay (Gray, "Friends"; Henry 73–100; Regosin, *Matter* 7–29; Rigolot, *Les métamorphoses* 61–78). Another example occurs in "On Practice," the essay in which Montaigne recounts the near-death experience that tamed his fear of death. After being thrown from a horse, he lay immobile for over two hours, "dead, stretched on my back, my face all bruised and skinned . . ." (269; 2.6). His companions, thinking him dead, were carrying him back to his house when he slowly began to recover consciousness. In retrospect, he says that he was absent from the scene—"I was not there at all" (271)—viewing it more as an onlooker than as a participant, and that, most important, he felt neither fear nor pain: "It would, in truth, have been a very happy death . . ." (272). The remainder of the essay in its first published version (1580) is a meditation on his state of mind during his slow return to awareness. This is Montaigne at his most transparent, an unmediated expression of subjectivity. Or is it? The account is peppered with quotations from Virgil, Ovid, and Lucretius. He refers directly to the poets' portrayals of lingering death and, in an epic simile, compares the passage between life and death to "the early stages of sleep" when we "sense as in a dream what is happening around us" (271). It is enlightening here to show students two passages in the *Aeneid* where Virgil artfully describes the approach to death: Dido's at the end of book 4 and Turnus's in book 12. Montaigne's debt to Virgil becomes clear, especially in the simile conveying Turnus's waning strength (908–12). Students can point out the similarities as well as the differences between the two similes. They will be having hands-on experience with Renaissance *imitatio*, because that practice involved both a copy of and a departure from the model. In addition, they will have touched a particularly rich line in literary genealogy because Virgil's version of the simile is itself a reworking of both Homer and Lucretius (McKinley 67–73).

Do these readings diminish the *Essays* as a representation of the writing subject? Has intertextuality replaced intersubjectivity? Montaigne's reworking of the ancients' texts in these examples reflects the intersection of literary and lived experience that is the home of his writing endeavor. Recent discussions of intertextuality focus on the literary axis of that intersection. By emphasizing the process of textual production, *écriture*, intertextuality challenges received notions of the writing subject as author.

Here it is well to point out a difference between contemporary notions of intertextuality and *imitatio*. Renaissance imitation was theorized as a conscious, willed process. Authors chose to imitate and were judged for their skill in manipulating and controlling the process. One might argue that since it was such a dominant literary convention, authors had little choice except to practice it. Nevertheless, the very existence of so many treatises encouraging and prescribing it implies that those writers could conceive of other, albeit less desirable, ways of generating literature. *Imitatio* was a matter of conscious choice and rhetorical skill. Theoreticians of intertextuality argue, on the other hand, that *all* writing occurs as a reaction to precursor texts, that the process may be conscious or unconscious, involving more or less skill, but that it is universal and unavoidable. In coining the term, Kristeva argued that it described "any text." That view of writing challenges the primacy of human agency in literary creation. By diminishing the role of the writing subject as the source of the text, it undermines the notion of the author. Defining the words *author* and *subject* has been the focus of often heated debate in recent theoretical polemics, engaging critics of many different persuasions: psychoanalytical, deconstructionist, phenomenological, and others, including the advocates of intertextuality. Witness Barthes's "The Death of the Author" and Foucault's "What Is an Author?" as well as, more recently, Paul Smith's *Discerning the Subject*. I mention this dispute with no pretense of entering the fray but simply as a means of returning to the question, How can theories of intertextuality stimulate us and our students in our reading of the *Essays?*

If ever a book proclaimed that the author is alive and well, it is Montaigne's *Essays*. Tradition has seen in it, if anything, the coming of age of the author. It presents itself from the outset as an authorial self-portrait and never abandons that mission: "whatever I make myself known to be, provided I make myself known such as I am, I am carrying out my plan" (495; 2.17). In "On Some Verses of Virgil," as if to dispel any doubt, Montaigne declares: "Enough, then. I have done what I wanted. Everyone recognizes me in my book, and my book in me" (667; 3.5). A recent work by a prominent scholar has reasserted Montaigne's and other Renaissance writers' belief in language's power to represent the self and to foster a relationship between the individual and God that we might call intersubjective (Defaux, *Marot*). It would seem that the author of the *Essays*, while embracing intertextuality, is a clear counterexample to the retreat of intersubjectivity, if it weren't for Montaigne's own intriguing comments on his experience of himself as author.

The essays repeatedly reflect on writing, especially on the writing that produced them. We might say that they become their own intertext, Montaigne both his own precursor and his own imitator. His descriptions of that process show his book taking on a life of its own. "Of Presumption," "Of Vanity," and "On Some Verses of Virgil" are particularly rich in such commentaries, but they occur in many chapters. Often, Montaigne's remarks about writing seem protointertextual: "there are more books about books than about any other subject: we do nothing but write glosses about each other. The world is swarming with commentaries; of authors there is a great scarcity" (818; 3.13). Primacy of the self or primacy of the text? Montaigne has a novel response: "I have no more made my book than my book has made me—a book consubstantial with its author, concerned with my own self, an integral part of my life" (504; 2.18). The notion of the book somehow composing the author intrigues the postmodern imagination, and Montaigne's relentless probing of his own process of textual production invites readings that foreground the essays as writing and investigate their "relation . . . to other texts" (Culler 139). To sample such readings, graduate and advanced undergraduate students can be directed to books by Terence Cave, Robert Cottrell, Patrick Henry, Lawrence Kritzman (*Destruction*), John Lyons, Richard Regosin (*Matter*), François Rigolot (*Les métamorphoses*), and André Tournon, among others.

Does the *Essays* represent the author's self in all its plenitude and power? Or do the essays illustrate the process of writing as mosaic making? As Rabelais's Trouillogan might say, "Neither one nor the other and both together."

En-gendering the *Essays*

Julia Watson

Simone de Beauvoir has observed, "Montaigne understood clearly how arbitrary and unjust was woman's appointed lot: 'Women are not in the wrong when they decline to accept the rules laid down for them, since men make these rules without consulting them. No wonder intrigue and strife abound.' But he did not go so far as to champion their cause" (50). Beauvoir identifies a central paradox of the *Essays*: Montaigne both speaks from within a system of fixed gender relations in the sixteenth century that is patriarchal and hierarchical and critiques the binary opposition of gender arrangements by which women become the other of a masculine subject with established but arbitrary authority.

A feminist analysis argues that gender is a socially constructed category that extends identity beyond the biological and sexual configuration to the cultural and historical specificity of the subject. As Beauvoir suggests, not all persons have enjoyed equal access to the status of the subject who is culturally empowered to speak. Indeed, in the Western tradition the agency of the subject has been claimed primarily by those who are white and male, indicating the importance of gender as well as race and class in inflecting identity. From the point of view of the late twentieth century this is an asymmetrical arrangement. Increasingly we are called upon to reread the Western tradition differently, "other-wise," considering what places were assigned to the others of the Western self.

A feminist analysis of gender is one such perspective for reading the *Essays* as a historically specific text. In Montaigne's text we may observe how discourses of the humanist recovery of antiquity, which upheld traditional gender arrangements, are intersected by Montaigne's semiotic interrogation of binary oppositions as an inadequate representation of the complexity of personal experience. To situate the *Essays* in a gendered context is a project that may be new to many Montaigne scholars accustomed to reading the work as a locus of tolerance for diversity, in which gender—and women— seem largely invisible. But a feminist reading of gender in the *Essays* may both display the relation of sexuality and textuality, an interest of many Montaigne scholars, and show the ideological crossroads at which Montaigne locates this category, like other categories, of social identity.

Locating the coordinates of gender in the *Essays* may also stir students to productive rereadings. If the contention of humanist scholars is true—that the great works of Western literature not only can withstand interrogation by new methods of reading but will be illumined by them to display their own multi-faceted richness—then posing for students the *problem* of reading the *Essays* "other-wise" should prove instructive. Gendered reading reminds us that no reading is genderless; all readings are informed by how both writer and reader are ideologically positioned. I accordingly sketch out a model of gendered reading, describe several levels at which it might be applied both to examine and to deconstruct the *Essays'* apparent gynephobic discourse, and propose reading Montaigne's text as an en-gendered body, inscribed in acts of maternal nurturance.

When we speak of gender in the *Essays*, what do we mean? Certainly we need to consider the literary and historical female figures scattered throughout the *Essays* and the rhetorical stances Montaigne adopts toward them. These include Montaigne's attitudes expressed toward women as a whole and his addresses to specific women, particularly Marie de Gournay. Thinking about gender involves other considerations, such as how Montaigne represents and critiques masculinity, his own and that of others, and how the "I" of the *Essays* articulates his relationship to his own body as a de-gendered site of self-communion that he fashions as an embodied text. Montaigne's critique of such dichotomous structures as male/female creates a new model of relationship to the reader, one that rejects hierarchy and proposes a nondominating discourse of exchange.

Gender and Gynephobia

Women are largely absent from the dense network of citations and allusions to historical and literary figures in the *Essays*, as they are from many humanist texts. In those places where an essay refers to a woman or women, it is often to paraphrase or cite commonplaces from antiquity or the Middle Ages that have a misogynistic cast. Renaissance conceptions of women as insatiably lustful and of love and marriage as incompatible build on this misogyny and may have contributed to an explicit antifeminism in Montaigne (Insdorf 92). In those traditions, women are typically located below men and with animals, lack rationality, and are prized for passivity and dutiful obedience.

In "Of Idleness," for example, Montaigne develops an elaborate simile for his mind, comparing it to fertile women. Left to themselves, they produce only shapeless monsters; they require "orderly" insemination with a male seed to produce useful children (20–21; 1.8). Some of his most vituperous denunciations occur in "Of the Affection of Fathers for Their Children," where he justifies patriarchal asymmetry: "It seems to me . . that no kind of mastery is due to women over men except the maternal and natural." He goes on to denounce women as having disordered judgment because they lack the "force of reason to choose and embrace what deserves it"; they "let themselves be carried away" (290; 2.8). In "Of Three Good Women," Seneca's wife, Paulina, is praised for the stoical self-abnegating virtue that leads her to follow her husband in everything, including attempted suicide (567; 2.35). In "Of Three Kinds of Association," books are valued as higher than men, women devalued as lower. In such passages Montaigne is echoing a patriarchal bias that kept most women disenfranchised because they were viewed as physically and mentally inferior to men, largely uneducable, ruled by nature, and valuable primarily for reproduction and domestic comfort.

Such commonplaces and exemplary stories assume a universal and divinely ordained patriarchal order. Undeniably, one discourse of the *Essays* is this combination of casual misogyny and silence on the accomplishments of historical women, typical of the literary gynephobia that has characterized much of the "great tradition" in both antiquity and the Renaissance. In a patriarchal world the otherness of women is less questioned than that of, for example, cannibals.

But Montaigne differs from his contemporaries in the numerous discourses through which reflections on gender circulate in the *Essays*—masculinity, the body and the senses, the destabilizing of oppositions. Indirectly, these discourses critique and subvert the norms of conventional gynephobia, unexamined by many in the great tradition, and show Montaigne's mistrust of all stereotypical thinking, even his own. His many discussions of sexuality, for example, may be read metatextually as displacing the gynephobic discourse; although to the extent that Montaigne's sexual discourse depends on a notion of unquestioned male privilege, it cannot efface his misogyny (Tetel, "Of Women").

Pedagogical suggestion   As part of a reading journal, ask students to keep a list of commonplaces on women and, where possible, to identify their sources. Doing so will acquaint them with the concepts of discourse and of woman as other. Students may note how some of these claims about women are either internally contradictory or at odds with those of other discourses in the *Essays*.

Women Readers of the Essays

Although various essays at points echo the Western discourse of silencing and marginalizing women while validating a universal, transcendent male subject, they also resituate some women who are Montaigne's contemporaries and make a case for women as identified and invited readers. Montaigne refers, for example, to the accomplishments of such sixteenth-century French writers as Marguerite de Navarre and dedicates several essays to French noblewomen. He especially praises his spiritual daughter, Marie de Gournay, though it is uncertain whether he is the author of this praise. Cathleen M. Bauschatz has noted the irony of critics' characterization of Montaigne as a "man's man" writing a canonically masculine text when Montaigne has been read enthusiastically in private by women for centuries ("Qualité"). More striking, several of his essays are dedicated to particular, named women, and only women (among the living) are specifically addressed in the *Essays*. Examining the dedicated essays, Bauschatz concludes that Montaigne both protected himself from public perception of his book's subversive intent by dedicating essays to women and saw women as ideal readers of the essays' intimate, private form, especially on the topics of parenting and education (101).

In the dedicated essays, Montaigne adopts a more courtly and formal address, which indicates his respect for each woman's social position and education. The dedications are, however, not unambiguous. In "Of the Affection of Fathers for Their Children," Montaigne's omission of references to his mother has occasioned speculation about his resentment of her and whether that resentment was directed primarily at her or his father. The "Apology for Raymond Sebond" concludes with an address to a specific woman, possibly Marguerite de Valois, on how a desperate devotionalist may defend Sebond by using reason to defeat reason. In "Of the Education of Children," dedicated to a mother-to-be, Montaigne praises Virtue as a Socratic woman, criticizes strict rote education, and calls for a more nurturant development that would form, rather than fill, the child's mind. Yet he sees no contradiction between calling for this "feminization" of education and insisting that Mme de Duras will bear a son because she is "too noble-spirited to begin otherwise than with a male" (109; 1.26). "Of the Resemblance of Children to Fathers," where Montaigne considers how he inherited his father's kidney stones and decries doctors, is dedicated to a noblewoman with the hope that the essay will "lodge . . . in a solid body" (595; 2.37), arguably as a fetus lodges in a mother rather than as a stone lodges in the body, and will thus evoke him in her memory. In this essay, which concludes by praising diversity as the most universal opinion (598), Montaigne points to difference as underlying all perception of resemblance, thereby undoing claims to universalism, and suggests his need for a female reader and a "female" mode of reading that would be nurturant rather than appropriative or antagonistic.

One woman has special status in the *Essays*. At the end of "On Presumption," the essayist praises Marie de Gournay, his covenant daughter, for her promise of achieving the kind of sacred friendship that he had earlier enjoyed with La Boétie (502; 2.17). This is high praise indeed, for it implies their parity of intellect and refinement. The passage, however, is frequently discredited as Marie's posthumous interpolation, which the author's wife later forced her to retract. This anxious father-daughter relationship between Montaigne and Marie has interested some recent readers of the *Essays*, who argue for viewing Marie as the literary daughter inheriting the daughter's impossible position of being unable to speak unless she mimes the father. As Richard Regosin suggests, Marie has been faulted both for having "spoken," in inserting herself into the *Essays*, and for having "misspoken," in later retracting her remarks. But Marie is negotiating her own impossible position: to defend Montaigne's text and to demand her own right to speak as a literary voice. Marie must both speak over his text and deny her own right to speak, so as not to displace the father with whom she competes for textual space ("Dutiful Daughter" 125–27). Marie's self-criticism reflects the historical marginalization of the woman writer and speaks up for Montaigne as a kind literary father who, by claiming her, provoked the dutiful daughter's silenced admiration and her own production of such literary texts as her 1622 treatise *Egalité des hommes et des femmes.*

Pedagogical suggestions   Students might consider how a dedication embedded in an essay or Marie's interpolation at the end of "On Presumption" changes their reading of the essay. They might describe that relation as a means of reflecting on the contradictory position of the Renaissance woman writer. An excerpt from de Gournay's writing could be contrasted with a Montaignian essay for evidence of both affiliation and the anxiety of influence.

Constructing a Masculine Subject

A related aspect of gender, one that has until recently been less scrutinized, is the construction of masculinity as a set of stances, values, and self-identifications. Montaigne's attitude toward masculinity is complex. He admires valor but sees some male assertion as foolhardy; he is conscious of how a strict code of masculinity can disrupt spontaneous responses. The signs of virile masculinity praised by the ancients—for example, potency, a warrior ethic, equanimity in the face of pain, a commanding physical presence—are "tried" in the *Essays* and tried on by Montaigne. The figures of public statesmen and warriors in Plutarch's *Lives* and other texts of antiquity pose models of masculine action. In such essays as "Of the Inconsistency of Our Actions," Montaigne's examples of worthy and unworthy action address how men have acted in dangerous and difficult situations and contrast that behavior with what a code of masculinity might require. In "On the Power of the Imagination" he contrasts public valor with the private timidity or inhibition that might overcome a man in intimate situations. In these essays Montaigne problematizes simple codes of masculinity and questions their "natural" or biological origin; anticipating twentieth-century critics, he views sexual identity as constructed by custom, situation-specific, and not controlled by the conscious mind. The essayist represents his own masculinity assertively yet nonstereotypically. As Marcel Tetel indicates, he sees himself as a good horseman both literally and metaphorically, one who rides loose in the saddle and flexes with the changing terrain (*Montaigne* 56–57). Several of the brief early essays, such as "On Riding Post" and "Of War Horses," show Montaigne establishing a firmly soldierly but nonheroic stance. In other passages, such as in his extensive self-portrayal in "Of Presumption," he defines himself against the extremes of both masculine and feminine stature, physique, and gait. A living example of the paradoxical "middle way" in his self-description of his moderate stature and voice, Montaigne praises naturalness as an ideal and a strategy that subverts social adherence to a strict ideology of gender differentiation.

In citing examples of masculine shyness, lack of valor, and impotence in men who look or have acted courageously in other situations, Montaigne unmasks the social construction of gender. Its binary oppositions—male/ female, heterosexual/homosexual, active/passive—are broken down into a fertile field of ambivalence that refigures stereotypes of macho masculinity as well as the exclusionary power of gender. In this critique the essayist antici- pates some recent feminist theorists who have discussed the "natural" system of oppositions in human sexuality as arbitrary and hierarchical (Butler 148– 49) and called for women to walk out of the patriarchal frame of reference that (re)produces gender (de Lauretis 17). For Montaigne masculinity is irreducibly performative. His speculations on sexuality in "On Some Verses of Virgil" figure him simultaneously as voyeur and "impertinently genital in his approaches" (679; 3.5), moving in and out of a panorama of possibilities in his solitary text.

Pedagogical suggestions Considering how masculinity is critiqued should stimulate copious discussion and provide insight into gender as an asymmetrical and arbitrary construction. Contrasting a brief early essay with an essay in book 3 will show how Montaigne both assumes masculine roles and interrogates "masculinity."

The De-gendered Body

In the essays of book 3, Montaigne moves increasingly toward a self- representation in which the body becomes a site for testing and "digesting" ideas, concepts, and systems. He writes both of and on the body, writing its dismemberment and separation as well as retreating to it as a haven (Mathieu-Castellani, "Discours"). Representing his body as a site whose or- gans have minds of their own, Montaigne suggests that his body is pregnant with its own text. To speak so extensively of his body as the locus of the "living" words of the book, Montaigne must in a sense give birth to himself, refigure his relation to language as nurturant rather than appropriative. As a self-creating and self-perpetuating subject the essayist subverts the oppo- sition of gendered subjects. His desire for fullness and self-enclosure is arguably both maternal and prior to assigned social roles—in that sense pre-Oedipal.

Montaigne may conflate contradictory bodily processes, making his text into "body," to show the unrepresentability of his self-experience; he desires to inhabit his text corporeally, with words of flesh. In "Of Giving the Lie," for example, he takes back the consubstantiality of self and book that he had celebrated by comparing self-experience to a digestive process that eludes the sight of any other and is pleasurable for just that reason (504; 2.18). In taking himself as both exemplary and deviant, Montaigne "makes trouble" for dualistic or objectified conceptions of the human being and the dichot- omy of words and things. He thereby suggests a model of textuality in which gender is both conceived in essentialist terms and deconstructed. The social custom and linguistic practices of gendering are as ripe for testing as are other categories of cognition and custom.

Nondominating Differences and Feminist Pedagogy

Finally, an analysis of gender needs to shape altered reading practices. In their nonlinear composition and associative mode of movement among topics to create a dialogue, Montaigne's essays interlace multiple discourses into a play of voices. For centuries they have been appreciated for their palpable language and nondominating address to the reader. Indeed, few canonical texts are as genuinely discursive. This dialogic quality of the *Essays* realizes some of the aims of feminist pedagogy and theory and opens up those feminist principles to wider applicability in reading texts. Following are some examples of the application of those principles to Montaigne's *Essays*:

1. Feminist critics have called for a model of *nonauthoritarian pedagogy* to empower students as participants in the classroom dialogue and restructure its "power relationship" of authority-figure teacher to passive students. Both the discursive style of the *Essays* and its adaptability to a participatory classroom suggest that it anticipates a model of nonauthoritarian pedagogy, particularly in the revision of educational practice described in "Of the Education of Children."

2. While *relational thinking* has been claimed by some feminists as a distinctively feminine mode of cognition, others consider it an essentialist fallacy because all humans have the capacity for relational or nonlinear thinking. In their associative movement of tracing a circle of possibilities rather than a linear argument, the *Essays* shows some aspects of "relational thinking." For example, in *Cassandra*, novelist Christa Wolf connects the repression of associational thinking with the establishment of a patriarchy that represses prophetic speech (273–77). But Wolf also notes that there is no simple return for either women or men to a matriarchal dream of the past; rather, as cultural subjects, we need to forge dialogic texts that engage the reader in an ongoing interrogation. This Montaigne has done.

3. The essay form, as no other fixed form in its engagement of multiple topics, might be considered in terms of Virginia Woolf's call for women's writing to "break the sentence and break the sequence" (95). While Woolf's notion of consciousness is very different from Montaigne's, the essayist's circular and circulating text defers and interrupts the expected linear sequence of narrative.

4. The *Essays* celebrates difference as a way of undermining hierarchical, authoritarian justifications of domination by any group. The call for revising asymmetrical power relationships into nondominating differences informs many multicultural critiques, not just a feminist analysis of gender.

5. Finally, the *Essays* has great potential for groups interested in analyzing the contradictions and complexities of masculinity as a privileged term within gender that carries its own burden of repression and silencing.

Pedagogical suggestions   Teachers might engage one of these models of feminist revision of the great tradition by inviting students, in discussion and writing assignments, to "talk back" to the *Essays* and to write their own essays, as voyages of exploration.

Montaigne and Deconstruction

Jerome Schwartz

Teaching the *Essays* through the lens of deconstruction permits students to see Montaigne's pertinence to many of the ethical and intellectual problems of the late twentieth century, in part, I believe, because Montaigne's project was protodeconstructionist in its own time. What I concentrate on in this essay are: first, resemblances between Montaigne's intellectual itinerary and that of contemporary deconstructionists, as well as the limits of those similarities; second, particular examples that demonstrate how a deconstructive approach can be accessible to undergraduates. In using this approach with undergraduates, I never use the term *deconstruction* and its derivatives; it is tautological to use these terms to explain what a deconstructive analysis entails. Indeed, in teaching literature to undergraduates, I make it a general rule to avoid the jargon of contemporary critical theory, while at the same time attempting to devise pedagogical strategies that help make its insights available to students.

Thus I believe that contemporary critical concern with the problematics of "writing" and "reading" brings our students straight to the core of what Montaigne's book is all about. "Writing" puts in question stable notions of self and authorial authority and focuses instead on the rhetoric of the *Essays*, on such notions as plurality and indeterminacy of meaning in a self-reflexive text that refuses coherence and unity, that is constantly playing with itself and with the reader (see Regosin, "Trends" for a useful critical summary). Indeed, the affinities between problems of writing in the sixteenth century and in the twentieth constitute the first important link between the *Essays* and deconstruction: "The consequences of Babel, the uncertainties of the 'logocentric' model (according to which language is presumed to have a natural and, ultimately, a supernatural grounding), were as pervasive then as now" (Cave xvi).

Simply and briefly defined, deconstruction is, in practice, twofold: it is an analytic, critical method, something a critic does to a text by revealing or exposing the discordant thread that will unravel its argument; it is also something a text does to itself at those moments when it simultaneously asserts and denies, thereby undermining the referentiality or the rhetorical authority of its discourse (de Man; Schwartz, "Moment"). The subversiveness and self-subversiveness of Montaigne's rhetoric in the *Essays* have been a major focus of recent work on Montaigne (e.g., Cave; Kritzman, "Destruction"; McKinley; Cottrell; Defaux, "Rhétorique"), but it is not my concern here to summarize or assess the merits of these particular studies.

Apart from the problems of writing and rhetoric, a second major affinity between Montaigne and deconstruction is provided by the challenge of Pyrrhonian skepticism to the Platonic foundation of Western metaphysics: "The closest contemporary analogue of the Pyrrhonist inquirer would be the deconstructionist strategy of someone such as Jacques Derrida" (Hiley 14). That challenge consists in an opposition to Platonic philosophy's claim that, like the prisoners in the allegory of the cave, we can emerge from darkness into light by escaping our condition of fallibility, finitude, and contingency through the practice of philosophy. Montaigne's skepticism, which, like deconstructionist skepticism, challenges philosophy's presumption to knowledge by denying any firm foundation to its epistemological claims, entails nonetheless a concept of philosophy as process—as the act of critical thinking inseparable from the processes of reading and writing.

One strategy I have found particularly useful in teaching the *Essays* is to focus on specific "deconstructive moments," that is, those nodal points when two rhetorical modes or ideological moves intersect and undermine one another. I have discussed elsewhere at greater length several of these instances ("Moment"). Foremost among them is the preface, "To the Reader," in which the text, hesitating between irony and direct statement, creates conditions of undecidability that constitute the reader's role as one of interactive process. This preface in its very undecidability defines the ideal Montaignian reader as one who is alert to the problematic relations between ideological content and rhetorical form.

An early protodeconstructionist move of Montaigne's is found in the essay "Of Custom, and Not Easily Changing an Accepted Law" where, well before the more systematic discussion in the "Apology for Raymond Sebond," Montaigne analyses cultural practices as arbitrary "signs" masquerading as natural and rational behavior: "For in truth habit ["la coustume"] is a violent and treacherous schoolmistress. She establishes in us, little by little, stealthily, the foothold of her authority; but having by this mild and humble beginning settled and planted it with the help of time, she soon uncovers to us a furious and tyrannical face against which we no longer have the liberty of even raising our eyes" (77; 1.23). The accumulations of examples and counterexamples in this chapter constitute a parody of argument by example, exposing the hollowness of custom's claims to be the arbiter of reason and nature. In robbing custom of any rational and natural legitimacy, Montaigne comes close to revealing it to be nothing more than *ideology* in that word's modern senses: "And the common notions that we find in credit around us and infused into our soul by our fathers' seed, these seem to be the universal and natural ones" (83). In contrast to the attitudes typical of the French nobility in Montaigne's time, which associated custom with nature and history as opposed to the fictions of law and theory (Nakam, *Les Essais*), the essayist states on the contrary that usage—the customs, beliefs, and practices of a social group—"robs us of the true appearance of things. . . . Once, having to justify one of our observances, . . . by tracking it to its origin, I there found its foundation so weak that I nearly became disgusted with it" (84). In thus dismantling the notion of custom, Montaigne is asserting the intuition, shared by deconstruction and psychoanalysis, that the true face of things is a lack, an absence of a recoverable point of origin that might serve as a solid foundation for knowledge.

Montaigne's exposing of ideological subjection hiding behind the mask of nature and reason does not lead to revolutionary consequences, however, but instead calls for an ironic doubleness, an inner, private reserve and an outer, public conformity: "the wise man should withdraw his soul within, out of the crowd, and keep it in freedom and power to judge things freely; but as for externals, he should wholly follow the accepted fashions and forms" (86). This essay may thus also be read as a "deconstructive moment" in which two opposing movements, the denunciation of custom and the upholding of custom, subtend and subvert each other. After the private subject is enjoined to perform an act of lucid consciousness ("when this mask is torn off, and he refers things to truth and reason" [85]), the public subject is enjoined to deny the evidence of rationality and to don again the mask of ideology and illusion. Consistently throughout its 1580, 1588, and 1595 editions, this supposedly rationalist essay is traversed by a profound irrationality, for there is nothing else beyond the diversity of social practices, no principle of universal truth that would transcend contingency.

The philosophical heart of the *Essays* is the "Apology for Raymond Sebond." It is here that Montaigne's innate skepticism, buttressed by his reading in Sextus Empiricus, both affirms and denies the arguments of Sebond. The counterpart of the earlier essay on custom, insofar as it exhibits both the radical questioning and the apparent acceptance of political or religious authority, the "Apology" is reciprocally undermined by a rational deep structure belying its attack on reason and an anti-intellectualism that subverts its own rational strategies. The essay as apology or defense rests on two objections to Sebond to which Montaigne is ostensibly replying. The first rejects reason in favor of faith alone as a foundation for Christian belief; the second attacks Sebond's arguments on the grounds that they are rationally inadequate. The response to the second objection—constituting the bulk of the essay—humbles reason, makes it subservient to faith, thus undercutting Sebond's arguments and the very rationality on which Montaigne's own strategy rests. Montaigne's rhetorical attack on the pretensions of philosophy develops into a scathing assault on the anthropocentrism characteristic of Sebond and typical as well of Montaigne's own contemporaries such as La Primaudaye and Duplessis-Mornay. While "defending" Sebond by attacking reason, he is undermining the anthropocentric foundations of "natural theology" and suggesting less piously that it is also of the very nature of Christian ideology that it be homocentric, hierarchical, privileging human beings over beasts. In his long romp with the animals, he overturns these hierarchies and relativizes them, as in the memorable personal example where he plays with his cat and wonders whether his cat may be making more sport with him than he with her (331; 2.12). Thus, while appearing to argue for faith over reason in matters of religion, Montaigne is in the process of undermining the very bases of Christian belief.

The crucial skeptical ploy comes toward the end of the "Apology" when Montaigne makes use of Sextus's case against the Stoic theory of "indicative" and "suggestive" signs:

> To judge the appearances that we receive of objects, we would need a judicatory instrument; to verify this instrument, we need a demonstration; to verify the demonstration, an instrument: there we are in a circle. Since the senses cannot decide our dispute, being themselves full of uncertainty, it must be reason that does so. No reason can be established without another reason: there we go retreating back to infinity. (454)

Montaigne's version of the problem of the criterion, while it adds nothing new to Sextus and even compresses the latter's demonstration considerably, is, perhaps for that very reason, a forceful restatement of the problem that is effectively coupled, at the essay's close, with a meditation on the problem of time. The two arguments, taken together, bring us very close to the standpoint of deconstruction with respect to its critique of presence and the consequent endless postponement of full meaning.

The infinite regress to which reason is condemned by the skeptical argument of the criterion is supplemented by a long conclusion borrowed from Plutarch in Amyot's French translation. This text dismantles the concept of being in time and the notion of full presence: "And as for these words, *present, immediate, now*, on which it seems that we chiefly found and support our understanding of time, reason discovering this immediately destroys it" (456). Montaigne's critique of presence and the lack of a criterion of judgment announce Derrida's concepts of the incompleteness, the supplementarity, and the infinite deferral of meaning in time (*la différance*). The skeptical argument for the infinite regress of interpretation also implies that meaning is never fixed and stable but always capable of engendering new meanings ad infinitum, as the American semiotician C. S. Peirce proposed in his definition of the sign as a triadic structure of *representamen-object-interpretant*, according to which the interpretant can always become a new sign in an infinite series.

The negative conclusions of the "Apology" concerning an epistemologically based linkage of philosophy and virtue have far-reaching implications. The critique of presence and knowledge bears on the nature of Montaigne's project of self-study and self-portraiture. The Montaignian subject can consequently not be a constitutive subject of the Cartesian kind— endowed with the certainty of its self-identity and its mimetic resemblance to its own self-representations. It is never fully present to itself but rather the site of contradiction, change, and otherness, as much the product of the text as its producer: "I have no more made my book than my book has made me" (504; 2.18).

The short essay that opens book 2, "Of the Inconsistency of Our Actions"—note that Cotgrave's French and English dictionary translates the French word *inconstance* variously as "inconstancie, unsteadfastnesse, ficklenesse, lightnesse, wavering, mutabilitie, changeablenesse"—enacts the mobility and contradiction that Montaigne lays down as the very conditions of human existence. The fragmentation of his book is the rhetorical and palpable figure of the fragmentation of human life and thought as always deferred in temporal terms, and the project of self-portrayal is continually undermined by the mediations of writing, which undo the stability and oneness of the writing subject.

This fragmentation is in part linguistic. Words and things are related to one another arbitrarily, by convention and not by nature: "There is the name and the thing. The name is a sound which designates and signifies the thing; the name is not a part of the thing or of the substance, it is an extraneous piece attached to the thing, and outside of it" (468; 2.16). This nominalist critique denounces the duplicities of language in its false complicities with reality. Montaigne is conscious of a "semiotic crisis" (Rigolot, *Les métamorphoses* 45) in the system of representation upon which humanism rested. This is seen in the following passage from "Of Experience":

> Our disputes are purely verbal. I ask what is "nature," "pleasure," "circle," "substitution." The question is one of words, and is answered in the same way. "A stone is a body." But if you pressed on:"And what is a body?"—"Substance."–"And what is substance?" and so on, you would finally drive the respondent to the end of his lexicon. We exchange one word for another word, often more unknown. (818–9; 3.13)

The nature of interpretation as endless gloss follows from this closed linguistic system in which signs refer only to other signs. Montaigne's project of self-portrayal had suffered this infirmity from the start. If the observer of his own self does not already possess his own self-image, how can he proceed to represent it in a portrait? The self-portrait must ultimately serve as the standard against which Montaigne will measure himself, but it is a fictive one, because the reality of his own being is out of reach, is unknowable itself, and is only glimpsed by mediations (interpretants) whose ontological status—relative and partial—is subtended by an infinite regress.

Despite the skeptical arguments against the validity of self-portrayal and self-knowledge, despite Montaigne's nominalist view of language as tautological (Compagnon, *Nous*), the *Essays* remains at the same time resolutely mimetic. He proceeds with even greater self-confidence in his project of self-representation as though the sheer force of desire and belief outweigh any merely logical strictures (Defaux, "Rhétorique"). Thus, although the logic of Pyrrhonian skepticism subverts the project of self-portrayal, it does not preclude or negate it.

In the final chapter of the *Essays*, "Of Experience," the arguments of the "Apology" against the epistemological value of the senses seem to be overturned. Here the body in its finiteness and its mortality appears to displace the argument of infinite regress. "I study myself more than any other subject. That is my metaphysics, that is my physics. . . . In this universe of things I ignorantly and negligently let myself be guided by the general law of the world. I shall know it well enough when I feel it" (821; 3.13). The metaphysical would appear to make room for the physical; mind to yield to body. The bodily trivia that Montaigne recounts in this essay would constitute the "intellectually sensible" and "sensibly intellectual" representation of Montaigne's individual selfhood in which the hierarchized, linguistic dichotomies of mind/body, reason/senses, life/death, and so on, would appear to collapse in holistic union. However, "Of Experience" performs a verbal enactment that is but a symbolic gesture of desire for the transcendence that, intellectually, Montaigne rejects.

Montaignian deconstruction, if such a term be permitted, is neither nihilism nor negation. The method of the essay—the testing or trying-out of the judgment, the weighing against one another of truth fragments, the ironies of mimesis and self-representation—is the textual and rhetorical analogue of experience itself. To write the *Essays* is not merely in the end to deconstruct other texts but to construct the self as a text that itself resists closure.

If Montaigne were alive and writing today, he might very likely be a deconstructionist—along the lines of a Paul de Man in literary criticism or a Jacques Derrida or a Richard Rorty in philosophy. Like the deconstructionists, Montaigne did not erect a philosophical system of his own but drew the life of the *Essays* from encounters with other texts: texts of the humanist tradition, which he subjected to corrosive analysis in order to reveal their hidden contradictions and their false truth-claims; texts constituted by the discourse of his contemporaries, as for example, the discourse of custom, the mask that when torn away leaves the judgment "all upset." But apart from this Socratic role as gadfly, that properly deconstructive role, Montaigne diverges from the concerns of the deconstructionists in his desire not only to pursue to the limit the critical differences in all things but as well to seize hold of the elusiveness of his own being in the "airy medium of words" (274; 2.6).

In teaching undergraduates, I would not propose as a simple model of deconstructive analysis that, say, a 1595 addition "deconstructs" an earlier text. Rather, students should be taught to be alert to the text's inconsistencies quite apart from the obvious ones explainable by chronology. From the standpoint of deconstruction, inconsistencies inside each stratum of composition and consistencies among all three are more challenging to the interpreter because the argument from evolution is no longer available. Such a reading strategy could help give students a feel for the deconstructive method as a "teasing out of warring forces of signification" (Johnson 5).

TEACHING SPECIFIC ESSAYS

"By Diverse Means We Arrive at the Same End": Gateway to the *Essays*

Frieda S. Brown

Unless reading excerpts or selected chapters of a particular work, students normally expect to start a book at the beginning. Yet the first chapter of Montaigne's *Essays* is rarely taught or anthologized, and, typically, the only reference made to it by teachers or, until very recently, by scholars, relates to the continuing theme of human inconstancy that both begins and ends the edition of 1580. With the notable exception of the celebrated sentence "Truly man is a marvelously vain, diverse, and undulating object" (5), the chapter that Montaigne placed as the first among a final 107 has generally been relegated to the fate shared by most of the early essays, so that, in classrooms and criticism, those essays have become the last to be taught and studied.

Composed largely of brief exempla taken from antiquity and contemporary history—which, for Montaigne, will always be a way of learning about human behavior—and with the apparent Stoical emphasis of the 1580 version, "By Diverse Means We Arrive at the Same End" shares some of the obvious features of the earliest essays written between 1572 and 1574. Despite these similarities, it was probably written at a later date (1578) and was then expanded to twice its original length during subsequent periods of composition. Pierre Villey's suggestion that the idea of human diversity rather than the date of composition explains the essay's placement seems eminently plausible (1:336–37). While it would not make sense to propose that this chapter, even with its additions, possesses the rich development and fullness of later and better known essays, it does nonetheless convey approaches, ideas, and attitudes that we readily consign to the mature Montaigne. It introduces the structure and philosophy to come, justifying its liminal position, and warrants the serious attention of students who might otherwise fail to appreciate not only the development of the *Essays* but also the presence of Montaigne in all his work, including those chapters too long seen as derivative and lacking in interest and originality.

The limits on this study forbid anything resembling a full discussion of the many parallels to be drawn with other essays. Nor is there any attempt to respond to recent commentaries on the chapter, which range from Gabriel Pérouse's reading of the 1580 text as a paean to Stoicism to David Lewis Schaefer's analysis of it as a demonstration of Montaigne's rejection of Christian compassion. My primary objective in presenting and teaching this essay is to have students work directly with the text and to recognize thereby that "in the small compass of three pages, some of Montaigne's most pressing, most inalterable concerns crowd upon us *in nuce*" (Gutwirth, "Means" 186). In broader terms, a close reading helps students see in the very first chapter of the *Essays* characteristic ways in which Montaigne's language and style reveal both his thought and his art. We also find here the first use of the personal pronoun *I* as well as the word *essayé* in its essential meaning of "testing."

The title of the essay is, of course, a general, even an axiomatic, one. The student already aware of Montaigne's early, almost obsessive concern with death—a matter clearly not absent from this essay—might well be inclined to view it as the "end" to be discussed. In his own war-torn era, Montaigne's contemporaries might have derived the same conclusion for different reasons. Still, unlike those of later and more complex chapters, this title does point to the conspicuous subject of the text, a subject given a particular orientation by the very first sentence: the end to be achieved is "softening the hearts of those we have offended" (3). Of equal if not more interest in the context of the whole work is the admirable balance struck in the title by the antithetical "diverse" ("divers") and "same" ("pareil") and by "means" ("moyens") and "end" ("fin").

The idea of diversity emerges implicitly in the text with the opening superlative, which necessarily suggests alternative ways of behavior. "The commonest way" to win over those who, "vengeance in hand . . . hold us at their mercy, is by submission to move them to commiseration and pity" (3). But that said, Montaigne immediately turns his and the reader's attention away from this apparently (given its commonness) successful method: "However, audacity and steadfastness—entirely contrary means—have sometimes served to produce the same effect" (3). With what will become a characteristic "however" and with the explicit "entirely contrary means," the second sentence provides the first indication in the *Essays* of the antithetical structure that will prevail throughout the book. Montaigne's method of presenting an argument only to refute it or of offering an example only to counter its truth (Kritzman, *Destruction* 18–33)—a process eminently well suited to the relativist and skeptic—is thus in evidence from the first page of the *Essays*. Even the inclusion of "sometimes" keeps the door open to other possibilities.

By contrast, of the examples that make up the 1580 edition, all but one—the last—demonstrate how the display of "audacity and steadfastness" succeeded where supplication failed to obtain mercy from those angrily determined to avenge harm done them. The first recounts the story of Edward, prince of Wales, whose vengeance against the Limousins "could not be halted by the cries of the people and of the women and children abandoned to the butchery, who implored his mercy and threw themselves at his feet," until he encountered three French gentlemen who "alone" and "with incredible boldness" held out against his army. "Consideration and respect for such remarkable valor first took the edge off his anger; and he began with these three men to show mercy to all the inhabitants of the city" (3). It is worthwhile to note here that Froissart, from whose chronicles Montaigne borrowed this account, reports that the Black Prince spared only the three men (*Œuvres*, ed. Thibaudet and Rat, 1431n). Clearly, the essayist's adaptation lends greater force to the effectiveness of exceptional courage and suggests, as does his use of hyperbole, his admiration for such behavior. Although, as he later adds, "Either one of these two ways would easily win me" (4), his expression of respect corresponds to his view of the action of the king's lieutenant in Guienne in the face of the mob that ultimately killed him. Montaigne tells us in "Various Outcomes of the Same Plan"—need we remark on the title?—that Moneins's mistake was to have taken a path of "submission and softness" rather than to have exhibited "a gracious severity . . . full of security and confidence . . . [that] would have succeeded better . . . or at least would have been more honorable and proper" (95; 1.24). Doubt about its success does not seem to nullify Montaigne's sense of the "honneur et . . . bien-seance" (130; 1.24) that belong to such audacity and courage. Indeed, seen in this light, Montaigne's own steadfastness in the face of danger (95–96; 1.24; 812–13; 3.12) assumes increased interest.

But neither the hyperbolic praise of the action of the three men from Limoges—"hardiesse incroyable . . . seuls . . . une si notable vertu" (7)—nor their success in attaining mercy for all through that action obscures the brutality and cruelty of the prince "who governed our Guienne so long" and "whose traits and fortune have in them many notable elements of greatness" (3). The description of Edward's pursuit of revenge, heightened by the picture of defenseless women and children "criants mercy, et se jettans à ses pieds" (7)—the impact of the present participles is unfortunately lost in the English translation—uncovers another concern at the heart of this essay, a concern that will figure prominently in many chapters: Montaigne's very real horror of bloodshed and cruelty. The reference to "notre Guienne" certainly had to prompt his compatriots' private memories and bring the event home to them. The mental leap to the bloody ravages of the civil wars they had been experiencing for sixteen years could hardly have been a broad one. The themes of vengeance—a passion whose "sweet," even "natural," attraction Montaigne would later explicitly acknowledge while claiming "no experience of it in myself" and recounting his own efforts "to lead a young prince away from it" (634; 3.4)—and of cruelty—"among other vices, I cruelly hate cruelty . . . the extreme of all vices" (313; 2.11)—unquestionably owe much to the violent events of the times and perhaps, as Géralde Nakam has observed (*Montaigne* 100), to the massacres of 1572 about which Montaigne remains forever silent.

In the examples that follow, Edward's "anger" ("cholere") becomes, respectively, Prince Scanderbeg's "fury" ("furie") and Emperor Conrad III's "bitter and deadly hatred" ("toute cette aigreur d'inimitié mortelle et capitale") (3–4; 7–8), a gradation that provides still another indication of Montaigne's regard for what audacity and courage can achieve. In contrast to his elaboration of women and children pleading with the Prince of Wales for their lives, Montaigne says of the soldier fleeing death at the hands of Scanderbeg only that "after trying ["ayant essayé"] every sort of humility and supplication . . . [he] resolved in the last extremity to await [his pursuer] sword in hand"; the prince, in turn, responded to that resolve and to "such an honorable stand," receiving him "into his favor" (3; 7). The account is brief and straightforward except for the superlatives, which accent the soldier's exceptional but unsuccessful attempt to mollify the prince by submission, thereby undermining and casting additional doubt on the efficacy of "the commonest way." Indeed, the exemplum itself seems to be undermined by Montaigne's inclusion of the possibility of another interpretation. The inference is clear: to "those who have not read about the prodigious strength and valor of that prince" (3)—or who may doubt what they read? (Kritzman, *Destruction* 25)—Scanderbeg may have acted out of fear and cowardice. Two conclusions, then, are possible: the prince's mercy was or was not achieved by the soldier's show of courage. Despite the ambiguity of this event, Montaigne affirms the appropriateness of his first three examples: "these examples seem to me more to the point, inasmuch as we see these souls, assailed and tested ["essayées"] by these two means, hold up unshaken against one and bow beneath the other" (4; 8). Submission, in any case, and despite its "commonness," remains futile.

In the third example, Conrad, consumed by his hatred of the duke of Bavaria, "would not come down to milder terms, no matter what vile and cowardly satisfactions were offered him, than merely to allow the gentlewomen who were besieged with the duke to go out, their honor safe, on foot, with what they could carry on them" (3). Montaigne's language so minimizes Conrad's gesture that the temptation to see in it anything but an insignificant concession is forestalled. Moreover, the intensification of anger in the three examples finds a dramatic complement in the devaluation of efforts at appeasement, which Montaigne now describes as "vile and cowardly satisfactions" (3). Finally, where the first two exempla have shown the audacity and courage of men, it is the courage and cleverness of women—noblewomen, to be sure—that dominates the scene, "as they great-heartedly decided to load their husbands, their children, and the duke himself on their shoulders" (3), thus subduing the hatred of the emperor, who henceforth "treated him and his humanely" (4). What better adverb to accentuate, by contrast, the bestiality of uncontrolled hatred and cruelty?

Looking back at the chapter sometime between 1580 and 1588, Montaigne added, after the third exemplum, a telling personal remark, clearly separating himself from the Stoics whose position seems to dominate the examples, and implicitly revealing his natural antipathy toward cruelty: "I am wonderfully lax in the direction of mercy and gentleness. As a matter of fact, I believe I should be likely to surrender more naturally to compassion than to esteem. Yet to the Stoics pity is a vicious passion" (4). The interpolation seems to place him among the "weaker natures, such as those of women [surely not those women who outsmarted Conrad!], children, and the common herd" of whom "[i]t may be said" that they are more susceptible to pity and compassion than those "strong and inflexible soul[s]" who revere "the sacred image of valor . . . and honor a masculine and obstinate vigor" (4). But no, still another "however" introduces the Theban people and their treatment of Pelopidas "who bowed under the weight of [their] accusations and used only pleas and supplications to protect himself" and barely escaped with his life, whereas Epaminondas, facing the people "in a haughty and arrogant manner," received only great praise for "the loftiness of [his] courage." Thus, "astonishment and admiration" may also move "less lofty souls" (4).

With their emphasis on the success of "audacity and steadfastness," these four exempla weight the 1580 version toward the Stoical bias that Villey long ago attributed to the early essays. Readers must not lose sight, however, of the fundamental uncertainty engendered by these same examples. The theme of diversity in human action, whatever the measure of its success or failure, and Montaigne's insistent affirmation that "[i]t is hard to found any constant and uniform judgment on [man]" (5) are clearly manifestations of the essayist's lasting skepticism. Moreover, the example that ends the 1580 edition shatters, in a single sentence, the promise of defiance and courage. In fact, the example is doubled as we see "Pompeius pardoning the whole city of the Mamertines, against which he was greatly incensed, in consideration of the valor and magnanimity" of one man. "Yet Sulla's host, who displayed similar valor in the city of Praeneste, got nothing out of it, either for himself or for the others" (5). The absence of submission here, combined with Montaigne's pairing of the two events, gives quite a different cast to the essay and to its title, since by the same means we have arrived at different ends.

Submission plays no role in either of the exempla Montaigne added after 1580. The story of Dionysius, although a later addition than that of Alexander, is placed directly after the example of the Theban people. Perhaps the best explanation for its placement also reflects—in this first chapter—Montaigne's sensitivity to his own text, become intertext, as Dionysius's case reinforces the effect of boldness and valor on "less lofty souls." Witnessing the stubborn courage of Phyto in the face of Dionysius's cruelty, "the rank and file ["la commune"] of Dionysius' army . . . , disregarding their leader and his triumph, . . . were softened by astonishment at such rare valor" (4, 9). Dionysius, however, would not be placated. By the mere mention of the "extreme delays and difficulties" that held up Dionysius's victory over Rhegium, Montaigne implicitly points to the heightened rage of the conqueror, who, determined to make Phyto, the defender of the city, "a tragic example of vengeance" (4), subjects him, step by step, to psychological as well as physical violence. Montaigne's description, the longest and most elaborate to this point in the essay, leaves no doubt as to the cruel excesses perpetrated by Dionysius:

> Il luy dit premierement comment, le jour avant, il avoit faict noyer son fils et tous ceux de sa parenté. . . . Apres il le fit despouiller et saisir à des bourreaux et le trainer par la ville en le foitant tres ignominieusement et cruellement, et en outre le chargeant de felonnes paroles et contumelieuses. (9)

> First he told him how the day before he had had his son and all his relatives drowned. . . . After that he had him stripped and seized by executioners, who dragged him through the town, whipping him very ignominiously and cruelly and, in addition, heaping on him slanderous and insulting words. (4)

Beyond the highly subjective language that underlines the brutality and ignominy of Dionysius's actions, the adverbs "premierement," "apres," "en outre," the insistent series of infinitives ("despouiller," "saisir," "trainer"), and the present participles ("foitant," "chargeant") lend to the horror of the total picture a sense of continuing, even interminable, abuse. Phyto responds with a constancy and courage that effectively matches Dionysius's cruelty but to no avail. Dionysius's rage is beyond control; his heart cannot be "softened," or at least not by the show of exemplary courage. And, in light of its futility in the earlier examples, there is little reason to believe that submission might have subdued his fury.

In the final form of the essay, this is the first exemplum that unambiguously presents a situation in which "audacity and steadfastness" have no calming effect on the vengeful conqueror. Indeed, his fear of mutiny and of losing Phyto to his recalcitrant army only leads Dionysius to the more ignoble act of "secretly send[ing] him to be drowned in the sea" (4). Left unstated, but clearly implied, is the possibility that such violent rage may be unstoppable.

The example of Alexander goes far in validating such a conclusion. If the accounts of Sulla's host and Pompeius reveal the uncertainty and diversity among men, Alexander affords us the example of that same inconstancy in one man. Here, "the bravest of men and one very gracious to the vanquished" exhibits in two separate instances an inordinate capacity for cruelty. "Blood," "wounds," "torment," "slaughter," and "death" fill these passages, which constitute fully one-third of the entire essay. Montaigne's graphic images compel us to see Alexander's brutality; his use of direct discourse makes us hear his threats against the valorous Bétis. An intransigent Alexander, "turning his anger into rage," has Bétis's heels pierced, and "had him thus dragged alive, torn, and dismembered, behind a cart" (5).

The "many great difficulties," "the dearly won victory," the "damage" and "fresh wounds" Alexander received magnify his rage, but his vicious actions remain baffling—is this the man known as Alexander the Great? The question ("Could it be . . . ?") that ended the 1588 edition and the two questions Montaigne later added ("Or did he . . . ?" "Or was the . . . ?") seek explanations for his cruelty. No answer is forthcoming. We are left even more keenly aware of man's "undulating" nature (5).

But the essay does not stop there. The general movement of the text has led to examples of vengeance fueled by greater and greater rage, which, in turn, produces greater and greater cruelty. Thus, the theme of cruelty dominates the final addition. "In truth," Montaigne asserts, had Alexander's anger been capable of restraint, it is likely that it would have been "bridled" in the devastating capture of Thebes. But the carnage wrought there by Alexander "went on to the last drop of blood that could be shed, and stopped only at the unarmed people, old men, women, and children, so that thirty thousand of them might be taken as slaves" (5). Montaigne here pits vengeance against vengeance, for "not one" of the valiant Thebans fails "to try even in his last gasp to avenge himself, and . . . to assuage his death in the death of some enemy" (5).

"Softening the hearts of those we have offended," which the beginning of the chapter announced as attainable by diverse means, becomes, at its conclusion, unattainable by any means, when, as with Alexander, an irrepressible rage and anger seizes the heart. Not surprisingly, Montaigne offers no solution to this problem, but he will return to it again and again.

"By Diverse Means We Arrive at the Same End" is, in fact, the gateway to the *Essays*, and our students' impulse to start Montaigne's book at the beginning is the right one. Following that impulse in the classroom, I have found it most useful to approach the teaching of this essay in much the same way as I have addressed it in this study. That is, I encourage my students to pay particular attention to Montaigne's language, to his use of exempla, and to the movement and structure of the essay as a whole, emphasizing that it is only through an appreciation of the specific elements of his writing that we may discern the general tenor of Montaigne's thinking. Finally, in teaching this chapter, as well as other chapters to which the essayist added appreciably, I urge my students to read the essay with a conscious awareness of the strata and of what the additions may teach us not only about Montaigne's response to his own text but also about the development of his thought and his art.

"Of the Education of Children": Knowledge and Authority

Steven Rendall

When teaching the *Essays*, I often begin with "Of the Education of Children" (1.26), not only because students find it more accessible than chapters dealing with less familiar subjects, but also because it raises questions about knowledge and authority that go to the very heart of Montaigne's discourse. For this reason, it is also a good choice if the teacher must select only a few chapters for study; I suggest reading it along with "Of Repentance." The approach I propose here has proved useful in undergraduate courses on French literature, on the essay, and on autobiography.

Montaigne begins this essay by declaring that both he and his book are ignorant: "I myself see better than anyone else that these are nothing but reveries of a man who has tasted only the outer crust of sciences in his childhood, and has retained only a vague general picture of them" (106). When the essayist finally turns to the topic of education, he insists that he understands nothing about it—except that "the greatest and most important difficulty in human knowledge seems to lie in the branch of knowledge that deals with the upbringing and education of children" (109). This opening section of the essay could be seen as an extended variation on the "modesty formulas" frequently used by orators and writers from late antiquity onward. But Montaigne's profession of ignorance (or as he calls it in "Of Physiognomy," "*inscience*" [1057; 3.12]) is more than a rhetorical ploy designed to win the reader's good will. It is integral to his definition of a discourse grounded not in knowledge but in an individual's peculiar perspective on the world.

The conception of oral or written discourse as the transmission of knowledge or information is so familiar as to seem almost unproblematic. The most salient model for such discourse in Montaigne's day was the writing of the Renaissance humanists. The encyclopedic range of their learning, their mastery of foreign languages, and their massive erudition lent their works an immense authority. Montaigne was familiar with the humanists; as he points out in this essay, "Nicholas Grouchy, who wrote *De Comitiis Romanorum*, Guillaume Guerente, who wrote a commentary on Aristotle, George Buchanan, that great Scottish poet, Marc-Antoine Muret, whom France and Italy recognize as the best orator of his time" (129) were his private tutors, and Adrianus Turnebus and Pierre Bunel were among his friends. Montaigne's declaration of his ignorance is designed in part to make it clear that he does not seek to compete with the humanists in scholarship and learning. "I have no authority to be believed," Montaigne writes, "nor do I want it, feeling myself too ill-instructed to instruct others" (109).

As an alternative to such "scientific" discourse, Montaigne outlines, perhaps for the first time, a conception of discourse as the representation, not of what *is* the case but of what the speaker *believes* to be the case. Whatever "absurdities" he may have put in his book, Montaigne writes:

> I have had no intention of concealing them, any more than I would a bald and graying portrait of myself, in which the painter had drawn not a perfect face, but mine. For likewise these are my humors and opinions; I offer them as what I believe, not what is to be believed. I aim here only at revealing myself, who will perhaps be different tomorrow, if I learn something new which changes me.   (108–09)

This can be fruitfully compared with the famous passage in "Of Repentance," in which Montaigne notes, "[M]y history needs to be adapted to the moment," and thus "I may indeed contradict myself now and then; but truth, as Demades said, I do not contradict" (611; 3.2). Truth is here redefined not as generally valid propositions about the world but as the sincere expression of the speaker's beliefs at the moment he expresses them. Even if these beliefs are "false," the speaker is still telling the truth in expressing them *as his beliefs*.

Montaigne's argument may seem very close to that of his English contemporary Sir Philip Sidney, who wrote—in *An Apology for Poetry*, first published in 1583—that the poet "nothing affirms, and therefore never lieth[,] . . . though he recounts things not true, yet because he telleth them not for true, he lieth not" (168). Sidney is arguing, however, that poets may write what they know to be false as long as they do not "affirm" it—that is, present it as true and seek to persuade others to believe it. His definition of lying— "to lie is to affirm that to be true which is false" (168)—ignores the difference between asserting something one knows to be false and asserting something false one believes to be true. The distinction Sidney neglects to make here is fundamental to Montaigne's view of his book as a representation of his ideas and opinions. Sidney points toward conceptions of fictional discourse as composed of "pseudo-statements" having the form of propositions about reality but referring to imaginary worlds; Montaigne inaugurates modern autobiographical writing by shifting the reference of discourse from its object (whether real or imaginary) to its subject—that is, to the speaker or writer.

While Montaigne's discussion of these points is no doubt important for the understanding of the *Essays*, one might well ask what it has to do with the education of children. On closer inspection, however, we can see that his own practices of reading and writing, as he describes them in the opening pages of the chapter, closely resemble those he goes on to prescribe for his ideal pupil.

In both cases, the discourse of others serves primarily as a whetstone for honing one's own judgment, not as a source of information to be stored up in the memory. And in both the emphasis falls on appropriation, on digesting ideas and making them one's own; for clearly Montaigne's claim that his book represents his ideas and opinions assumes that they are in some sense truly *his*. Appropriation depends upon thinking ideas through for oneself—if the pupil "embraces Xenophon's and Plato's opinions by his own reasoning, they will no longer be theirs, they will be his" (111)—and cutting them loose from their "source"; that is why the pupil may be allowed to "forget . . . where he got them" (111). Reverting to the first person, Montaigne explains that "[t]ruth and reason are common to everyone, and no more belong to the man who first spoke them than to the man who says them later. It is no more according to Plato than according to me, since he and I understand and see it in the same way" (111). Thus while Montaigne insists that he may reformulate ideas found in other authors, and even repeat their words, he also maintains, "I do not speak the minds of others except to speak my own mind better" (108).

Citing Cicero, Montaigne suggests that the authority of teachers and master-texts is an obstacle to the student's freedom of judgment in selecting and appropriating ideas (110). He laments that "[o]ur mind moves only on faith, being bound and constrained to the whim of others' fancies, a slave and a captive under the authority of their teaching" and urges the tutor to "make his charge pass everything through a sieve and lodge nothing in his head on mere authority and trust" (111). This applies as well, of course, to what the tutor himself says, and by extension, to Montaigne's own discourse. Montaigne is well aware that in writing about teaching (or any other subject) he seems to be casting himself in the role of master, and from the outset he seeks to throw off the mantle of authority by proclaiming his ignorance and positioning himself not over but alongside or even beneath the pupil: "there is not a child halfway through school who cannot claim to be more learned than I" (107). Like the pupil, Montaigne's reader should feel free to accept or reject what he says. Hence the tutor will take Montaigne's advice "only as far as it seems good to him" (110). This implies, of course, that the *Essays* can also be regarded as a source of ideas to be critically evaluated by the reader and put to his or her own uses.

Similar conceptions of reading and writing can be found in other sixteenth-century authors, Erasmus and Sidney among them. But perhaps the most influential statement on this subject was that of Montaigne's favorite author, Plutarch, who had been recently translated into French by Jacques Amyot. In his essay "How a Young Man Should Study Poetry," Plutarch urges readers to explore the moral implications of a text, without regard to its author's intentions, and in "On Listening to Lectures," he says that one should not be a passive listener but, rather, "taking the discourse of another as a germ and seed, develop and expand it." And he goes on:

> Imagine, then, that a man should need to get fire from a neighbour, and upon finding a big bright fire there, should stay there warming himself; just so it is if a man comes to another to share the benefit of a

discourse, and does not think it necessary to kindle from it some illumination for himself and some thinking of his own.   (258–59)

This latter passage is reproduced in Montaigne's "Of Pedantry," where it is associated with the metaphors of reading as digestion and appropriation that we have encountered in "Of the Education of Children" ("We are just like a man who, needing fire . . ." [101; 1.25]). The emphasis falls not on the speaker's discourse but on what the listener makes of it. Similarly, reading is oriented less toward the author than toward the reader's production of a personal discourse.

What this might mean in practice is indicated in "Of the Education of Children" when Montaigne discusses the way he reads "historians":

> I have read in Livy a hundred things that another man has not read in him. Plutarch has read in him a hundred besides the ones I could read, and perhaps besides what the author had put in. . . . There are in Plutarch many extensive discussions, well worth knowing . . . but there are a thousand that he has only just touched on; he merely points out with his finger where we are to go, if we like. . . . We must snatch these bits out of there and display them properly.   (115)

This suggests that as a reader-writer, Montaigne elaborates on particular passages in his own way and in relation to his own interests, without much regard for their relation to the rest of the work or for the author's intentions. Indeed, a study of the way he recontextualizes passages from other authors in the *Essays*—for instance, through the use of quotations—tends to bear this out, and he encourages students to do the same. The discourse of others will not lend the student's discourse authority, but it will provide materials the student can appropriate and reuse. From this point of view, reading and writing constantly regenerate each other; they are moments in the endless circulation and recycling of words and ideas.

Montaigne depreciates the role of authority, faith, and trust in education only in order to relocate and redefine it. The authority grounded in the tutor's knowledge of the "sciences" is displaced by the authority of the pupil's self-knowledge. The student's thoughts are best known to the student, and this is the authority necessary for the kind of discourse Montaigne describes—which is, as I have been suggesting, the same kind he claims to practice in the *Essays*. In a famous passage in "Of Repentance" he writes that "no man ever treated a subject he knew and understood better than I do the subject I have undertaken; and . . . in this I am the most learned man alive" (611; 3.2). Similarly, although Montaigne warns his ideal pupil not to rely on faith or trust in assessing the truth of what is read or heard, tutors must trust pupils to express their own beliefs faithfully, just as the reader must trust the sincerity of Montaigne's statements about his "humors and opinions." In the passage just quoted from "Of Repentance," Montaigne claims that to accomplish the task he has set himself in writing the *Essays*, he need only "bring to it fidelity; and that is in it, as sincere and as pure as can be found" (611). Similarly, he begins his preface, "To the Reader," by insisting that "[t]his book was written in good faith . . ." (2).

Yet there is a fundamental asymmetry between the kind of reading Montaigne practices and recommends to students and the kind he expects from his own readers. For if the pupil is the correlate of Montaigne as a reader of other texts, the tutor seems to be the correlate of the reader implied by the essays themselves. The pupil's reading gives little attention to determining the original intent of any given passage and still less to treating the text as a portrait of its author's "humors and opinions" (108). The tutor, on the other hand, listens to the pupil's responses, not merely to use them as a springboard for formulating the tutor's views but to understand the pupil's views and to determine the pupil's character. And when the tutor breaks the silence to address the pupil, the tutor's words are oriented toward the pupil's horizon, not the teacher's own: "he should have his pupil trot before him, to judge the child's pace and how much he must stoop to match his strength" (110). If tutors lack a sense of this "proportion" (110), they cannot enter into a genuine dialogue with their pupils and end up "bawling into our ears, as though they were pouring water into a funnel" (110).

Montaigne makes it clear that he wants his reader to respond *to him*; that is implicit in his description of his book as a self-portrait. Toward the end of the chapter "Of the Resemblance of Children to Fathers," he tells Mme de Duras: "I want to derive nothing from these writings except that they represent me to your memory as I naturally am. These same traits and faculties you have been familiar with . . . I want to lodge (but without alteration or change) in a solid body that may last a few years, or a few days, after me . . . ." (595; 2.37). The essays are to be a monument that faithfully preserves their author's image. Those who, unlike Diane de Foix or Mme de Duras, cannot *remember* Montaigne must *infer* his "traits and faculties" from the *Essays*. Readers for whom Montaigne's book was no more than a collection of commonplaces to be used in elaborating their own ideas would satisfy this demand no more (but perhaps no less) than those who used its pages to wrap butter (504; 2.18).

Thus to this new conception of writing corresponds a new conception of reading, one that sees the text as an authoritative representation of its author's perspective on the world. In this respect, Montaigne's argument anticipates the fundamental premises of a program of literary education radically different from the one he proposes in "Of the Education of Children." Teachers of the *Essays* might ask their students to reflect on the irony of that outcome.

"Of Three Kinds of Association":
In the Library, Looking Out

John D. Lyons

From the library, Montaigne writes, he could look out the window in three directions while flipping through books between moments of daydreaming. Is this not a familiar experience to a college student? My teaching of parts of Montaigne's *Essays* has been in the context of an introduction to comparative literature in a medium-sized undergraduate college. This course had as one of several themes the collective definition of what reading is and how the process of reading is affected by personal experience and by surroundings. The course emphasized reading as an activity and tried to overcome the tendency of some students to see their relation to books as a merely accumulative phenomenon, as the passive contact with reading material. Texts for this course included accounts of important scenes of reading and of contact with books, as related by such authors as Augustine, Dante, Descartes, Lafayette, Proust, and Nabokov. On the theme of reading, Montaigne's "Of Three Kinds of Association" (3.3) runs against the ideal of attentive, purposeful reading implicit in almost every American college syllabus. Montaigne's reading was definitely not "homework," and his comments in this essay have been mentioned as evidence of "a fundamental transformation in the use of books" (Regosin, "*Matter*" 92). This essay serves as a reminder of the larger nonacademic traditions of reading as a lifelong experience. In defining this experience, the chapter examines other ways of defining oneself in terms of gender and society.

As a preliminary to studying the *Essays*, the issue of Montaigne's self-presentation had to be discussed. Without abandoning the idea that Montaigne intended to give as faithful a representation as possible of the concrete reality of life—that is, without treating the *Essays* simply as fiction—students had to confront two related aspects of the first-person text. First, in "Of Three Kinds of Association" the narrator very pointedly reminds us of his name—"my house is perched on a little hill, as its name indicates" (629). He is describing not the average person but a specific individual. However, each chapter selects certain experiences and traits of this individual while condensing and omitting others. Students were invited to look at the character-narrator as a creation of this text. Second, this character is called "I," "me," and "myself." Since "Of Three Kinds of Association," like most other chapters, frequently and minutely describes "myself," class discussion was always hesitating over the term to use in speaking about this character. "Montaigne" was possible but did not always seem to fit the intimate, microscopic view of the character presented in the essay. Our solution—like that of most scholars—was to speak, rather impersonally, of "the self."

On close examination of the chapter, we found these preparatory considerations to coincide with Montaigne's thematic questioning of what "myself" is and where it is located or displayed. A constant of the *Essays* is the concept of the unstable nature of the self, unstable in the etymological sense of something that does not *stay* (Latin *stare*). Expressions such as "I do not portray being: I portray passing" (611; 3.2) turn up throughout Montaigne's book. The self is definable less by its location in a place than by its movement from one place to another and back again. To the extent that the self identifies with a place and begins to take that place's boundaries as the self's own limits, the self seems to elect borders only to experience the change that comes from crossing them. In such a situation we are forced to pay special attention to boundaries in attempting to track the elusive, moving self. In "Of Three Kinds of Association," Montaigne first evokes boundaries of the self in social situations, contrasting what is within a personality and what appears on the outside, before culminating with a description of his library whose walls and windows offer a satisfactory resolution to the problems of social surfaces.

One last preliminary before a detailed discussion of the essay is a clarification of Montaigne's chapter title. While "association" is a fine overall solution to the problem of translating Montaigne's French *commerce*, at times other English terms are necessary to point out that Montaigne is writing not about clubs, organizations, or societies but rather about interaction with, negotiation with, or simply dealing with men, women, and books. While shifting from term to term may not seem consistent, no other approach is faithful to the variety of meanings in Montaigne's title.

The apparent disorder of the opening page of this chapter is not untypical of the *Essays*. Yet a clear and strong progressive organization is retrospectively evident. The chapter's careful placement in the *Essays* is suggested by the insistence on the number three in its location, its title, and in numerous details (Conley, "*De Capsula*"). After mentioning the three *commerces*, or kinds of association, in the title, Montaigne does not return explicitly to the idea that there are three kinds of interaction until three-quarters of the way through the chapter. Yet the three associations are mentioned in an order that is evaluative (from two imperfect associations to a satisfactory one), temporal (from earlier in the speaker's life to an association that suits late maturity), and spatial (from outward exposure to other people toward protective enclosure). The concept of commerce stresses the contact between independent entities that do not lose their identities through their relation. Each preexists the association and coexists within it. By describing commerces, Montaigne allows himself to characterize the points of contact—the boundaries—between the partners to commerce and thus to investigate the way each partner affects the other—in particular how it affects the self known as Montaigne or "I."

We can see this boundary definition emerge in three sections of the chapter, sections that I present as heuristically valuable even though they are not explicitly designated by Montaigne. In the first section (621–22, up to "not my memory"), Montaigne presents the danger of an entirely stable and self-centered self and mentions reading as a way of anticipating the concluding passages of the essay. In the second section (622–28, up to "the affairs of the world"), he describes two social commerces, compares them, and depicts their effects on him. The third and concluding section describes the library and how Montaigne uses this place for contact with books, with the world outside, and with himself.

The first part begins with the paradox that the self is most free when it is not bound too closely to itself. While Montaigne's approach can be rightly characterized as generally introspective, his own argument here seems to hold that the inward turn must be balanced by a contrary movement: "We must not nail ourselves down so firmly to our humors and dispositions" (621). No sooner, however, has Montaigne stated the need to move outward toward other objects of perception than he announces his tendency to be excessively attracted to the outside: "Most minds need foreign matter to arouse and exercise them; mine needs it rather to settle down and rest . . ." (621). Montaigne explicitly proposes himself as different, as naturally finding sufficient stimulation in himself. Meditation is a full and powerful study "for anyone who knows how to examine and exercise himself vigorously" (621–22). But it quickly appears that Montaigne is describing a much less stable and self-sufficient personality than at first appears. No sooner does he describe the pleasures of self-study than he mentions the stimulating power of reading, "to arouse my reason" (622).

Thus the perplexing, truly borderline status of reading appears early in the chapter, as neither clearly outside nor inside the self. In a passage on meditation, Montaigne writes, "It is the occupation of the gods, says Aristotle, from which springs their happiness and ours. Reading serves me particularly to arouse my reason by offering it various subjects to set my judgment to work, not my memory" (622). The way reading relates to self-examination ("se taster" [819]) in meditation is left in suspension. Does reading form the outward boundary of meditation, an additional stimulus imported from the outside? Or is reading so internalized as to be part of the self? Even though reading does not reappear until late in the chapter, as the third kind of association, its mention here establishes it as a pivot for the upcoming discussion of Montaigne's relationship to others.

The second part of the essay is devoted to the speaker's apparently contradictory tendency to *withdraw* from contact and to *seek* contact with other people. The two social associations, with both men and women, have in common the danger that the movement back and forth across the boundary of the self will be replaced by a mask or mirror that allows a purely exterior and false version of the self to dominate. The risk is that nothing come from the inside and that the prevailing social discourse rule. Montaigne sees this as a fall—terms of descending and weighing-down are frequent, for example, "more need . . . of lead than of wings" (624)—and he comes close to using the modern cliché of the lowest common denominator: "crawl along the ground, if they want" (624). This lower, exterior world is designated as a place for role playing. You act as if you understand—"act knowing among those who are not" (624)—while others also put on the same airs. Or you pretend to be ignorant—"and sometimes affect ignorance"—when you are not ignorant.

Montaigne describes women as being coerced into putting on appearances in society, preventing their internal nature from being seen. "At least they have the appearance of it," he says of women and pedantic learning; "[t]hey conceal and cover up their own beauties under foreign beauties" (624). Erudite learning does not penetrate their external mien to awaken any interior response or understanding ("The learning that could not reach their mind . . ." [624]), but the wish to conform to the commerce with learned men prevents them from letting their true nature, their "own natural riches" appear outwardly. While to a twentieth-century reader Montaigne will certainly seem to take here an essentialist view of women as not being capable of erudition, the situation of women is a subcategory of the general deformity imposed on the self by society. The learned men whom women attempt to imitate are themselves presented by Montaigne as falling into the trap of an excessive exteriority, an attempt to impress the people around them: "Learned men are prone to stumble over this stone. They are always parading their mastery . . ." (624).

Soon, however, a paradox appears in Montaigne's comments on the surface we show other people. The crucial problem that Montaigne presents is that he is not, after all, simply calling for greater introspection and thus a withdrawal from interaction with other people. In his comments on women, first, and then in his self-description, Montaigne promotes a certain kind of external show as being the best way to be true to one's own nature. Of the kind of learning appropriate for women, he selects first of all poetry: "poetry is an amusement suited to their needs; it is a wanton ["follastre" (823)] and subtle art, in fancy dress, wordy, all pleasure, all show, like themselves" (624).

Only a few sentences later, Montaigne says that he too is more inclined to be opened outward than to be retiring: "There are private, retiring, and inward natures. My essential pattern is suited to communication and revelation. I am all in the open and in full view, born for company and friendship" (625). Therefore, women are "all show" (624) and Montaigne is "all in the open and in full view" (625). In describing his association with men, Montaigne reveals values surprisingly close to the qualities he appreciates in women. Weight and depth ("le pois et la profondeur" [819; 824]) do not attract him as much as beauty. At first, this preference seems strange, even contradictory. Even though "weightiness" has frequently negative connotations for Montaigne, despite the social importance of weight as synonym for authority, depth would seem to correspond to the inward sources of desire, like the women's "natural riches" against which the social facade is so often imposed as a surface. However the writer values in men nonutilitarian qualities, ones not associated with the achievement of substantial civic enterprises—for example, the work of magistrates deciding "lineal substitutions" (625). Instead he enjoys "charm and pertinency" (625; cf. in women "the charm of their eyes" [624]), that is, the charm that is oriented toward the social situation and thus turned outward rather than inward toward the self and its hidden qualities. He favors occasions where the mind "shows its beauty" (625). Therefore in men and women Montaigne seeks nonutilitarian interaction, aiming merely at "intimacy, fellowship, and conversation ["privauté, frequentation et conference" (824)]: exercise of minds, without any other fruit" with "kindliness, frankness, gaiety, and friendliness" (625) just as in the poetic nature of women he appreciates the quality of an art that is playful and subtle, all oriented toward pleasure.

The resolution of this paradoxical valuation of appearance after an earlier denigration of appearance and surface seems to be in the movement from inside out or at least an integrity of the surface of the self with something deeper. The "show" therefore is not a concealment of something else, not a barrier to the passage between inside and out. It is neither a slavery of the self, as denounced in the opening sentences of the essay, nor a mere reproduction of the prevailing social discourse. However, this ideal result is not available to Montaigne. Even more than women confronted by a male display of learning—or of flattering desire (626)—Montaigne's contact with society prevents the manifestation of his nature. When he is in the crowd at the royal court in the Louvre, he notes, "I withdraw and contract into my skin; the crowd drives me back to myself" (625). When there is no one there, his self is displayed: "Solitude of place, to tell the truth, rather makes me stretch and expand outward" (625). This description of Montaigne's reaction to two different situations, social and solitary, emphasizes the boundary of the self, its expansion and contraction *on the outside* and in respect to its *skin*, its physical boundary with the outside world.

This problem of the boundary of the self appears in acute form in the interaction between women and men. As the mature Montaigne experiences it, the company of women is a sweet association (*doux commerce* [824]). Yet as a young man, he found it dangerous in the way it absorbed him. This is one of the two extreme positions without a middle that seem to characterize erotic attraction between the sexes. On one hand, the young Montaigne allowed himself to be fully absorbed by passion, suffering all the rages described by poets. Rejecting this full engagement of the self, he considers it "madness to fasten all our thoughts upon it and to become involved in a furious and reckless passion" (626). On the other hand, withholding one's inner feelings and performing a social role for the purpose of physical satisfaction seems even worse. Montaigne makes the theater metaphor explicit in describing the male creation of a surface detached from an inner nature: "to go into it without love and without binding our will, like actors, to play the standard role of our age and customs and put into it nothing of our own but the words" (626). In contact with this exhibition of the male outward boundary beyond which they cannot see, women either reject all interaction with men or imitate men by creating in turn an impenetrable barrier of social pretense and "fall in line with this example that we give them, play their part in the farce, and lend themselves to this negotiation, without passion, without interest, and without love" (627). For Montaigne only self-investment in an erotic relationship produces pleasure. In other words, the self must be engaged deeply and not only on the surface for such an association to be worthwhile; yet excessively deep engagement is painful. Both kinds of social interaction have drawbacks. The self is either constrained behind an opaque border or excessively exposed in such a way that it is soon thrust back behind its defenses. After youthful excess in association with women, Montaigne claims to have learned that "we must keep a bit on guard" (626).

The third part of the chapter is the most crisply demarcated—"These two kinds of association are accidental and dependent on others" (628)—and recalls the framework established by the title. The concluding pages are most explicit in the need to provide for the contradictory needs of the self for openness and enclosure at the same time. The library, place of interaction with books, offers the seemingly impossible opportunity for an association without constraint, where the self can receive stimulation from the outside without putting on a front. The association with books depends entirely on the self. This assertion of the intermediate status of books—not identical with the self, yet not foreign and independent—recalls the first mention of reading in this chapter, where reading is associated with meditation (621). In this third part reading is presented at first in terms of temporal alternation. The social associations with men and women are defective because one is infrequent (with men of quality) and the other deteriorates with age. Books are more constant ("the constancy and ease of [their] service" [628]). The availability of books at all times is not, however, their sole advantage. They may be picked up and put down at the sole option of the self. Not constancy or continuity but controllability is a major advantage of books.

Books provide a stimulus to the self while protecting the self against intrusion. Their association "relieves me of the weight of a tedious idleness, and releases me at any time from disagreeable company" (628). These words recall the fear of slavery to the self and the intrusiveness of the other interactions. *Some* interaction seems necessary for pleasant meditation provided that it not become an uncontrollable pressure from the outside against the fragile self. Although Montaigne never uses the simile of the mollusk, this might be an apt comparison. The third part of the essay corresponds to the need of a tender, easily bruised animal for a shell that is not too heavy to carry. And, indeed, portability is one of the great advantages of books. They are available *when* he wants them: "I'll do it soon, I say, or tomorrow, or when I please"; and *where* he is: "I do not travel without books, either in peace or in war. . . . [T]hey are at my side to give me pleasure at my own time" (628).

This praise of interaction with books is, on closer inspection, a rather astounding one. The books' presence is alone sufficient, even without reading. Montaigne claims not to make much more use of books than the illiterate do: "Actually I use them scarcely any more than those who do not know them at all" (628). Although books are a refuge, Montaigne does not, in this particular essay, propose the elaborate justification of reading on the basis of communion with other thinkers or refinement of thought through the intellectual struggle and emulation provided by outstanding texts (as in "Of the Education of Children"). It seems enough to be where the books are. Terence Cave has written of Montaigne's "dismissive gesture towards books" ("Problems" 160). Yet Montaigne distances himself also from the material bibliophile by pointing out that he abandoned ostentatious book purchases and the use of books as furniture (629–30). This curious description of a "commerce" that differs both from reading and collecting is the culmination and the resolution of the chapter.

Montaigne's description of his library here shows that it affords both stimulation and protection from outside pressure. Being stuck, being nailed down, was the problem that opened the chapter, and the library has enough space to keep Montaigne moving so that his thoughts do not fall asleep. Even getting to the library is a source of stimulation. Montaigne notes that one advantage of the tower room is "the benefit of the exercise" (629). The library is out of the way and hard to get to, so that most people will not bother him there. In the library Montaigne displays his flight from other people in a compromise with his desire to watch others, his love of enclosure and of outwardness combined. In this place, he does not necessarily read but walks around and looks away from his books: "There I leaf through now one book, now another, without order and without plan . . ." (629). This is a space for studying *without books*, and that is why walking is so important: "Those who study without a book are all in the same boat" (629). Montaigne emphasizes that the library provides a view of almost every part of his house and that he can look out in three different directions. By accentuating so strongly the activity of walking around and looking *out* the windows of his library, Montaigne recalls the essay's opening call to avoid excessive self-absorption. The books and the windows of the library have a somewhat similar function of distracting the self, or at least providing the occasions of distraction. Books were said, in the first part of the essay, to be for Montaigne's mind "one of the kinds of occupations which entice it away from its study" (621). The surroundings of Montaigne's tower are not therefore rivals with books for his attention but instead quasi-equivalents of books as outlets from his laborious self-study. This equivalency is clear in the juxtaposition of sentences concerning the different parts of his property that Montaigne can see from the library with the description of his disconnected way of reading: "I am over the entrance, and see below me my garden, my farmyard, my courtyard, and into most of the parts of my house" (628–29). Montaigne seems to page through his house, glancing freely and without necessary connection, from one place to another as he would through a book.

Books, windows, and walking are the opportunities provided in the library for shaking the self out of slavery to the self without enslaving it to anything else. Interaction, *commerce*, is a way of keeping the self going. Books, like the windows of the tower, are the openings, the enticements that keep the mind from idleness. Books are therefore in themselves no more important than windows or stairs. They are opportunities for interaction, expansion, and self-study.

"Of the Art of Discussion":
A Philological Reading

Jules Brody

To read Montaigne philologically is to describe and analyze his use of language—repetitions, imagery, rhetorical embellishments, quoted matter—rather than attempt to divine his intentions or his meaning by recourse to his biography, personal relationships, and putative opinions or through reference to such abstractions as the Renaissance, humanism, and the baroque. The philological reader fastens on the individual essay as unit of study, marked off as it is from the others by white space, a distinctive title, its number and position in the volume, and, most important, by a unique set of words arranged in a unique order. As a pedagogical tool, philological reading recommends itself for at least two reasons: first, it compels the student to face up to Montaigne's most conspicuous quality: his unprecedented and inimitable way of writing; second, by privileging each essay's objective property, the configuration of words that it alone contains, the philological approach offers the inexperienced, ignorant, and culturally deficient readers who fall into our nets a significant degree of control over a text whose density and richness continue to confound even the most learned and accomplished among the Montaigne experts.

My first concern in teaching Montaigne is to convince my subjects that, if they will refrain, especially at the outset, from trying to drag out of him clear, firm ideological statements, they will find that the actual text of the *Essays* is quite reader-friendly. To make this point with "Of the Art of Discussion," I ritually begin my reading by asking the students to describe the most salient stylistic feature of the essay's first few paragraphs. Whether we are working from the original or a translation, someone always directs attention to the string of polar oppositions that characterize the style from the opening sentence onward: "some"/"others," "done"/"undone," "correct"/"incorrigible," "imitable"/"evitable," "self-accusation"/"self-commendation," "by flight"/"by pursuit," "the fools"/"the wise," "bad way of speaking"/"good one," "what stings"/"what pleases" (703; 3.8). My eventual aim is to establish, whether through Socratic prodding or professorial intervention, that the word "stings" in the last example initiates a sequence of "stimulation" passages that runs through the essay from beginning to end. But before listing these, I explain what it is in the context of the "poind"/"plaist" binary that makes me want to single it out for special scrutiny:

> [A] bad way of speaking reforms mine better than a good one. Every day the stupid bearing of another warns ["m' advertit"] and admonishes me. What stings ["poind"], touches and arouses us ["touche et esveille"] better than what pleases ["plaist"]. (703; 922)

I note, to begin with, that the expression "way of speaking," Montaigne's first explicit mention of his announced subject, marks a deferred transition

between the title and the body of the essay. This evidence of continuity is
further reinforced when we observe that the word "warns" ("m' advertit")
refers back to the "warning" ("advertissement") in the opening sentence—"It
is a practice of our justice to condemn some as a warning to others" (703)—
while at the same time launching the tautological series: "warns" > "stings"
> "touches" > "arouses." The contextual function of this sequence, in turn,
is to actualize an antithetical dialogic model that undergoes elaborate development on the very next page:

> The study of books is a languishing and feeble activity that gives no
> heat, whereas discussion teaches and exercises us at the same time. If
> I discuss with a strong mind and a stiff jouster, he presses on my flanks,
> prods me right and left; his ideas launch mine. Rivalry, glory, competi-
> tion, push me and lift me above myself. And unison is an altogether
> boring quality in discussion.   (704)

This comment presents "the art of discussion" in one of its most conspicuous aspects as an "exercise" in the physical and sportive, and in sharp
opposition to the academic and scholastic, sense of the word. Montaigne
likens *conference* (etymologically, the bringing together of people or ideas)
to what modern French calls a *joute oratoire* or *joute d'esprit*. For Montaigne's first readers, however, this still current courtly metaphor would have
denoted a socially upscale form of verbal skirmishing and intellectual spar-
ring, a battle of wits as exhilarating to wage and to witness as book learning
and any of its one-sided, monologic variants are dull and boring.

It is at this juncture that I distribute the first of several handouts, an
anthology of excerpts containing expressions from the overlapping semantic
fields of sport, contest, single combat, and the like, whose common denominator is some literal or figurative connection with the idea of "stimulation" or
"pointiness." In skeletal form:

stings; *poind* (703; 922)
prods; *pique* (704; 923)
touch, arouse; *touche, esveille* (705; 924)
treat roughly; *gourment* (706; 925)
blows; *atteintes* (706; 925)
fencing; *escrime* (707; 927)
hit the ring; *mettra dedans* (708; 928)
weapons; *armes* (709,716; 929,937)
point, dagger; *pointe, poignard* (715; 936)
sword; *enferrons* (715; 936)
ripostes; *revirades* (715; 936)
sharp repartee; *devis pointus* (717; 938)
pluck; *pinçons* (717; 939)

pointed fashion; *façon pointue* (719; 941)
pointed; *aigu* (719; 941)
describing, decrying; *peint, pince* (719; 941)

With this anthology in hand, students can be made to see at a glance how a confusing, ostensibly disjointed and digressive piece of writing actually exhibits, even if only in the primitive content of its lexicon, an unsuspected coherency. In the synoptic, philological perspective that I have drawn here, the essay may be taken, if only provisionally and minimally, as a metaphorical construct generated at one end from the word *poind* and bounded at the other by the word *pince*. At all events, it is a source of strength and reassurance to the student to observe how the essay hangs together, even makes an odd kind of sense as a verbal continuum, in ways and to a degree seldom apparent in the usual content-centered, ideological readings of the *Essays*.

Given the constraints of space, this philological reading touches just a few of the high points of Montaigne's inquiry into the subjects of eloquence, persuasion, and communication, sighted exclusively along the parallel or coincidental semantic lines of "stimulation," "competition," "pungency." When made to channel their reading in this narrowed perspective, students are particularly pleased—and instantly won over to the virtues of the philological method—when they are able to see, for example, how the opposition *verbal jousting/book learning* is further reinforced and raised to thematic prominence in the following development:

> Now who will not begin to distrust learning . . . ? Who has acquired understanding from logic? . . . I would rather have my son learn to speak in the taverns than in the schools of talk. . . . Take a Master of Arts, converse ["conferez"] with him. . . . Why does he not dominate and persuade us at will? Why does a man with such advantages in matter and method mix insults, recklessness, and fury with his fencing ["escrime"]? (707; 927)

It is especially satisfying to note here that the contemptuous challenge— "Take a Master of Arts [i.e, a professor in the Faculty of Arts], converse ["conferez"] with him"—marks the one and only joint recurrence of the essay's two operative title-words. This striking injunction, with its emphasis on the negative aspects of the *art de conferer* (erudition, technique, authority), poses two discrepant modes of *conference*, as inalterably exclusive of each other as understanding and logic, talent and learning, proletarian good sense and academic rigidity, aristocratic good humor and bourgeois distemper. Reduced to its nuclear expression, the distinction between bad and good, artificial and artistic *conference*, is subsumed in Montaigne's confrontation of two disparate models of competitive interaction: the learned disputation, singled out for its acrimonious resistance to contradiction, and the sporting elegance of the aristocratic fencing match. It should be observed finally, in this connection, that the irascible debating style ascribed to the bungling master of arts is the complete obverse of the relaxed position Montaigne had earlier staked out for himself—"When someone opposes me, he arouses my attention, not my anger"—in emulation of the sublime Socrates, "who always smilingly welcomed the contradictions offered to his arguments" (705).

As we travel down the stations on the semantic line of stimulation/pointiness described by the texts in my handout, a compelling property of the philological approach becomes increasingly apparent: it enables us to see in the form of the message certain ideological and didactic constants neither readily perceptible nor fully articulated in its propositional content. What is slowly emerging from this philological reading of the essay are the lineaments of a typology or a sociology of communication, in which eloquence and persuasiveness are a function not of what one knows, nor even of what one says or does, but, rather, of what one *is*.

Toward the end of the essay there is a pivotal passage that recapitulates and expands Montaigne's concept of the best kind of *conference* as a verbal duel, an aristocratic pastime conducted in a relaxed, jocular spirit of gentlemanly reciprocity:

> May we not include under the title of discussion . . . the sharp, abrupt repartee ["les devis pointus et coupez"] which good spirits and familiarity introduce among friends . . . ? An exercise for which my natural gayety makes me rather fit; and if it is not so . . . serious as that other exercise I have just been speaking of, it is no less keen ["aigu"] and ingenious. . . . And when a sally ["charge"] is made against me . . . I do not go wasting my time pursuing the point ["pointe"] with a boring and lax argumentativeness ["contestation ennuyeuse et lasche"]. . . . In this gay mood we sometimes pluck ["pinçons"] the secret strings of each other's imperfections . . . and we profitably give one another a hint ["entre-advertissons"] of each other's defects.   (717; 938–39)

I note in passing that the words "charge" ("sally") and "ennuyeuse" ("boring") direct attention back along the verbal chain to that first passage (704) in which the excitement of dialectical jousting and the monotony of scholastic pontification were originally set forth as *the* defining, polar types in "the art of discussion." I would point out too that the expression "entre-advertissons" throws back to the early passage, marked by the seminal presence of "poind" (703), that first set this investigation in motion and, from there, to the theme of stimulation-as-warning that was enunciated in the essay's opening sentence. But by far the most noteworthy verbal property of Montaigne's tribute to the spontaneous discourse of good-fellowship is the striking way in which it overlaps, proleptically, at the words "pointu," "aigu," and "pincer," with his discussion of the style of Tacitus:

> He always pleads with solid and vigorous arguments, in a pointed and subtle fashion ["façon pointue et subtile"]. . . . He rather takes after Seneca's writing; he seems to me more meaty, Seneca more pointed ["aigu"] . . . ; you would often say that it is us he is describing and decrying ["qu'il nous peint et qu'il nous pince"].   (719; 941)

Montaigne's recourse to the verbal cluster "pointu"-"aigu"-"pincer" in these two disparate contexts is enormously suggestive. For one thing, it opens up the possibility of explaining his otherwise unmotivated shift in subject matter in the essay's final section (717–21) from the colloquial to the literary manifestations of *conference*. It is as if he were saying that whether composing speeches, writing history, debating weighty matters, or conversing casually, we should frame all discourse on a unitary stylistico-aesthetic model: stimulation, excitement, spontaneity, exhilaration, these are what the "art of discussion"—an art of verbal and intellectual jabbing and stabbing, pricking and sticking—is really all about.

It soon will be obvious as well that Montaigne's praise of the pointy, pinchy Tacitean manner intersects the larger question of the relative roles of subjectivity and objectivity in writing. The last few pages of the essay are in fact given over to the comparison of two basic kinds of book: the author-oriented—as opposed to the subject-oriented—those in the first category being prized for their "own power and fortune" and those in the second "by reason of their subjects" (718; 939). Unlike the *Essays*, many well-reputed books purvey borrowed riches. This string of examples and quotations follows next:

> When some years ago I read Philippe de Commines . . . I noted this remark as uncommon: That we must be very careful not to serve our master so well that we keep him from finding a fair reward for our service. I should have praised the idea ["l'invention"], not him; I came across it in Tacitus not long ago: *Benefits are agreeable as long as they seem returnable; but if they go much beyond that, they are repaid with hatred instead of gratitude.* And Seneca says vigorously ["vigoreusement"]: *For he who thinks it is shameful not to repay does not want the man to live whom he ought to repay* ["Nam qui putat esse turpe non reddere, non vult esse cui reddat"]. Q. Cicero, in a weaker vein ["*d'un biais plus lache*"]: *He who thinks he cannot repay you can by no means be your friend.*   (718; 940)

This laconic exercise in comparative stylistics marks the only place in the essay where Montaigne gets down to cases and illustrates, with instances drawn from actual performance, what we are to understand by resourceful, effective, artistic *conference*. His examples fall into three categories. Commines and Tacitus, who merely exploit an attractive idea, stand somewhere in the middle in a qualitative limbo, whereas the limp or weak ("lâche") rendering of Quintus Cicero, the orator's brother, receives clearly bad marks. Seneca alone is credited with having expressed the thought in question with proper force ("vigoureusement"). In the scheme of value that Montaigne is applying here, *vigoreux* and *lâche* are coded terms, charged with designating metonymically the collective attributes of the two styles, the pointed and the dull, the dialectic and the monologic, the stimulating and the boring, that have been pitted and played off against each other throughout the course of the essay.

Although Montaigne does not give us a clue as to what Seneca's superiority consists in, the "vigor" of his utterance is clearly a function of its antithetical, "pointed" form. What seems to distinguish Seneca from the others, to judge from Montaigne's examples, is his special way of reinforcing the *invention* he shares with them by making the very syntax of his aphorism ("esse . . . non . . . reddere," "non . . . esse . . . reddat") mirror, structurally, the ideas of duplicity and perversity that inform it. A writer of this stripe, Montaigne goes on to specify, allows us to see "the strength and beauty of his mind" in "the choice, arrangement ["disposition"], embellishment, and style ["langage"] that he has supplied" (718; 940). What Montaigne does not quite come out and say is that the energetic, personal "disposition" that he has singled out for praise in Seneca happens also to be the very model of his own. And in the teaching situation, one need only ask at this point what other instances we may have seen of the antithetical, self-reflexive *style vigoureux* exemplified by Seneca, and more than one student—in absolute ignorance of Latin or, for that matter, of French—will point back triumphantly to the essay's opening, specifically to the sentences: "the good that worthy men do the public by making themselves imitable, I shall perhaps do by making myself evitable" and "I . . . learn better by contrast than by example, and by flight than by pursuit" (703; 922).

If we were now to inventory the other occurrences of *vigueur* and its derivatives, we would find that they crop up, not surprisingly, in exactly those places where the best forms of *conference*, wedded to the ideas of contention, virility, and innate mental power, stand in an antagonistic relation to bookishness, pedantry, and mere technical skill. The uses of *lâche*, the contextual antonym of *vigoureux*, trace a slightly more complex and sinuous pattern. The fact that *lâche* appears in the essay's final sentence, and in connection with Tacitus into the bargain, lends it special prominence: "That is what my memory of Tacitus offers me in gross, and rather uncertainly. All judgments in gross are loose ["lâches"] and imperfect" (721; 943). This marginal self-reproach actually echoes the main criticism that Montaigne had earlier leveled at Tacitus: his subordination of personal to public concerns, notably his "mean-spirited" ("láche") reluctance to talk about his private affairs. Tacitus's tendency to sacrifice personal authenticity to respect for external niceties betrays a moral slackness, Montaigne suggests, that is the counterpart, at the level of content, to the laxity of expression of which Q. Cicero stands guilty at the level of style.

Our circuitous return to Tacitus via the word *láche* illustrates Montaigne's casual, deft way of promoting himself from narrator to chief actor and of skewing the discussion of his announced topic toward the interrogation and often, as in the present instance, toward the affirmation and celebration of selfhood as an autonomous value. The critique of Tacitus, with which the chapter concludes, confronts the attentive reader with an astonishing fait accompli. By shifting the primary reference of *conference* from the oral to the written, by denouncing the traditional dichotomy between author and book, manner and matter, and, finally, by having the essay culminate in a commentary on the differences between the *Essays* and the histories of Tacitus, Montaigne is investing his polysemic title, retrospectively, with a new dimension, the notion of "literature" itself. With Tacitus, his style, his authorial attitudes and narrative practice targeted as a potential model of excellence, Montaigne joins the larger question, that was to dominate early modern discussions of poetics, of what Erasmus called "the best way of writing" ("de optimo genere dicendi"). In the essay "Of the Art of Discussion" Montaigne orients this debate on the essence of art and the purpose of communication toward a unique connivance of opposites, the general and the particular, the public and the private, the written and the spoken, which in the histories of Tacitus, he suggests, had been left incomplete and which was at length to be consummated in the *Essays*, the founding examplar of the new genre that Richard Regosin has called "The Book of the Self" ("*Matter*").

"Of Physiognomy": The Staging and Reading of Facial Narrative

Raymond C. La Charité

Capable students I have taught, both in undergraduate senior seminars (classics) and master's-level graduate courses (Renaissance survey), generally do not find Montaigne an easy read. While they favor close readings of individual essays, they find it difficult to pull an essay together, to see and discuss it as a concrete, identifiable, and relatable whole, as they might a play or a novel. The essay's mobile, centrifugal structure deprives them of the sense of grasp and contour they seek. As a teacher, I want my students to penetrate, understand, and enjoy the *pleasure* of discovery that is the dynamic of the Montaignian form. To that end I stress the need for multiple readings and the pursuit of linkage.

"Of Physiognomy" (3.12), one of Montaigne's best essays, is one whose matter seems but remotely related to its title. However, concentration on the essay's manner, on how it produces itself, shows that it is energized discursively and theatrically through the staging of faces. As a "facial" narrative, "Of Physiognomy" emblematizes the act of reading, penetration, and the retrieval of meaning. The cornerstone of this deployment is Socrates, whose wisdom and inner character—considered beautiful and divine—emanate from a body and face said to be ugly. The essay's examination and reconciliation of these disparates brings about the proliferation of faces to be read.

The facial linkage of the essay rests on three generating loci: the first is the mention of Socrates's "so mean a form" ("si vile forme") (793; 1037) in the opening lines; the second, some twenty pages later, is the indication of a possible rubric for the description of the writing, that is, borrowing "enough to bedeck this treatise on physiognomy" (808); the third is the writer's own "favorable bearing" ("port favorable") (811; 1059), which brings the critical excursion and structure full circle. As the discussion moves from certainty to uncertainty, the semantic field of *face*, comprising "form," "physiognomy," "bearing" ("port"), "face" ("mine"), "face" and "visage," orchestrates its own instability and elusiveness and comes to rest in a game of chance, the writer taking refuge in a game of cards as the lowest of the face cards, as a "jack of clubs" (814). Socrates's "si vile forme," recast twenty pages later as "a body and face ["visage"] so ugly ["vilain"]" (809; 1057), is the pivot of the text, its organizing figure and metaphor, the bleak shape that will cover an examination of being in the guise of a panegyrical topos, the elaborate encomium in turn reversing itself in a most engaging praise of the ugly.

As in most of Montaigne's late chapters, so much is going on in "Of Physiognomy" that the reader is apt not only to forget that Socrates stands as a compositional model, a collocation of contrastive faces (physical, metaphorical, esthetic), with appeal to the visualizing eye and the cover, on the one hand, and the critical eye and enclosed thought, on the other, but also to forget that the distance between inner and outer is the spark that energizes the text's conceptual and formal schema. In other words, a text has a scriptural, shaping face or form, an exterior that enables us to see within. This is brought about here by Socrates's "si vile forme," his "vileness," that which seemingly repulses rather than attracts.

Socrates's "vile forme" engenders textuality and creates textual faces—precisely because it is "vile." Unlike Erasmus and Rabelais, Montaigne does not elaborate on Socrates's features; there is no mention of the traditional trinity of nose, bovinity, and yokel's face, and the term *ugliness* is reserved for others. "Vile," on the contrary, allows for full etymological play and the parade of faces that passes in review. Socrates's shape is thus not only homely but also apt to be depreciated, undersold in the marketplace, of little or no value. But because he is *vilis* (cheap), rather than *carus* (costly), he can be "purchased at a low rate" and circulated far and wide so that, ultimately and poetically, he will be "found in great quantities, abundant, common" (Lewis and Short s.v. *vilis*). And while the chapter plays on his simplicity, glossing on how what he does have can be obtained inexpensively, it fills its canvas with what he has in abundance, form and faces. As a result, the essay becomes a face from beginning to end.

All the faces that flow from Socrates's cornucopian and perambulating form—for he is a living book whose oral utterances, mediated by others, must be read and restaged—are assembled in the tragic space and spectacle of the essay as *theatrum mundi*. Most of its faces—"charms that are not sharpened, puffed out, and inflated" (793); Socrates himself; "the poor people" (795); knowledge; "this state" (797); "those who were not yet born" (798); "every Frenchman" (800); the face of France itself ("my country" [800], "a whole nation" [803]); nature, which has in fact "lost her own constant and universal countenance" ("visage") (803; 1050); and the face of the writer—are imperiled and threatened with loss of property, security, freedom, sanity, either through a putrid, ulcerated, cancerous, and consuming dis-figurement ("no part is free from corruption" [796]) or, alternatively and more completely, through extinction. Disease, insanity, and anarchy reign supreme. Indeed, "no worse state ['visage'] of things can be imagined" (798; 1043).

This "storm" (800), "confusion" (800), "collapse" (801), this horrible face, more frightening even than the plaguish face of death, mutilates itself internally ("eats . . . itself . . . tears and dismembers itself" [796]), while its external features undergo "the worst of deformations" (798). The fiend virtually erupts on the page in an exclamatory burst: "Monstrous war!" (796). Gone are the wartlike excrescences and bloated figures of the human love of ostentation and masquerade that thread the text and strut on the boards in the rhetorical flourish of the opening. Harbingers of defacement though they may be, they are now replaced by a terrifying facial shape, whose religious etymology—"a divine omen indicating misfortune, an evil omen" (Lewis and

Short, s.v. *monstrum*)—plays itself out in "this notable spectacle of our public death" (800).

In this crumbling, tumbling world-upside-down, where everyone is imperiled, in which "wickedness" drapes itself in "the cloak of virtue" (798) and in which moral ugliness radiates from the core and ironically outshines Socrates's surface appearance, beauty and Socrates's "secret light" (793) are conversely found in the observed faces and behavior of the "common people" (805). We see them singly, in crowds, in various postures. Indeed, their flesh becomes articulate as the writer observes their body language. Poetically, the text brings them closer and closer to the ground and the earth from which they sprang and to which they are about to return: "Here a man, healthy, was already digging his grave; others lay down in them while still alive" (802); another pulls the earth over him as though it were a blanket in order to sleep better, and so on. While the writer pictures the untroubled, unfrightened face of constancy and courage, their individual and collective presence and faces are etched in the text through a figural vocabulary: "humble people" (797), the "people" (798), "a family astray" (801), "the group" (802), "this caravan" (802), "children, young people, old people" (802), "one of my laborers" (802), "that rustic, unpolished mob" (803), "the simplest" (794), "a peasant" (794), "one of my peasant neighbors" (805), the "living" (798), the "common people" (805), the "vulgar" (805), "the poor people" (795).

Like their model Socrates, they have become teachers, and in their "stupid simplicity" (803) and "school of stupidity" (805) they are showing up knowledge for the beggar it is and restoring nature to its magisterial state. Whereas the human tendency is to put on the face of others, an insistent subtheme of the essay, the "rustic, unpolished mob"—like Socrates—has *itself*, "the pure and primary impression and ignorance of Nature" (807) stamped on its face. And lest we forget the specular bond they and Socrates share, the essay's general concern for visualization insists imperatively on this union: "See these people" (802) echoes and recalls the earlier "See him [Socrates] . . . , see . . ." (793–94).

However many individual and personified faces there may be throughout the essay, its title is not a limiting "Of Faces" but the more interesting "Of Physiognomy," an expression that appears only four times in all of Montaigne (Leake 2: 963): in the title; in another possible title, "this treatise on physiognomy" (808); and in the qualified "There are favorable physiognomies" (811). The fourth instance—not found in this chapter—is fittingly linked in "Of Cruelty" to Socrates and the critical discourse of "Of Physiognomy": Socrates "admitted to those who recognized in his face ["physionomie"] some inclination to vice that that was in truth his natural propensity, but that he had corrected it by discipline" (313; 429; 2.11).

While there is no question that the whole text of "Of Physiognomy" calls on the eye and mind to examine and read faces and surfaces in order to penetrate and interpret an inner core, the physiognomic umbrella gathers under it all possible ramifications of the Socratic facial/compositional model. As we know, the study of physiognomy, an ancient art, was popular in the sixteenth century. The names of Barthélemy Coclès (*Physiognomania*, 1533), Michel Lescot (*Physionomie*, 1540), and Jean d'Indagine (*Chiromance*, 1549), for example, are well known. They and others were convinced that character could be made to surface, so to speak, through an examination of the face, and their works were often accompanied by illustrative woodcuts and engravings, whose inspiration is both fascinating and comic. In Coclès, for instance, the bust-type figures are grouped in pairs, with countenances facing each other, sometimes contrastively (a crafty man, a simple man), sometimes as representations of a similar trait, but always including a part of the head (foreheads, mouths, teeth, noses, hair, and so on, and especially eyes).

Similarly, although "[t]he face ["la mine"] is a weak guarantee," "Of Physiognomy" outlines several such faces, for, in all likelihood, the subject "deserves some consideration" (811; 1059). Moreover, there is undoubtedly "some art to distinguishing the kindly faces ["visages"] from the simple, the severe from the rough, the malicious from the gloomy, the disdainful from the melancholy, and other such adjacent qualities. There are beauties not only proud but bitter; others are sweet, and even beyond that, insipid" (811; 1059). In fact, the essay has been engaging in this oppositional construct throughout, framing it between opening portraits of Cato and Socrates, Plutarch and Seneca (depicted as "hot and impetuous" [795]) and the closing portrait of the writer, whose contrastive twin is Socrates. While it is something that does "not fall very directly and simply under the heading of beauty and ugliness" (810), the gallery of portraits is, nevertheless, inventoried because the essay's avowed project is the depiction and discussion of "physiognomies" and because the inventory serves as (1) a reminder that the "art" of physical and moral portraiture is neither simple nor easy to pin down, (2) a way of blurring and ultimately jettisoning the beauty/ugliness pattern that the critical discourse has been deconstructing all along, (3) a shifting down of the intensity with which the faces to this point have been highlighted and read, and (4) a passage at last to the writer's own face: physical, moral, and writerly.

The shift to the art of reading and the interpretation of untold numbers of "physiognomies" allow the writer in turn to move from general categories to specifics and to stress and link his face *and* his "frankness" (813) and "firmness" (814). Moreover, the presence of "physiognomy" colors the entire essay and allows Montaigne to put on it the exact face and interpretation he wants it to have. This is not one of those instances in which the reader needs to be reminded that "[t]he titles of [Montaigne's] chapters do not always embrace their matter; often they only denote it by some sign" and that the thread of it all will be found "off in a corner" (761). On the contrary, the subtle play of alternative titles in the text shows with what care the choice was determined. Other options would have been either too general, "this general and principal chapter on knowing how to live" (805), too antithetically restrictive, "the heading ["chapitre"] of beauty and ugliness" (810; 1058), or too bookish, "this treatise on physiognomy" (808), the word "treatise" calling for the same sanction cast on bookish knowledge throughout the essay.

"Of Physiognomy" is in search of form, figures, faces, inward configurations, and outward designs that add up to the nature of things and faces, to individual nature. Short of "In Search of a Face," Montaigne could not have come up with a better directional title. The optics of the essay illuminate the reading of formation and design. Etymologically, *physiognomy* collocates "nature" (*physis*) and "knower" (*gnomon*), that is, a knower of nature. Therefore, "Of Physiognomy" emerges in all its parts, from beginning to end, as the depiction and analysis of fundamental constitution, of figure, and it is precisely because of this that the writer can rightly say, "We naturalists judge that the honor of invention is greatly and incomparably preferable to the honor of quotation" (809). In terms of a neologism, a "naturalist" writer *physiognames*, that is, the writer fashions faces, makes faces come to the fore, and both writer and reader label and read them.

As a naturalist writer, Montaigne disguises his readings, his "borrowings" (809). To give them *his* corporeality, he de-forms them, and, through the alteration of their faces, his book takes on its face, a different face. The important discussion of borrowings throughout the essay makes of them a kind of facial binding for the book, and it is in this way that the chapter puts on stage another of its colorful "physiognomies," that is, writing and book as faces to be read.

Finally, while it is true that Montaigne does not say anything as explicit as Shakespeare's "Read o'er the volume of young Paris' face / . . . . Find written in the margent of his eyes" (*Romeo and Juliet* 1.3.81,83) or "I'll read enough / When I do see the very book indeed / Where all my sins are writ, and that's myself. / Give me the glass, and therein will I read" (*Richard II* 4.1.273–276), it seems clear that the topos of "face as book" is implicit throughout because the Socratic construct is a metaphor for reading and because the writer reads his face in the book-mirror that is Socrates. Moreover, the exchange between the book as face—through the discussion of borrowings—and the face as book becomes clear as the writer reads feminine faces: "Those who accuse the ladies of belying their beauty by their character do not always hit the mark. . . . I have sometimes *read* ["lu"] between two beautiful eyes threats of a malignant and dangerous nature" (810–11; 1058; my emphasis).

For the topography of the face to be complete, there remains but one important face for the essay to read, that of the writer. The final section of the essay casts him in life-threatening situations. This new setting is not unlike the perilous one confronting Socrates at the moment of his "loftiest test" (807), and it thus extends and revitalizes the dramatic structure associated with the war, the plagues, and Socrates's predicament. In the immediacy of the account, grandiloquence—"I speak ignorance pompously and opulently, and speak knowledge meagerly and piteously, the latter secondarily and accidentally, the former expressly and principally" (809)—is set aside, and the rhetorical struts of much of the essay disappear.

The moral portrait of Socrates and Montaigne, encased in an examination of "disposition" ("complexions") (811; 1059) in relation to "training" (810), not only allows the writer to bask in the glow of the philosopher but also brings about a distancing and some uncertainty involving formation and reformation. The "assay" has not managed to resolve the very crux of the essay, that is, the vexing question of correction ("Socrates . . . if he had not corrected it" [810]; "I have not, like Socrates, corrected my natural disposition" [811]), and the excursion into the unpredictability of physiognomics and aesthetics has been equally marked by uncertainty. For this reason the writer's facial portrait now looms as necessary, not only to fulfill the terms of the construct and bring about closure, but also to create writerly refuge.

Indeed, the discrepancy between the writing stance of the moral face and that of the physical one seems best accounted for as an effort to foreclose on the former through an enterprising and entertaining flow of stories. Throughout the final section of the essay, the shift in narrative voice from moralist to storyteller accompanies the production of narrative, as the writer takes the full measure of his facial reading in the guise of storytelling as a problem-solving structure.

Like Aeneas, the fictional hero whose courage and steadfast heart he recalls in a 1595 addition (813), the writer is imperiled, not once but twice, one tale authenticating and glossing the other. In each anecdote, he is threatened with loss: "my house" (812) in the first and "my life" (813) in the second. In both instances, suspense builds to the breaking point; the "neighbor" (812) of the first incident and the "leader" (813) of the second then back off, somewhat like a deus ex machina, reconsider their actions, and transform themselves from thieving cutthroats to "natural" readers. The first tells him that his "face" ["visage"] and . . . frankness" (813; 1061) have dissuaded him, the second that his "face ["visage"] and the freedom and firmness of [his] speech" (814; 1062) deserve better.

Unlike Socrates's mediators—"We have light on him from the most clear-sighted men who ever lived; the witnesses we have of him are wonderful in fidelity and competence" (793)—the writer's facial readers are hesitant, unsure of themselves to say the least. Hesitancy is also encoded in the episodes in other ways. In the forest episode, for example, the writer has trouble with numbers: were there "three or four groups," was he pounced on by "fifteen or twenty masked gentlemen," was he unhorsed for "two or three hours," was he guarded by "fifteen or twenty musketeers," did they travel "two or three harquebus shots away" together (813)? Moreover, validation of the facial readings requires repetition, as though one reading does not suffice to prove the point. The neighbor's reading is punctuated by the statement, "He has often said since" (813), while the hostage-taker "repeated to [Montaigne] then several times" (814).

At the outset of the storytelling, the writer speaks of his "favorable bearing ["port"], both in itself and in others' interpretation" (811; 1059) and says that he has often been trusted strictly on the basis of "the mere credit of [his] presence and manner" ("air") (811; 1060). In addition to the fact that the "bearing" ("port") is now self-glossing, what is the reader to make of the shift from "bearing" ("port"), "presence," and "manner" ("air"), all having to do with "bearing," in this case pleasing and imposing, to "visage," a "visage" whose features are no longer so much "in themselves" ("en forme") (811; 1059) as they are "frankness" and "firmness"? With reason, the writer declares, in the second instance, "The true cause of so unusual an about-face . . . , I truly do not even now well know" (813–14). And what of his steadfastness? He admires it in Socrates, he alludes to it in the name of Aeneas, and his aggressors consider it his asset, but in the final sentence of the essay he admits to vacillation and claims that he is in fact irresolute: "As I do not like to take a hand in legitimate actions against people who resent them, so, to tell the truth, I am not scrupulous enough to refrain from taking a hand in illegitimate actions against people who consent to them" (814). This admission is prepared by an equally fascinating wart on the facial canvas when, in the preceding sentence, he states that, as in the case of the king of Sparta, it would be said of him that "'He could not possibly be good, since he is not bad to the wicked.' Or else . . . 'He must certainly be good, since he is good even to the wicked'" (814). Like the poacher and the highwayman, the writer wavers, reverses himself, and folds his hand, appropriately referring to himself as the "jack of clubs" (814) in this whole chancy business of "physiognomy," of facial reading. Hence, the inability to conclude on the level of critical discourse is resolved—inconclusively—in storytelling, as the account of firmness and the statement about firmness accentuate the cleavage between the narrating of face and the revelation of face.

In the contrastive configuration of faces, "Of Physiognomy" has found a generating principle for both critical discourse and performance. For the essay writer, the proliferation of "physiognomies"—moral, material, physical—gives life to the inseparability of face and writing, of reading and revelation. As the various "physiognomies" confront one another, the writer reveals and unmasks his own.

CONTRIBUTORS AND SURVEY PARTICIPANTS

Listed below are the names and affiliations of the contributors to this volume and of the scholars and teachers who graciously took time from their work to participate in the survey of approaches to Montaigne's *Essays*. Their ideas and information were an invaluable contribution.

Josette B. Ashford *Brigham Young University*
Cathleen M. Bauschatz *University of Maine, Orono*
Barbara C. Bowen *Vanderbilt University*
James G. Beaudry *Indiana-Purdue University, Indianapolis*
Richard Bell *Cambridge University*
Jules Brody
Frieda S. Brown *Michigan State University*
Craig Brush *Fordham University*
Elisabeth Caron *University of Kansas*
Tom Conley *University of Minnesota, Minneapolis*
Michel Dassonville *University of Texas, Austin*
Gérard Defaux *Johns Hopkins University*
Philippe Desan *University of Chicago*
Colin Dickson *Washington College*
Ann W. Engar *University of Utah*
William Engel *Vanderbilt University*
Donald M. Frame *Columbia University*
James F. Gaines *Southeastern Louisiana University*
Perry Gethner *Oklahoma State University*
Timothy Hampton *University of California, Berkeley*
George Hoffmann *Boston University*
Jefferson Humphries *Louisiana State University, Baton Rouge*
Abraham Keller *University of Washington*
Lawrence D. Kritzman *Dartmouth College*
Raymond C. La Charité *University of Kentucky*
Deborah N. Losse *Arizona State University*
John D. Lyons *University of Virginia*
Mary B. McKinley *University of Virginia*
Marianne S. Meijer *University of Maryland, College Park*
Donald Nash *Roberts Wesleyan College*
Janis L. Pallister *Bowling Green State University*
Michael G. Paulson *Kutztown University of Pennsylvania*
T. A. Perry *University of Connecticut*
Betty T. Rahv *Boston College*
Richard L. Regosin *University of California, Irvine*
Steven Rendall *University of Oregon*

Regine Reynolds-Cornell *Agnes Scott College*
François Rigolot *Princeton University*
David Lewis Schaefer *College of the Holy Cross*
Jerome Schwartz *University of Pittsburgh*
Edwina Spodark *Hollins College*
Donald Stone *Harvard University*
Alice J. Strange *Southeast Missouri State University*
Marcel Tetel *Duke University*
Constantin Toloudis *University of Rhode Island*
Julia Watson *University of Montana*
John H. Williams *Ohio Valley College*
Colette Winn *Washington University*
Ian Winter *University of Wisconsin, Milwaukee*

WORKS CITED

Adorno, Theodore W. "The Essay as Form." *Notes to Literature*. Trans. Shierry Weber Nicholsen. New York: Columbia UP, 1991. 3–23.

Anderson, Richard C., and P. David Pearson. "A Schema-Theoretic View of Basic Processes in Reading Comprehension." Carrell, Devine, and Eskey 37–55.

Armaingaud, Arthur. "Etude sur Michel de Montaigne." Montaigne, *Œuvres complètes,* ed. Armaingaud. 1: 1–257.

———. *Montaigne pamphlétaire: L'énigme du "Contr'un"*. Paris: Hachette, 1910.

Auerbach, Erich. "L'Humaine Condition." *Mimesis: The Representation of Reality in Western Literature*. Trans. Willard R. Trask. New York: Doubleday, 1957. 249–73.

Bakhtin, Mikhail M. *Esthétique de la création verbale*. Paris: Gallimard, 1979.

———. "Forms of Time and of the Chronotope in the Novel." *The Dialogic Imagination*. By Bakhtin. Trans. Michael Holquist. Austin: U of Texas P, 1981. 84–258.

Ballaguy, Paul. "La sincérité de Montaigne." *Mercure de France* 245 (1933): 547–75.

Baraz, Michaël. *L'être et la connaissance selon Montaigne*. Paris: José Corti, 1968.

Barthes, Roland. "The Death of the Author." *Image, Music, Text*. Trans. Stephen Heath. New York: Hill, 1977. 142–48.

———. *Roland Barthes*. Paris: Seuil, 1975.

Bauschatz, Cathleen M. "'Leur Plus Universelle Qualité, C'Est la Diversité': Women as Ideal Readers in Montaigne's *Essais*." *Journal of Medieval and Renaissance Studies* 1 (1989): 83–101.

———. "Montaigne's Conception of Reading in the Context of Renaissance Poetics and Modern Criticism." *The Reader in the Text: Essays on Audience and Interpretation*. Ed. Susan Suleiman and Inge Crosman. Princeton: Princeton UP, 1980. 264–91.

Beaujour, Michel. *Miroirs d'encre*. Paris: Seuil, 1980.

Beauvoir, Simone de. *The Second Sex*. Trans. H. M. Parshley. New York: Knopf, 1952.

Benjamin, Walter. "Epistemo-Critical Prologue." *The Origin of German Tragic Drama*. By Benjamin. Trans. John Osborne. London: Verso, 1985. 27–56.

Bensmaïa, Réda. *The Barthes Effect: The Essay as Reflective Text*. Minneapolis: U of Minnesota P, 1987.

Bishop, Morris, ed. *A Survey of French Literature*. New York: Harcourt, 1965.

Bitton, Davis. *The French Nobility in Crisis, 1560–1640*. Stanford: Stanford UP, 1969.

Blanchard, Marc Eli. "'Of Cannibalism' and Autobiography." *MLN* 93 (1978): 654–76.

Bowen, Barbara C. *The Age of Bluff: Paradox and Ambiguity in Rabelais and Montaigne*. Urbana: U of Illinois P, 1972.

Bowman, Frank. *Montaigne*: Essays. London: Arnold, 1965.

Brody, Jules. "'Du Repentir' (III: 2): A Philological Reading." *Montaigne: Essays in Reading. Yale French Studies* 64 (1983): 238–72.

———. *Lectures de Montaigne*. Lexington: French Forum, 1982.

Brown, Frieda. "'De la Solitude': A Re-examination of Montaigne's Retreat from Public Life." *From Marot to Montaigne: Essays on French Renaissance Literature*. Ed. Raymond La Charité. *Kentucky Romance Quarterly* 19 (1972): 137–46.

———. *Religious and Political Conservatism in the* Essais *of Montaigne*. Genève: Droz, 1963.

Brunel, Pierre, et al. *Histoire de la littérature française*. Paris: Bordas, 1972.

Brush, Craig. "The Essayist Is Learned: Montaigne's *Journal de voyage* and the *Essais*." *Romanic Review* 42 (1971): 16–27.

———. "Montaigne Tries Out Self-Study." *L'Esprit Créateur* 20 (1980): 23–35.

Burckhardt, Jacob. *The Civilization of the Renaissance in Italy*. Trans. S. G. C. Middlemore. New York: Harper, 1958.

Burke, Peter. *The Italian Renaissance*. Princeton: Princeton UP, 1986.

———. *Montaigne*. Oxford: Oxford UP, 1981.

Busson, Henri. *Le rationalisme dans la littérature française de la Renaissance*. Paris: Vrin, 1952.

Butler, Judith. *Gender Trouble*. New York: Routledge, 1990.

Butor, Michel. *Essais sur les* Essais. Paris: Gallimard, 1968.

Butrym, Alexander J., ed. *Essays on the Essay: Redefining the Genre*. Athens: U of Georgia P, 1989.

Cameron, Keith. "Montaigne and 'De la Liberté de Conscience.'" *Renaissance Quarterly* 26 (1973): 285–94.

Carrell, Patricia L., Joanne Devine, and David E. Eskey, eds. *Interactive Approaches to Second Language Reading*. Cambridge: Cambridge UP, 1988.

Castiglione, Baldesar. *The Book of the Courtier*. Trans. Charles S. Singleton. New York: Anchor-Doubleday, 1959.

Castor, Graham. *Pléiade Poetics: A Study in Sixteenth-Century Thought and Terminology*. Cambridge: Cambridge UP, 1964.

Cave, Terence. *The Cornucopian Text: Problems of Writing in the French Renaissance*. Oxford: Clarendon–Oxford UP, 1979.

———. "Problems of Reading in the *Essais*." McFarlane and Maclean 133–66.

Chambers, Frank M. *Prosateurs français du XVIe siècle*. Lexington: Heath, 1976.

Chastel, André. *La crise de la Renaissance*. Genève: Skira, 1968.

Clark, Carol E. *The Web of Metaphor: Studies in the Imagery of Montaigne's Essais*. Lexington: French Forum, 1978.

Clark, Kenneth. "Protest and Communication." *Civilisation: A Personal View*. New York: Harper, 1989. 139–65.

Clouard, Henri, and Robert Leggewie, eds. *Anthologie de la littérature française*. Vol. 1. New York: Oxford UP, 1975.

Coleman, Dorothy Gabe. *Montaigne's Essays*. London: Allen, 1987.

Colie, Rosalie. *Paradoxia Epidemica: The Renaissance Tradition of Paradox*. Princeton: Princeton UP, 1966.

Colie, Rosalie. *The Resources of Kind: Genre-Theory in the Renaissance.* Ed. Barbara K. Lewalski. Berkeley: U of California P, 1973.

Compagnon, Antoine. *Nous, Michel de Montaigne.* Paris: Seuil, 1980.

———. *La seconde main; ou Le travail de la citation.* Paris: Seuil, 1979.

Conley, Tom. "*De capsula totoe*: Lecture de Montaigne, 'De trois commerces.'" *L'Esprit Créateur* 28 (1988): 18–26.

———. *The Graphic Unconscious: The Letter of Early Modern French Writing.* Cambridge: Cambridge UP, 1992.

Cotgrave, Randle. *A Dictionarie of the French and English Tongues.* 1611. New York: Da Capo, 1971.

Cottrell, Robert. *Sexuality/Textuality: A Study of the Fabric of Montaigne's Essais.* Columbus: Ohio State UP, 1981.

Culler, Jonathan. *Structuralist Poetics: Structuralism, Linguistics, and the Study of Literature.* Ithaca: Cornell UP, 1975.

Curtius, Ernst Robert. *European Literature and the Latin Middle Ages.* Trans. Willard R. Trask. Princeton: Princeton UP, 1953.

Davis, Natalie Zemon. *Society and Culture in Early Modern France.* Stanford: Stanford UP, 1975.

Defaux, Gérard. *Marot, Rabelais, Montaigne: L'écriture comme présence.* Etudes montaignistes 2. Paris: Champion; Genève: Slatkine, 1987.

———. *Montaigne: Essays in Reading. Yale French Studies* 64 (1983).

———. "Readings of Montaigne." *Montaigne: Essays in Reading* 73–92. Expanded French version: "Lectures de Montaigne." *Saggi e ricerche di letteratura francese* 22 (1983): 49–78.

———. "Rhétorique et représentation dans les *Essais*: De la peinture de l'autre à la peinture du moi." *Rhétorique de Montaigne.* Ed. Frank Lestringant. Paris: Champion, 1985. 21–48.

de Gournay, Marie. *Egalité des hommes et des femmes.* Paris: n.p., 1622.

de Lauretis, Teresa. *Technologies of Gender.* Bloomington: Indiana UP, 1987.

de Man, Paul. "Semiology and Rhetoric." Harari 121–40.

Demonet, Marie-Luce. *Michel de Montaigne: Les Essais.* Paris: PUF, 1985.

Derrida, Jacques. "La structure, le signe et le jeu . . ." *L'écriture et la différence.* Paris: Seuil, 1967. 409–28.

———. *La vérité en peinture.* Paris: Flammarion, 1978.

Desan, Philippe, ed. *Humanism in Crisis: The Decline of the French Renaissance.* Ann Arbor: U of Michigan P, 1991.

Dickens, A. G. *Reformation and Society in Sixteenth-Century Europe.* New York: Harcourt, 1966.

Dickson, Colin. "L'invitation de Montaigne au banquet de la vie: 'De l'experience.'" *Mélanges sur la littérature de la Renaissance à la mémoire de V.-L. Saulnier.* Genève: Droz, 1984. 501–09.

Dresden, Sem. "Het herkauwen van teksten." *Forum der Letteren* 3–4 (1971): 142–72.

Dubois, Claude-Gilbert. *Le maniérisme.* Paris: PUF, 1979.

Duby, Georges, and Robert Mandrou. *Histoire de la civilisation française.* 2 vols. Paris: Colin, 1958.

Duval, Edwin M. "Rhetorical Composition and 'Open Form' in Montaigne's Early Essays." *Bibliothèque d'humanisme et Renaissance* 43 (1981): 269–87.

Edgerton, Samuel, Jr. *The Renaissance Rediscovery of Linear Perspective.* New York: Basic, 1975.

Eisenstein, Elizabeth. *The Printing Press as an Agent of Change.* 2 vols. Cambridge: Cambridge UP, 1979.

Erasmus, Desiderius. *Adages Ivil to Ix100.* Trans. and annotated R. A. B. Mynors. Vol. 32 of *Works.* Toronto: U of Toronto P, 1989.

———. *The Ciceronian.* Ed. A. H. T. Levi. Vol. 28 of *Works.* Toronto: U of Toronto P, 1986.

———. *The Collected Works of Erasmus.* 42 vols. to date. Toronto: U of Toronto P, 1974– .

Erlanger, Philippe. *Le massacre de Saint-Barthélemy.* Paris: Gallimard, 1960.

Etiemble, René. "Sens et structure dans un essai de Montaigne." *Cahiers de L'Association Internationale des Etudes Françaises* 14 (1962): 267–74.

Evennett, H. Outram. *The Spirit of the Counter-Reformation.* New York: Cambridge UP, 1968.

Felman, Shoshana, ed. *Literature and Psychoanalysis.* Spec. issue of *Yale French Studies* 55–56 (1977): 1–507.

Fleuret, Colette. "Montaigne et la société civile." *Europe* 50 (1972): 107–23.

Fontaine, Marie-Madeleine. "Images littéraires de l'escalier." Guillaume 111–16.

Foucault, Michel. "What Is an Author?" Harari 141–60.

Frame, Donald M. *Montaigne: A Biography.* New York: Harcourt, 1965.

———. *Montaigne's Discovery of Man: The Humanization of a Humanist.* New York: Columbia UP, 1955.

———. *Montaigne's Essais: A Study.* Englewood Cliffs: Prentice, 1969.

———. "Specific Motivation for Montaigne's Self-Portrait." *Columbia Montaigne Conference Papers.* Ed. Frame and Mary B. McKinley. Lexington: French Forum, 1981. 60–69.

France, Peter. *Rhetoric and Truth in France: Descartes to Diderot.* Oxford: Clarendon–Oxford UP, 1972.

Friedrich, Hugo. *Montaigne.* 1949. Trans. Robert Rovini. Paris: Gallimard, 1968. Ed. Philippe Desan. Trans. Dawn Eng. Berkeley: U of California P, 1991.

Genette, Gérard. *Introduction à l'architexte.* Paris: Seuil, 1979.

Glauser, Alfred. *Montaigne paradoxal.* Paris: Nizet, 1972.

Good, Graham. *The Observing Self: Rediscovering the Essay.* New York: Routledge, 1988.

Grabe, William. "Reassessing the Term 'Interactive.'" Carrell, Devine, and Eskey 56–70.

Grafton, Anthony, and Lisa Jardine. *From Humanism to the Humanities.* Cambridge: Harvard UP, 1986.

Gray, Floyd F. *La balance de Montaigne: Exagium/essai.* Paris: Nizet, 1982.

———. "Montaigne's Friends." *French Studes* 15 (1961): 203–11.

———. *Le style de Montaigne.* Paris: Nizet, 1958.

Greene, Thomas M. *The Light in Troy: Imitation and Discovery in Renaissance Poetry.* New Haven: Yale UP, 1982.

Grendler, Paul F. *Schooling in Renaissance Italy: Literacy and Learning, 1300–1600.* Baltimore: Johns Hopkins UP, 1989.

Guillaume, Jean. "L'escalier français dans l'architecture française: La première moitié du XVIᵉ siècle." *L'escalier dans l'architecture de la Renaissance.* Ed. Guillaume. Paris: Picard, 1985. 30–47.

Guizot, Guillaume. *Montaigne: Etudes et fragments.* Paris: Hachette, 1899.

Gutwirth, Marcel. "'By Diverse Means . . .' (1:1)." Defaux, *Montaigne* 180–87.

———. *Michel de Montaigne ou le pari d'exemplarité.* Montréal: PU de Montréal, 1977.

Hale, J. R. *Renaissance Europe: Individual and Society, 1480–1520.* Berkeley: U of California P, 1971.

Hallie, Philip P. "The Ethics of Montaigne's 'De la Cruauté.'" *La Charité, O un Amy!* 156–71.

Hampton, Timothy. "Montaigne and the Body of Socrates: Narrative and Exemplarity in the *Essais.*" *MLN* 104 (1989): 880–98.

———. *Writing from History: The Rhetoric of Exemplarity in Renaissance Literature.* Ithaca: Cornell UP, 1990.

Harari, Josué V., ed. *Textual Strategies: Perspectives in Post-structural Criticism.* Ithaca: Cornell UP, 1979.

Hayden, Hiram. *The Counter-Renaissance.* New York: Scribner's, 1950.

Henry, Patrick. *Montaigne in Dialogue.* Saratoga: Anma, 1987.

Hiley, David R. *Philosophy in Question: Essays on a Pyrrhonian Theme.* Chicago: U of Chicago P, 1988.

Hollier, Denis, ed. *A New History of French Literature.* Cambridge: Harvard UP, 1989.

Huguet, Edmond. *Dictionnaire de la langue française du seizième siècle.* 7 vols. Paris: Champion, 1925–35; Didier, 1944–67.

Huppert, George. *Les Bourgeois Gentilhommes: An Essay on the Definition of Elites in Renaissance France.* Chicago: U of Chicago P, 1977.

———. *The Idea of Perfect History: Historical Erudition and Historical Philosophy in Renaissance France.* Urbana: U of Illinois P, 1970.

Insdorf, Cecile. *Montaigne and Feminism.* Chapel Hill: North Carolina Studies in the Romance Languages and Literatures, 1977.

Johnson, Barbara. *The Critical Difference: Essays in the Contemporary Rhetoric of Reading.* Baltimore: Johns Hopkins UP, 1980.

Jonas, Hans. *The Phenomenon of Life.* New York: Harper, 1966.

Kahn, Victoria. *Rhetoric, Prudence, and Skepticism in the Renaissance.* Ithaca: Cornell UP, 1985.

Kelley, Donald R. *Foundations of Modern Historical Scholarship: Language, Law and History in the French Renaissance*. New York: Columbia UP, 1970.

Keohane, Nannerl O. "Montaigne's Individualism." *Political Theory* 5 (1977): 363–90.

———. *Philosophy and the State in France*. Princeton: Princeton UP, 1980.

Kerrigan, William, and Gordon Braden. *The Idea of the Renaissance*. Baltimore: Johns Hopkins UP, 1989.

Kingdon, Robert M. *Myth and Massacre in Sixteenth Century Europe: Reactions to St. Bartholomew's Massacres of 1572*. Cambridge: Harvard UP, 1988.

Knecht, R. J. *Francis I*. Cambridge: Cambridge UP, 1982.

Kristeller, Paul Oskar. *Renaissance Thought: The Classic, Scholastic, and Humanist Strains*. 2 vols. New York: Torchbooks-Harper, 1961–65.

Kristeva, Julia. *Black Sun*. Trans. Leon Roudiez. New York: Columbia UP, 1989.

———. *The Kristeva Reader*. Ed. Toril Moi. New York: Columbia UP, 1986.

Kritzman, Lawrence D. *Destruction/découverte: Le fonctionnement de la rhétorique dans les* Essais *de Montaigne*. Lexington: French Forum, 1980.

———. "Montaigne's Family Romance." *The Rhetoric of Sexuality and the Literature of the French Renaissance*. Cambridge: Cambridge UP, 1991. 73–92.

La Boétie, Etienne de. *Discours de la servitude volontaire*. Ed. Simone Goyard-Fabre. Paris: Garnier, 1983.

Lacan, Jacques. "The Mirror Stage as Formative of the Function of the I as Revealed in Psychoanalytic Experience." *Ecrits*. Trans. Alan Sheridan. New York: Norton, 1977. 1–7.

La Charité, Ramond C. "The Coherence of Montaigne's First Book." *L'Esprit Créateur* 20 (1980): 36–45.

———. *The Concept of Judgment in Montaigne*. The Hague: Nijhoff, 1968.

———. "Montaigne's Early Personal Essays." *Romanic Review* 42 (1971): 5–15.

———, ed. *O un Amy! Essays on Montaigne in Honor of Donald M. Frame*. Lexington: French Forum, 1977.

———, ed. *The Sixteenth Century*. Vol. 2 of *A Critical Bibliography of French Literature*. Rev. New York: Syracuse UP, 1985.

Lagarde, André, and Laurent Michard, eds. *XVIe siècle*. Paris: Bordas, 1963.

Lanham, Richard. *The Motives of Eloquence: Literary Rhetoric in the Renaissance*. New Haven: Yale UP, 1976.

Lanson, Gustave. "La vie morale selon les *Essais* de Montaigne." *Revue des deux mondes* (1924): 603–25; 836–58.

Leake, Roy E. *Concordance des* Essais *de Montaigne*. 2 vols. Genève: Droz, 1981.

Lefranc, Abel. *La vie quotidienne au temps de la Renaissance*. Paris: Hachette, 1938.

Léonard, Emile G. *Histoire générale du protestantisme*. 1961. 3 vols. Paris: PUF, 1964.

Levin, Harry. *The Myth of the Golden Age in the Renaissance*. Bloomington: Indiana UP, 1969.

Lewis, Charlton T., and Charles Short. *A Latin Dictionary*. Oxford: Clarendon-Oxford UP, 1879.

Livet, Georges. *Les guerres de religion.* Paris: PUF, 1962.

Luthy, Herbert. "Montaigne; or, The Art of Being Truthful." *Encounter* 2 (1953): 33–44.

Lyons, John D. *Exemplum: The Rhetoric of Exemplarity in Early Modern France and Italy.* Princeton: Princeton UP, 1989.

Machiavelli, Niccolò. *The Prince.* Trans. Luigi Ricci and E. R. P. Vincent. *The Prince and the Discourses.* Ed. Max Lerner. New York: Modern Library–Random, 1950.

Mack, Maynard, gen. ed. *The Norton Anthology of World Masterpieces.* Vol. 1. New York: 1956.

Mandrou, Robert. *Introduction à la France moderne, 1500–1640.* Paris: Albin, 1961.

Marcu, Eva. "Quelques invraisemblances et contradictions dans les *Essais*." *Mémorial du 1er Congrès International des Etudes Montaignistes.* Ed. Georges Palassie. Bordeaux: Taffard, 1964. 238–46.

Martin, Daniel. Introduction. *Essais: Reproduction photographique de l'édition originale de 1580.* Vol. 1. Genève: Slatkine; Paris: Champion, 1976. 1–44.

Mathieu-Castellani, Gisèle. "Discours sur le corps, discours du corps dans le troisième livre des *Essais*." *Le parcours des Essais: Montaigne, 1588–1988.* Ed. Marcel Tetel and G. Mallary Masters. Paris: Aux Amateurs, 1989. 125–45.

———. *Montaigne: L'écriture de l'essai.* Paris: PUF, 1988.

McFarlane, Ian. *Renaissance France, 1470–1589.* Vol. 2 of *A Literary History of France.* New York: Barnes, 1974.

McFarlane, Ian, and Ian Maclean, eds. *Montaigne: Essays in Memory of Richard Sayce.* Oxford: Clarendon–Oxford UP, 1982.

McGowan, Margaret. *Ideal Forms in the Age of Ronsard.* Berkeley: U of California P, 1985.

———. *Montaigne's Deceits: The Art of Persuasion in the* Essays. London: U of London P, 1974.

McKinley, Mary B. "Montaigne's Reader: A Rhetorical and Phenomenological Examination." *Montaigne: Regards sur les* Essais. Ed. Lane M. Heller and Felix R. Atance. Ontario: Wilfred Laurier UP, 1986. 69–77.

———. *Words in a Corner: Studies in Montaigne's Latin Quotations.* Lexington: French Forum, 1981.

Ménager, Daniel. *Introduction à la vie littéraire du XVIe siècle.* Montreal: Bordas, 1968.

Montaigne, Michel de. *The Complete* Essays *of Montaigne.* Trans. Donald M. Frame. Stanford: Stanford UP, 1965.

———. *The Complete Works of Montaigne: Essays, Travel Journal, Letters.* Trans. Donald M. Frame. Stanford, Stanford UP, 1957.

———. *Essais.* Paris: Nouveaux Classiques Larousse, 1985.

———. *Essais.* Ed. Michel Butor. 4 vols. Paris: Union Générale, 1964.

———. *Essais.* Ed. C. Faisant. Paris: Bordas, 1978.

——. *Essais*. Ed. Alexandre Micha. 3 vols. Paris: Garnier, 1969.

——. *Essais*. Ed. Pierre Michel. 3 vols. Paris: Livre de Poche–Gallimard, 1965.

——. *Les* Essais *de Michel de Montaigne*. 5 vols. Ed. Fortunat Strowski. Bordeaux: Pech, 1906–19.

——. Essais *de Michel de Montaigne: Texte original de 1580 avec les variantes des éditions de 1582 et 1587*. Ed. Reinhold Dezeimereis and H. Barckhausen. 2 vols. Bordeaux: Féret, 1870.

——. *Les* Essais *de Montaigne: Edition réimprimée sous la direction de V. L. Saulnier*. Ed. Pierre Villey. Paris: PUF, 1965.

——. *Les* Essais: *Reproduction photographique de la deuxième edition*. (1582 ed.) Ed. Marcel Françon. Cambridge: Harvard UP, 1969.

——. Essais: *Reproduction photographique de l'édition originale de 1580*. Ed. Daniel Martin. 2 vols. Genève: Slatkine-Champion, 1976.

——. Essais: *Reproduction photographique du livre troisième de l'édition originale de 1588*. Ed. Daniel Martin. Genève: Slatkine-Champion, 1988.

——. *The* Essayes *or moral, politike and militarie discourses of Lo Michaell de Montaigne*. Trans. John Florio. London: V. Sims for E. Blount, 1603.

——. *Essays*. Trans. John M. Cohen. Baltimore: Penguin, 1959.

——. *The* Essays *of Michel de Montaigne*. Trans. and ed. Jacob Zeitlin. 3 vols. New York: Knopf, 1934–36.

——. *Journal de voyage en Italie*. Ed. Pierre Michel. Paris: Livre de Poche, 1974.

——. *Montaigne: Selected Essays*. Ed. Arthur Tilley and A. M. Boase. New York: St. Martin's, 1988.

——. *Montaigne's* Essays *and Selected Writings*. Bilingual ed. Trans. and ed. Donald M. Frame. New York: St. Martin's, 1963.

——. *Montaigne's Travel Journal*. Trans. Donald M. Frame. San Francisco: North Point, 1983.

——. *Œuvres complètes*. Ed. Arthur Armaingaud. 12 vols. Paris: Conard, 1924–41.

——. *Œuvres complètes*. Ed. Albert Thibaudet and Maurice Rat. Paris: Gallimard, 1962.

——. *Reproduction en phototypie de l'exemplaire avec notes manuscrites marginales des* Essais *de Montaigne appartenant à la ville de Bordeaux. . . .* 3 vols. Ed. Fortunat Strowski. Paris: Hachette, 1912.

Moore, Will. "Montaigne's Notion of Experience." *The French Mind: Studies in Honor of Gustave Rudler*. Oxford: Clarendon–Oxford UP, 1952. 34–52.

Nakam, Géralde. *Les* Essais *de Montaigne: Miroir et procès de leur temps. Témoignage historique et création littéraire*. Paris: Nizet, 1984.

——. *Montaigne et son temps: Les événements et les* Essais: *L'histoire, la vie, le livre*. Paris: Nizet, 1982.

Nilles, Camilla, and Ian Winter, eds. *Rabelais et Montaigne: Chapitres Choisis*. Lewiston: Mellin, 1991.

Ong, Walter J. "Latin Language Study as a Renaissance Puberty Rite." *Rhetoric, Romance and Technology: Studies in the Interaction of Expression and Culture*. Ithaca: Cornell UP, 1971. 113–41.

————. *The Presence of the Word: Some Prolegomena for Cultural and Religious History*. New Haven: Yale UP, 1967.

————. *Ramus: Method, and the Decay of Dialogue*. Cambridge: Harvard UP, 1958.

Panofsky, Erwin. *Studies in Iconology*. New York: Oxford UP, 1939.

Peirce, C. S. "Logic as Semiotic: The Theory of Signs." *Philosophical Writings of Peirce*. Ed. Justus Buchler. New York: Dover, 1940. 99–119.

Pérouse, Gabriel A. "Le seuil des *Essais.*" *Etudes montaignistes en hommage à Pierre Michel*. Ed. Claude Blum and François Moureau. Paris: Champion, 1984. 215–21.

Pertile, Lino. "Paper and Ink: The Structure of Unpredictability." La Charité, *O un Amy!* 190–218.

Plattard, Jean. *La Renaissance des lettres en France, de Louis XII à Henri IV*. Paris: Colin, 1967.

Plutarch. "On Listening to Lectures." *Moralia*. Vol. 1. Loeb Classical Library. Trans. F. C. Babbitt. London: Heinemann, 1927. 201–59. 14 vols.

Popkin, Richard. *The History of Scepticism from Erasmus to Spinoza*. Berkeley: U of California P, 1979.

Porteau, Paul. *Montaigne et la vie pédagogique de son temps*. Genève: Droz, 1935.

Pouilloux, Jean-Yves. *Lire les* Essais *de Montaigne*. Paris: Maspéro, 1969.

Quint, David. *Origin and Originality in Renaissance Literature: Versions of the Source*. New Haven: Yale UP, 1983.

Rabinowitz, Peter J. *Before Reading: Narrative Conventions and the Politics of Interpretation*. Cornell: Cornell UP, 1987.

Reed, Sue Welsh, and Richard Wallace. *Italian Etchers of the Renaissance and Baroque*. Boston: Museum of Fine Arts, 1989.

Regosin, Richard L. "Figures of the Self: Montaigne's Rhetoric of Portraiture." *L'Esprit Créateur* 20 (1980): 66–80.

————. *"The Matter of My Book": Montaigne's* Essays *as the Book of the Self*. Berkeley: U of California P, 1977.

————. "Montaigne's Dutiful Daughter." *Montaigne Studies* 3 (1991): 103–27.

————. "Recent Trends in Montaigne Scholarship: A Post-structuralist Perspective." *Renaissance Quarterly* 37 (1984): 34–54.

————. "Sources and Resources: The 'Pretexts' of Originality in Montaigne's *Essais.*" *Substance* 21 (1978): 103–15.

Reiss, Timothy J. "Montaigne and the Subject of Polity." *Literary Theory/Renaissance Texts*. Ed. Patricia Parker and David Quint. Baltimore: Johns Hopkins UP, 1986. 115–49.

Renaudet, Augustin. *Humanisme et Renaissance*. Genève: Droz, 1958.

Rendall, Steven. "Dialectical Structure and Tactics in Montaigne's 'Of Cannibals.'" *Pacific Coast Philology* 12 (1977): 56–63.

————. "Montaigne under the Sign of *Fama*." *Yale French Studies* 66 (1984): 137–59.

————. "*Mus in Pice*: Montaigne and Interpretation." *MLN* 94 (1979): 1056–71.

————. "The Rhetoric of Montaigne's Self-Portrait: Speaker and Subject." *Studies in Philology* 73 (1976): 285–301.

Rice, Eugene. *The Renaissance Idea of Wisdom*. Cambridge: Harvard UP, 1958.

Rider, Frederick. *The Dialectic of Selfhood in Montaigne*. Stanford: Stanford UP, 1973.

Rigolot, François. *Les métamorphoses de Montaigne*. Paris: PUF, 1988.

———. *Le texte de la Renaissance: Des rhétoriqueurs à Montaigne*. Genève: Droz, 1982.

———. "Montaigne's Purloined Letters." Defaux, *Montaigne* 145–67.

Ronsard, Pierre de. *Œuvres complètes*. Ed. Gustave Cohen. 2 vols. Paris: Gallimard, 1950.

Salmon, J. H. M. "Cicero and Tacitus in Sixteenth-Century France." *American Historical Review* 85 (1980): 307–31.

———. *Society in Crisis: France in the Sixteenth Century*. New York: St. Martin's, 1975.

Sayce, Richard A. "Baroque Elements in Montaigne." *French Studies* 8 (1954): 1–16.

———. *The* Essays *of Montaigne: A Critical Exploration*. London: Weidenfeld, 1972.

———. "L'ordre des *Essais* de Montaigne." *Bibliothèque d'humanisme et Renaissance* 18 (1956): 7–22.

———. *Style in French Prose: A Method of Analysis*. Oxford: Clarendon–Oxford UP, 1953.

Schaefer, David Lewis. *The Political Philosophy of Montaigne*. Ithaca: Cornell UP, 1990.

Schapiro, Meyer. *Late Antique, Early Christian, and Medieval Art*. New York: Braziller, 1979.

Schlossman, Beryl. "From La Boétie to Montaigne: The Place of the Text." *MLN* 95 (1983): 891–909.

Schutz, Alexander H., ed. *The Sixteenth Century*. Vol. 2 of *A Critical Bibliography of French Literature*. New York: Syracuse UP, 1956.

Schwartz, Jerome. "'La Conscience d'un Homme': Reflections on the Problem of Conscience in the *Essais*." La Charité, *O un amy!* 242–76.

———. "The Deconstructive Moment in Montaigne's *Essais*." *Stanford French Review* 9 (1985): 321–33.

Screech, M. A. *Montaigne and Melancholy: The Wisdom of the* Essays. Cranbury: Susquehanna UP, 1984.

Seigel, J. E. *Rhetoric and Philosophy in Renaissance Humanism, Petrarch to Valla*. Princeton: Princeton UP, 1968.

Sidney, Philip. "An Apology for Poetry." *Critical Theory Since Plato*. Ed. Hazard Adams. New York: Harcourt, 1971. 155–77.

Simone, Franco. *Culture et politique à l'époque de l'humanisme et de la Renaissance*. Turin: Accademia delle Scienze, 1974.

Smith, Barbara Herrnstein. *Poetic Closure: A Study of How Poems End*. Chicago: U of Chicago P, 1968.

Smith, Paul. *Discerning the Subject*. Minneapolis: U of Minnesota P, 1988.

Starobinski, Jean. *Montaigne en mouvement*. Paris: Gallimard, 1982.

———. *Montaigne in Motion.* Trans. Arthur Goldhammer. Chicago: U of Chicago P, 1985.

Stone, Donald. "Death in the Third Book." *L'Esprit Créateur* 8 (1968): 185–93.

Strauss, Leo. *Persecution and the Art of Writing.* Glencoe: Free, 1952.

Strowski, Fortunat. *Montaigne.* 1931. New York: Burt Franklin, 1971.

Supple, James J. *Arms versus Letters: The Military and Literary Ideals in the* Essais *of Montaigne.* Oxford: Oxford UP, 1984.

Telle, Emile. "A propos du mot *essai* chez Montaigne." *Bibliothèque d'humanisme et Renaissance* 30 (1965): 225–47.

Tetel, Marcel. "Les fins d'essais: Mise en question ou début du convaincre." *Rhétorique de Montaigne: Actes réunis par Frank Lestringant.* Paris: Champion, 1985. 191–99.

———. *Montaigne.* 1974. Rev. ed. Boston: Twayne, 1990.

———. "Of Women, of Father, of Mother." Unpublished essay.

Thibaudet, Albert. *Montaigne.* Ed. Floyd Gray. Paris: Gallimard, 1963.

Thompson, James W. *The Wars of Religion in France, 1559–1576.* 1909. New York: Ungar, 1957.

Thweatt, Vivien. "L'art de conferer: Art des *Essais,* art de vivre." *Romanic Review* 68 (1977): 103–17.

Tournon, André. *Montaigne: La glose et l'essai.* Lyon: PU de Lyon, 1983.

Trinquet, Roger. *La jeunesse de Montaigne.* Paris: Nizet, 1972.

Villey, Pierre. *Les sources et l'évolution des* Essais *de Montaigne.* 2 vols. Paris: Hachette, 1908; New York: Franklin, 1968.

Volochinov, V. N. "La structure de l'énoncé." *Mikhaïl Bakhtine: Le principe dialogique suivi de* Ecrits du cercle Bakhtine. Ed. Tzvetan Todorov. Paris: Seuil, 1981. 287–316.

Walker, D. P. *The Ancient Theology: Studies in Christian Platonism from the Fifteenth to the Eighteenth Century.* Ithaca: Cornell UP, 1972.

Weber, Max. *The Protestant Ethic and the Spirit of Capitalism.* Trans. Talcott Parsons. New York: Scribner's, 1958.

Weimann, Robert. "'Appropriation' and Modern History in Renaissance Prose Narrative." *New Literary History* 14 (1983): 459–95.

Weller, Barry. "The Rhetoric of Friendship in Montaigne's *Essais.*" *New Literay History* 9 (1978): 503–23.

Wilde, Alan. *Horizons of Assent: Modernism, Postmodernism, and the Ironic Imagination.* Baltimore: Johns Hopkins UP, 1981. Philadelphia: U of Pennsylvania P, 1987.

Wilden, Anthony. "'Par Divers Moyens On Arrive à Pareille Fin': A Reading of Montaigne." *MLN* 83 (1968): 577–97.

Winegrad, Dilys. "'Maistrise Engendre Mespris': Montaigne and the Generative Power of Language." *Symposium* 35 (1981): 168–80.

Winter, Ian. *Montaigne's Self-Portrait and Its Influence in France, 1580–1630.* Lexington: French Forum, 1976.

Wolf, Christa. *Cassandra.* Trans. van Heurck. New York: Farrar, 1984.

Woolf, Virginia. *A Room of One's Own*. 1929. New York: Harcourt, 1957.

Zeitlin, Jacob, ed. and trans. *The* Essays *of Michel de Montaigne*. 3 vols. New York: Knopf, 1935.

Zerner, Henri. *The School of Fontainebleau: Etchings and Drawings*. New York: Abrams, 1969.

INDEX